Wherever He Leads

Dear

I hope that you enjoy reading my journey, "Wherever He Leads." He is faithful & supplies our every need -

Millie Redding

Psalm 32:8

June 2013

Wherever He Leads

The Story of Elcho and Millie Redding

Led by God to India,
the Tibetan Border,
California, China, and Japan

Millie Redding

Wherever He Leads by Millie Redding
©2011 Millie Redding
Edited by Agnes Lawless Elkins
Cover design by Mastery Sheets and Michael Sheets
Design and layout by Mastery Sheets
Illustrations and additional design by Michael Sheets

ISBN-13: 978-1463622442
ISBN-10: 1463622449

https://www.createspace.com/3635870

With gratitude, I dedicate
this book to my late husband,
Elcho Zaire Redding, with
whom I shared this journey,
and to our dear family.

Contents

Part 1: Early Years

Part 2: India

Part 3: Tibetan Border

Part 4: Orange County

Foreword

It was a special day for me personally and for the ministry of International Students, Inc., when I met Elcho Redding at a stewardship conference at the Disneyland Hotel in 1968, and I later met his wife Millie. They not only had missionary experience, but they had missionary hearts and children who reflected the same spirit. My wife Betsy's and my hearts were knit with theirs in a common purpose of serving Christ.

During the years they were in Orange County, California, I enjoyed visiting and ministering with them. The lovely home that "Aunt Mary" Marshburn enabled them to use was an excellent setting in the "open house—open heart" ministry they developed. Never was I there on a weekend but the house was crowded with international guests. In the morning, I would find them sleeping on the floor, on the couches, and on any open spaces. That is how I met "Lee" Wichit Maneevone. I inadvertently kicked this Thai student, who was sleeping under the dining-room table. He became a believer and with a talented wife, Miriam Redding Maneevone, has become a premier missionary leader in international student ministry.

It was a blessing to relate to the Redding children as they grew into responsible Christian adults. Having been reared in their early years in India, they had a worldview that few of their American counterparts held. It has been rewarding to see Mary Ellen and Bert; LeRoy and Carol; and Miriam and Wichit retain the missionary spirit and love of internationals. They are a testimony to the Redding devotion to Christ and the ministry.

Through the Orange County years, it was my privilege to be with the Reddings in "friend-raising" contacts and events. These were opportunities for me to support their groundwork in sharing the biblical vision of reaching people away from home.

Orange County was never the same after the Reddings left for other fields. We remember those special years as demonstrating the ultimate in home hospitality being used for "friendship evangelism." I praise the Lord for Elcho and Millie Redding. As pioneers in missionary ministry, their loving touch has changed the lives of important people around the world.

Rev. Hal W. Guffey, D. D.
President, International Students, Inc. (1967–1985)

Preface

When my husband, Elcho, and I gave ourselves to the Lord for His service, He led us to exciting, challenging, and sometimes difficult places—India, the Tibetan border, China, Japan, California, and the Pacific Northwest. Through it all, He faithfully provided for us.

God tells us, "And you shall remember that the Lord your God led you all the way" (Deuteronomy 8:2). "Only take heed to yourself, and diligently keep yourself, lest you forget the things your eyes have seen, and lest they depart from your heart all the days of your life. And teach them to your children and your grandchildren" (Deuteronomy 4:9). My children, grandchildren, and great-grandchildren inspired me to tell this story of God's faithfulness wherever He led us.

Surrounded by our family as we sang, "I will sing of the mercies of the Lord forever," Elcho died on September 24, 2006. His long battle with Parkinson's disease was over, and he was with the Lord whom he loved and served. While I miss him, I'm thankful he is no longer suffering. I know he is "absent from the body but present with the Lord" (2 Corinthians 5:8).

I enjoyed a wonderful life by his side. I want to share that story with you in this book, *Wherever He Leads*.

Millie Redding
July 2011

Acknowledgments

Elcho and I believed that the people who sent us out to the mission field were as important to the work as those of us who went. Many friends and churches have helped us at various times on this journey. In particular, I want to thank the churches which have stood with us, some since 1949: Basin Bible Church in Tulelake, California; Eagle Point Community Church in Eagle Point, Oregon; First Presbyterian Church in Yakima, Washington; New Community Church in Vista, California; Village Bible Church in Garden Grove, California; and Williams Community Church in Williams, Oregon.

I also want to thank Westminster Chapel in Bellevue, Washington, my church since 1993—especially former Missions Pastor Mark Carlson and Senior Pastor Gary Gulbranson, for their encouragement in the ministry to international students and for financial help with our medical expenses.

When I first started writing my journey, Agnes Lawless Elkins and Marilyn Baxter edited the first manuscript, and they've assisted with this final edition as well. Thank you, dear friends, for your invaluable help.

During the last years of Elcho's life, he needed someone with him at all times. While taking care of him, I put together six books for our children, grandchildren, and friends, containing pictures and narrative compiled from old letters and memories. Now with the invaluable help of Mastery Sheets, I have condensed them into one book. Mastery has helped me produce this book for publication. Thank you, Mastery, for your endless hours of work in helping to make this dream a reality. I also appreciate the illustrations that Michael Sheets created for this book. They add just the right touch.

I am sorry that Elcho never lived to see this book published. He was a godly husband, father, grandfather, friend, teacher, and missionary. I am thankful to have walked by his side for nearly six decades. I also want to thank our three children, Mary Ellen Kubo, Miriam Maneevone, and LeRoy Redding, for encouraging me to write this story of our lives.

"You will show me the path of life; in Your presence is fullness of joy; at Your right hand are pleasures forevermore" (Psalm 16:11).

Part 1
Early Years

1

Growing Up in Washington State

World War I was about to break out, and my grandparents' lives, along with the rest of the world, were about to change forever. In 1914 my grandpa Kooistra left on the last ship from Holland to the United States without a word to my grandma or their three children. My father Bill, the eldest child, was ten years old when his father left. Aunt Sadie, Dad's only sister, told me that Grandpa didn't tell the family he was going because he thought Grandma would talk him out of it, and she probably would have. Grandpa left funds with his brother to give to the family after he had gone, but my uncle used the funds for himself, leaving Grandma destitute. Friends and other family members helped her until after the war ended and Grandpa could send the funds to repay them.

When the war ended four years later in 1918, the family departed on the first ship leaving Holland for America. Grandpa met them as they cleared immigration at Ellis Island in New York City, and took them by train to Yakima, Washington, where he had purchased an apple orchard.

Meanwhile, my mother, Margaret Esther Clithero, was born in Concordia, Kansas, in 1905. When she was three years old, she came by train with her parents and siblings to Yakima, Washington, where they bought a hotel. Both families attended the First Presbyterian Church in Yakima, where my parents met as teenagers, and they married on my dad's twentieth birthday. They soon moved to Beaverton, Oregon, and Mom was only nineteen when I was born on July 6, 1925. By the time I

The Kooistra sisters: Sadie, Millie, Jeane, and Polly. I was very close to my sisters. We all accepted Jesus as our Lord in junior high.

was five years old, I had three younger sisters, Sadie, Jeane, and Polly. We were the "Kooistra sisters."

Those Great Depression days that began when I was four were difficult for our folks, but I didn't realize it. Although we were poor, we had delicious fresh fruit from our orchard and vegetables from our garden. Mom canned the fruit and made our clothes from feed sacks. I remember once when Dad took a truckload of fruit to Seattle to sell, but he was unable to sell it for even the cost of the boxes. He had to dump his load and bring back empty boxes. That was the first time I saw him cry.

Grandpa Clithero owned the Donelley Hotel in Yakima. Soon after the stock-market crash in 1929, he traded the hotel for a big home on Queen Anne Hill in Seattle where he moved his family. He then bought the Savoy and the Rehan Hotels in downtown Seattle.

Although our parents were not active in church themselves, they took us to Sunday school, vacation Bible school, and other church activities. Dad hauled supplies and helped at our church camp so we could attend. My sixth-grade Sunday-school teacher, Florence Hull, and her husband became good friends and were a great encouragement to me.

During my high-school years, my sisters and I joined the Victory Club, a group of Christian young people from all over the Yakima Valley. Our motto was "Victory in Jesus," and our theme verse was, "Thanks be to God, who gives us the victory through our Lord Jesus Christ" (1 Corinthians 15:57). We met Saturday nights at a radio studio and helped produce half-hour radio programs, consisting of singing, testimonies, and short Bible lessons or missionary talks. We stayed after the broadcasts for more singing, Bible teaching, and fellowship. My sisters and I, along with many others, dedicated ourselves to the Lord for Christian service.

We were eager to know missionaries who came to our church. Dick and Margaret Hillis and their four young children were a missionary family who had been forced to leave China. Margaret's parents were good friends of ours, and the Hillis family was staying with them until they knew what to do next. Dick and Margaret were particularly positive influences in my life. I was fascinated with their exciting stories and the work that they had been doing for the Lord in China. Dick was a great storyteller and a gifted devotional speaker. He could keep us spellbound as he expounded on short Bible themes, such as, "Here Am I, Send Me," "Standing in the Gap," and "Occupy 'Til I Come." He challenged us to be missionaries in our own high school. Crossing the seas wouldn't make us missionaries, but we should begin where we were. He urged us to give our lives to the Lord, then go where He wanted us to go, whether here or overseas.

Dick told us that when he was in China during his first term, he wrote a letter to his girlfriend, Margaret, in Yakima, asking her to marry him. Letters went by ship, and the answer didn't arrive. He thought she had rejected him. One day many months later, he found a letter from Margaret that had arrived while he'd been away and had been mixed in with other papers. When he opened it, he found she had accepted his proposal. But until he read the letter, he didn't know the good news. "That's like the Bible," Dick said. "If we don't open it and read it, we don't know God's good news."

When I was sixteen, our parents divorced. My three sisters and I were devastated, but Dick Hillis told us, "This is your parents' problem, not yours. Since you're believers, the Lord will see you through this difficult time." My sisters stayed with Mom, and I lived with Dad during my senior year of high school.

For several months, our Bible-class teacher was Helen Cope, a young single woman who had spent two years in China on special assignment. Now she was planning to go there as a full-time missionary. "I will probably never marry," she said. "There are few single male missionaries in China." I admired her willingness to abandon the idea of marriage. Two years after her arrival in China, she did in fact marry a fine missionary named Walter Jespersen. Later, in my retirement years after Helen's death, I became good friends with Walter and his daughters, Linda Reed and Margie Nichols, in Bellevue, Washington.

Even though the missionaries we met lived most of the time in foreign countries far from home

In the photo with me is Wanda Cline (Ackley). We were among eighteen young people who went with Dick Hillis on a Greyhound bus from Yakima, Washington, to Biola. Most of us went into full-time Christian work. Wanda and I remain close friends to this day.

and in difficult situations, they had peace, contentment, and purpose in their lives. I believed that Christ had chosen me to be His ambassador in a foreign land too, but how should I prepare? Those who had influenced my life had all studied at the Bible Institute of Los Angeles (Biola). So after graduating from high school, I decided to study there too.

That fall, Dick Hillis was going to teach in the missions department at Biola, so in August 1943, eighteen of us traveled with him on a Greyhound bus to attend that school.

2

Elcho's Early Years

Elcho's father, Samuel Jacob Redding, was born in Illinois in 1900. When Samuel was a boy, the family moved to Oregon.

Elcho's mother, Mary Estelle Rollins, was born in California, also in 1900. The Rollins family moved to Maine, where her father died tragically when she was thirteen years old. Two years later, her mother moved to California, where she married her second cousin, Elcho Zaire Fowle. They moved to Beaver Hill, Oregon, when Mary was seventeen.

Elcho's parents met as teenagers. After a short courtship, they eloped. They had five children—Dallas, Robert, Elcho, Sammie, and Miriam. Elcho was born September 2, 1924, at home in Grants Pass, Oregon.

Elcho and his siblings went to church with his mother, who sang in the choir. He always admired her and thought she was the prettiest lady up there. Since his father was a baker and worked nights in a bakery, he didn't go to church. Each day he brought home a loaf of bread. Elcho's mother kept a pot of beans on the stove, and the boys had bean sandwiches for their school lunches.

One day when Elcho was nine years old, he saw a Bible in the window of the local secondhand store. He went in and asked the lady how much it cost. When she realized his disappointment at not having any money, she asked him, "Does your mother can? If she does, bring me a jar of her canned tomatoes." Happily, he hurried home and, with his mother's approval, gave a jar to the lady to buy his first Bible.

Elcho began taking accordion lessons when he was twelve years old. He learned quickly and played in many talent contests, usually winning first prize. He earned money picking blackberries and hops to buy his first accordion. When he was fourteen, he performed in a talent show where George Burns and Gracie Allen were the judges. They presented him with the first prize of fifty dollars—a lot of money for a teenager in 1938.

Later, Elcho's parents bought a dairy farm in Eagle Point, Oregon. He and his brothers milked the cows and helped with chores.

The summer he turned fifteen, someone invited him to an American Sunday School Union Bible camp at Lake of the Woods, Oregon. Because he had chores to do, he gave his brother Robert his newborn calf for doing his share of the work so he could attend camp. Robert agreed, and Elcho went to camp, where he accepted Christ as his Savior. When he asked the young leaders how they knew so much about the Bible, they said they attended the Bible Institute of Los Angeles (Biola). From then on, he was determined to go there when he finished high school. Oh, yes, Elcho's cow had twins, so he also had a calf to sell!

The summer after he graduated from high school, Elcho worked for Ginger Rogers on her Rogue River Ranch. He also played his accordion in a dance band on weekends. Ginger's mother wanted him to continue milking their cows and helping on their ranch. He was tempted to stay for the good money, but he had planned to go to Biola and study the Bible.

One day, as he pondered his decision, he stepped off a street curb and saw a bright-colored tract in the gutter. He picked it up and read, "Seek first the kingdom of God and His righteousness, and all these things shall be added to you" (Matthew 6:33). He knew what he should do. Soon after that, he took the bus to Los Angeles to study at Biola.

3

Meeting Elcho at Biola

One day in my second semester at Biola, I saw a handsome young man talking with some of my friends in the lobby. Eagerly, I joined them, and they introduced me to Elcho Redding.

In the course of conversation, he asked, "Can anyone here play a little pump organ?"

No one answered.

"You don't have to be a good musician," he continued, "just be able to play simple hymns."

"What's it for?" I asked.

"A street meeting."

"Sounds interesting to me," I responded. "I'll give it a try." This would be my chance to get to know this young man, I thought.

That Sunday afternoon, Elcho and I walked to Fifth and Wall, the sleaziest part of Los Angeles. I had seen hobos jumping on freight trains in Yakima during the Great Depression, but I had never seen drunks and homeless people on the streets like I saw that day on Skid Row.

When we arrived, a group of old people gathered around Elcho. "This is Millie Kooistra," he said. Much to my surprise, he added, "She's going to take my place today because I have to sing in a church with a men's quartet." Then he turned and walked off.

A few days later, Elcho played the hymn, "Great Is Thy Faithfulness," on his accordion for the school's chapel service. I had never heard the accordion played so beautifully, and that song became my favorite.

Elcho approached me a few days later after class. "Some of us are going to see the live broadcast of the *Old-Fashioned Revival Hour* in Long Beach," he said. "Would you like to go?"

"I'd love to," I replied. "I used to listen to that program in Yakima."

We rode a red trolley car to Long Beach and enjoyed hearing the quartet sing, Rudy Atwood play the piano, and Dr. Charles Fuller preach. It was the first time we'd been in such a large auditorium for a Christian service.

Our friendship grew as Elcho and I became more involved in the Student Missionary Union at school. On Wednesday evenings, we heard missionaries from all over the world or representatives of mission organizations. After listening to speakers, we went to prayer groups. Elcho and I divided our time between the China group and the India group.

One day, Elcho's roommate, Bill Ackley, asked him to type a term paper about Tibet for him. Part of Bill's research included an article from an issue of the *National Geographic* magazine about Tibet that inspired Elcho to want to go there. To me, Tibet was the mystical, hidden utopian place of Shangri-La depicted in James Hilton's novel and the movie, *Lost Horizon.*

Since Elcho and I were in the same classes, we often studied and ate our evening meal together in the school cafeteria. After dinner, we would study, and we sometimes played miniature golf or walked to the famous Biltmore Hotel for butterscotch sundaes. During the noon hours, we both worked in downtown upscale restaurants. I was fired from my waitress job in a very exclusive restaurant because I refused to treat the black guests differently from the white ones. I then got a job in a stationery store that I enjoyed until my graduation.

In those days, Biola was in downtown Los Angeles at Fifth and Hope Streets, and we enjoyed strolling past large department stores, looking at the latest fashions and windows decorated for various seasons and holidays. On Saturdays for lunch, we often went to Clifton's, an exotic cafeteria, or to a little French restaurant. Not only was the food reasonably priced, but we also could talk in a quiet booth.

Once we went ice-skating. As I struggled to stay upright, Elcho smiled and said, "My ex-girlfriend was the champion ice skater for the state of Wisconsin." Just then, I took a big tumble. That was our first and last ice-skating date.

We attended Youth for Christ rallies and various activities at large churches downtown. One day, we visited the famous Angelus Temple and saw evangelist Aimee Semple McPherson's dramatic theatrical style— very different from my Presbyterian background.

Elcho was handsome, and I was falling in love with him. But in those years, Biola had an "eighteen-inch rule." That meant that the young men and women could not be closer to each other than eighteen inches. We and other Biola couples used to walk hand-in-hand while we window-shopped or came home from an activity, but a few blocks from school, we walked apart. Teachers were on patrol as the eleven o'clock curfew neared.

During his years at Biola, Elcho played his accordion and sang in quartets on many Biola gospel teams. He also sang in the concert choir, the men's chorus, and the men's quartet. He taught Mexican Sunday-school classes and helped in the youth departments of several churches. In addition, he assisted Hubert Mitchell (author of the hymn, "He Giveth More Grace") in the Union Rescue Mission, where they occasionally played accordion duets.

I sang in the Biola glee club, trained with the Child Evangelism organization, taught a Bible class at juvenile hall and a sixth-grade girls' Sunday-school class in a Chinese church. I took the girls on picnics, to visit Biola, and to the zoo. One of those little girls, Dora Wong, has remained my good friend through the years.

One late afternoon in Santa Monica, Elcho and I sat on a park bench and watched the sun sink in a blaze of crimson and gold over the Pacific

Ocean. He put his arm around me, looked into my eyes, and said, "Millie, I love you. Will you marry me?"

"Oh, yes, I will," I said. "I've loved you for a long time."

He put his hand in his pocket, pulled out a small, velvet-covered box, and handed it to me.

I opened it to find a beautiful ring with three diamonds. "Oh, Elcho, it's lovely!"

As he put it on my finger, he said, "I designed it myself—just for you." Oblivious to bystanders, we sealed our engagement with an embrace.

By this time, I was studying at Biola's School of Missionary Medicine, and Elcho was in his last year of Biola's School of Theology.

Elcho and I courted for most of our time at Biola.

He helped in a church in Venice, California. Although he had little money, he decided one Sunday morning to put all the money in his wallet in the offering plate. He had memorized the Scripture verse, "My God shall supply all your need according to His riches in glory by Christ Jesus" (Philippians 4:19). He wanted to see if that promise was really true.

After the service, he walked, penniless, to the bus stop. He looked on the sidewalk and gutter for the needed dime for the fare but found none. "Dear Lord," he prayed, "here comes the bus! Please help me."

Just then a man ran towards him, calling, "Elcho! Elcho! Here, this is for you." The man handed him a five-dollar bill and shook his hand. "Thanks for all your help in the church. God bless you."

"Thank you, sir," he said, then climbed onto the bus. When he sat down, he prayed silently, "Lord, you really do mean what you say, don't you? Thanks for meeting my need."

Sometimes the need was met in a different way. Elcho met every morning with six other students for prayer. One senior couldn't graduate unless he finished paying his school bills, so he asked for prayer about that.

When Elcho went to the accounting office to pay his own bill, the clerk looked up his records and said, "You don't owe anything more. You're all paid up." Elcho was surprised but grateful. So, while he was at the office, he anonymously put money into his friend's account.

The next morning at prayer meeting, his friend reported that the Lord had provided, and he would be able to graduate after all. The others rejoiced with him.

Later that day, Elcho picked up his mail and found a bill for his board and room. He hurried to the accounting office. "I'd like to ask about this bill," he said. "When I was here yesterday, the girl told me I was paid up."

The clerk checked his records. "I'm sorry," she said. "The other girl must have looked at the wrong account when she told you that. You do owe money."

Elcho went to the superintendent of men and told him the story. The kind gentleman allowed him an extension.

The next week was the semester break. Elcho's younger brother Sammie came from Oregon to go with him for a week of special meetings in Globe, Arizona.

Since the pastor, Owen Douglas, had been Elcho's classmate at Biola, and they had sung in the Biola men's quartet together, he asked Elcho to help with the music. During that week, Sammie accepted Jesus as his Savior. At the close of the meetings, the church gave Elcho a check for twice the amount of his bill at Biola.

During the summer break of his senior year at Biola, Elcho went home to Eagle Point, Oregon. The family dog had had pups.

After our graduation in 1947, Elcho went with his roommate Everett Chambers to work on a mission in the back hills of Kentucky for the summer.

I returned home to Yakima to work as a practical nurse and to prepare for our wedding.

4

Beginning Our Journey Together

On August 22, 1947, we were married in the First Presbyterian Church of Yakima, surrounded by family and friends. Our sisters and brothers were our attendants, and the bridesmaids were lovely in their pastel-colored long dresses. Senior Pastor Dr. David Ferry performed the ceremony. He had known both sets of my grandparents since the early 1920s and had married my parents twenty-three years earlier.

We had a four-day honeymoon in a cabin in the Cascade Mountains near Yakima. Our happiness was complete. The Evangelical Alliance Mission (TEAM) had accepted us as candidates to go to the Tibetan border. Because we were both just twenty-two years old and recent Biola graduates, the mission asked us to get practical experience before we could go.

Central Presbyterian Church in Des Moines, Iowa, hired Elcho as youth director. When we drove to this assignment, we stopped by Yellowstone National Park for a couple of days on the way. Working with the junior and senior high school young people was a happy experience.

On Father's Day, June 20, 1948, Mary Ellen joined our family. That day was not only significant because of her birth but also because Peter Marshall, chaplain of the United States Senate, spoke at our church in Des Moines. The church asked us to stay on for another year, but we knew that if we were going to get to the mission field, we had to keep preparing for that.

Elcho had been having ear trouble for several years. An ear specialist, who was a member of the church, arranged for him to get a new radical mastoid operation at the University of Iowa Medical Hospital. Since Elcho was willing to let student doctors observe the surgery, all expenses were paid. He had to stay in the hospital for another month for recuperation and observation. Three-month-old Mary Ellen and I went to Yakima to stay with my dad.

When Elcho was released, he joined us, and we made plans to go with TEAM to the Tibetan border. Since we had to raise all our support before we could go, we presented our vision to friends, Sunday-school classes, and churches in Washington, Oregon, and California. While support slowly trickled in, we helped in my dad's day-care center to pay for our room and board.

Then we learned that I was pregnant again. Before my seventh month, my contractions began. I was hospitalized for ten days on complete bed rest in order to save the baby. When I was released, we moved to a small basement apartment in my mother's home.

Money was scarce, and we wondered if we would ever get to the mission field. However, the most important thing was to save our baby. I stayed in bed, and Elcho cooked and looked after Mary Ellen. Miriam Frances was born on July 22, 1949. "God gave you this baby girl," our Christian doctor told us. "Medically speaking, I didn't think we'd be able to save her." As the psalmist said, "Behold, children are a heritage from the Lord" (Psalm 127:3).

A month after Miriam was born, T. J. Bach, director of TEAM, interviewed us at a church in Yakima. "How much support have you raised so far?" he asked.

"Not nearly enough," Elcho answered.

Dr. Bach pulled a five-dollar bill from his wallet, held it up high, and asked the congregation to pray with him. "Dear Lord, bless this five dollars as you blessed the loaves and fishes many years ago. Multiply it to meet the needs of this family so they can minister for you in that dark land. In Jesus' mighty name, amen." Then he handed the five-dollar bill to Elcho.

God answered that prayer. Within the next nine months, all our support requirements and passage to the Tibetan border were at TEAM headquarters. Elcho was ordained as a minister of the gospel, and we were commissioned as TEAM missionaries in the Calvary Church of Placentia, California. God had multiplied that five-dollar bill.

Elcho called TEAM headquarters and talked to an official. "We're ready to go! What's next?"

"I'm so sorry, but because of a critical housing shortage, we're not sending any more families to the Tibetan border right now," the official said. "Would you be willing to go to India instead?"

"I guess so." Elcho was hesitant. "Let us pray about this."

As we prayed and discussed the matter, we knew God had led us this far. We telephoned the mission and said that we would go to India.

The official said, "Great! A freighter is leaving for India from San Francisco, California, in a few weeks. Can you be ready?"

"Yes, we can!"

Now we had to pack our clothes and supplies then say our good-byes. We distributed prayer cards with our picture and this verse, "As his part is who goes down to the battle, so shall his part be who stays by the supplies; they shall share alike" (1 Samuel 30:24).

Our family picture was in the July 1950 issue of TEAM magazine with this testimony:

PRAY FOR US

MR. AND MRS. ELCHO REDDING
MARY ELLEN AND MARIAM

The Evangelical Alliance Mission
2839 W. McLean
Chicago, Illinois

"But as his part is that goeth down to battle, so shall his part be that tarrieth by the stuff: they shall part alike."   I Samuel 30:24

Field Address
RASUL BAGH
Nasik, India

This was our prayer card as we set out for India in 1950.

He who created all things, even giving us new life in the Lord Jesus Christ, has now called us to tell others of the new creation, which is to be had in Him. Knowing Him as Lord of our lives, we are persuaded, even as Paul, that the gospel of Christ is truly "the power of God to salvation for everyone who believes" (Romans 1:16). Like Paul, we have asked ourselves, "How shall they believe in Him of whom they have not heard? And how shall they hear without a preacher?" (Romans 10:14). Isaiah 6:8 says, "Also I heard the voice of the Lord, saying, 'Whom shall I send, and who will go for us?' Then said I, 'Here am I; send me.'" So, we go.

Part 2

India

5

Adjusting to India

As we sailed under the San Francisco Bay Bridge and watched the shoreline of California disappear that beautiful June day in 1950, we were excited to be on our way to India. Yet, standing on the deck of the freighter with our two little girls, we had mixed emotions. While we were glad to be going, we were sad to say good-bye to our family and friends for six long years.

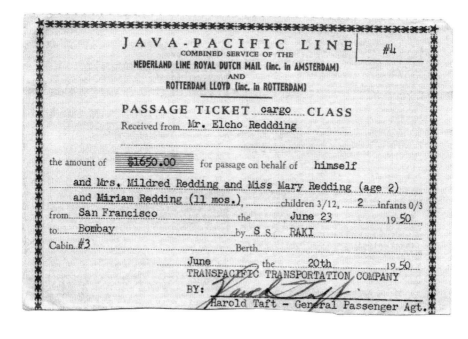

We celebrated Mary Ellen's second birthday on the day we sailed. Miriam's first birthday and my twenty-fifth birthday were also celebrated aboard ship as we traveled across the Pacific Ocean. Because we were on a freighter, our journey took two months, with the ship stopping in Manila, Singapore, Jakarta, Bali, Borneo, and Ceylon before reaching Bombay (modern-day Mumbai).

Only twelve passengers were on the freighter, including a veteran missionary couple that had spent twenty years in India. They found it difficult to leave their two teenage sons behind in the States for the first time.

We ate with the captain, his officers, and our fellow passengers. After fifteen days at sea, we docked in Manila. We visited missionary friends on the island of Luzon for three days. When we returned to Manila, Elcho took our cabin boy, Secup, to town to get him something special. As they rode along in a rickshaw, Secup smiled and pointed to a big prickly melon, indicating that was what he wanted. They stopped, and Elcho bought two melons—one for him and one for us. The melon was jackfruit, a foul-smelling but edible fruit with cream-colored pulp. Secup was glad when we tasted it, made faces, and gave the rest of ours to him. Later in India, we learned to like it.

In Indonesia, we saw the last ship leave with Indonesian war brides going to Holland. In Bali, Elcho bought two wooden hand-carved Balinese figurines for my twenty-fifth birthday. Those figurines haven't changed at all with the passing of the years, and I still enjoy them in my home today. When the ship stopped at the different ports, we went sightseeing but returned to the ship to eat and sleep. As we traveled from port to port, we read, wrote letters, and played games. It was a good transition from living in America to living a very different lifestyle in India.

Early on Sunday morning, August 20, 1950, we docked in Bombay. This was just one week after the signing of the constitution of the new Republic of India and exactly three years since England had granted independence to this country.

On our first day there, a missionary friend took us to Malabar Hill, where we had a panoramic view of the city and Marine Drive with its line of expensive apartments on the Arabian Sea. This is also called "the Queen's Necklace," because lights along the shore sparkle like jewels. Going up the hill, we passed large, beautiful homes. At the top are the Hanging Gardens, with shrubs artistically trimmed to look like big animals. Coming down the hill, we passed the Parsi "Tower of Silence." We were told that because Parsis are followers of Zoroaster, they believe in the purity of the elements (earth, water, fire, air). Since they do not want to pollute these elements, they do not cremate or bury their dead. Instead, they place corpses on cliffs, and let vultures do the rest.

Back in the city, we saw people cooking, bathing, eating, and sleeping on sidewalks and under bridges. Bombay is truly a city of contrasts. The richest and the poorest live close together.

That same evening, we were taken to visit the "fire god." Hindus especially worship this god at death, since they burn dead bodies on pyres. When we arrived, two bodies were burning. For another pyre, workers had piled twelve big logs on top of each other and placed a man's dead body in the middle. Then his oldest son lit the fire. We were told that a man's wife used to be put on the fire (called *suttee*) with her dead husband. Even though we were assured that this was no longer done, we later heard stories to the contrary. Through the years, we also heard numerous tales of women who died under mysterious circumstances. Many times the wife's sari "caught fire" while she was cooking, or she took poison "by mistake." This usually happened when the husband wanted out of the marriage.

Driving through Bombay to the home of our missionary hosts, we passed through an area where we saw hundreds of fancily dressed girls sitting in cage-like cubicles waiting to be "bought" for the night. We were saddened to see these young girls in prostitution, people living on the streets, and beggars everywhere.

The next day, our senior missionary helped us clear our goods through customs and load them onto the trailer of his Jeep. He brought along sandwiches and bottles of boiled water. But first, we stopped in a bazaar and purchased mosquito netting, water canteens, fruit, and vegetables.

We piled into the Jeep and set off on the one hundred twenty-mile journey to our new home in Nasik. We passed bullock carts loaded with people and supplies, cows strolling down the middle of the road, people walking with heavy loads on their heads, two or three people riding on one bicycle, and brightly painted trucks called lorries. There were no rest stops, so our driver periodically stopped the Jeep and yelled, "Men on the left, ladies on the right!"

After a hot, dusty, six-hour Jeep trip, we were glad to get to our new home at Rasul Bagh in the city of Nasik. The mission compound consisted of two old thatched-roofed bungalows. We lived in one with a married

The bullock cart was very important to families in India.

Rasul Bagh in Nasik City was our first home in India. We and ten other TEAM missionaries lived, studied Marathi, and began our missionary careers under the eyes of the senior missionaries.

couple and their three-year-old son. Another couple lived in the second bungalow with three single men.

Our living quarters were two small bedrooms and a so-called bathroom for our private use. Actually, the bathroom was just a small room with whitewashed walls and a gray stone floor. A faucet in the wall about eight inches from the floor provided cold running water. A washbasin sat on a table, and a portable commode stood in the corner of the room. A small tin tub served as our bathtub, and we poured dirty water down a hole in the floor. A sweeper—the lowest in the Hindu caste system—emptied our commode twice a day. Sweepers do the dirtiest work of India—sweeping streets and emptying portable potties. We heated water in a charcoal burner outside and carried it in buckets to the kitchen and bathroom.

The bungalow had stone floors, whitewashed mud walls, and a burlap ceiling. We shared two rooms in the middle and the adjoining kitchen with the Johnson family. One room had wicker furniture for our living room, and the other had a big table and two wooden cupboards, one for food supplies and the other for dishes. Since there was no electricity, we used kerosene lamps for lights and cooked on charcoal and kerosene stoves. The kitchen looked much like the bathroom, with a stone floor and a hole in the corner to pour dirty water. The kitchen had two wooden tables—one for basins to wash the dishes and the other for the charcoal and kerosene stoves.

We slept under mosquito nets with big flashlights next to our pillows. The netting kept out mosquitoes, rats, scorpions, and centipedes. When we got out of bed, we checked our slippers to make sure no creatures were in them. In the house, we followed the Indian custom of going barefoot because the cool stone felt good on hot days. In the evenings, the stone floor was cooler, so we usually wore slippers.

Outside we wore sandals called *chappales*. One time, when Elcho was traveling in the Jeep, he and his companions came to a river crossing the road. The men told him to get out and walk. He said, "Wait until I get my *chapatis* on." Everyone laughed because he'd used the word for bread instead of the word for sandals.

On our third wedding anniversary, all ten of our fellow missionary-language students gave us a surprise party. The next week we began studying the Marathi language along with them.

Mary Ellen and Miriam adjusted well to India. They loved playing with their dolls and having tea parties. The Johnson's young boy, Phil, had a little Jeep, and the girls took turns sitting in it and making noises like a car. They also liked to ride in his red wagon when we pulled them. Mary Ellen enjoyed riding her tricycle with her doll on the front of it.

We ate differently than we had in the United States. Fortunately, we all liked Indian food. In the interest of good health, we had a rule that if we could not peel it or boil it, we didn't eat or drink it. We ate lots of curry, rice, and different kinds of lentils. Indians told us that curry wasn't good unless it was so spicy hot that it made your eyes and nose run. Chilies were a good source of vitamin C.

Since wheat was plentiful in Nasik, we made our own whole-wheat bread with dry yeast from home—as well as chapatis—and ate lots of it. We couldn't buy flour, but we bought wheat, cleaned it, and took it to the mill to be freshly ground. Finely ground, it was flour; coarsely ground, it was hot cereal for breakfast.

We bought water-buffalo milk, and after we boiled and cooled it, cream came to the top. It made good whipped cream, butter, yogurt, and cottage cheese. We boiled the milk, and when it was warm, added a starter of yogurt, stirring it well. We left it covered for about twelve hours then our yogurt was ready. By wrapping yogurt in a gauze cloth and hanging it from a peg for several hours, we made cottage cheese. We bought raw brown sugar, called *gurl*, and made delicious syrup. Nothing tasted better than gurl, whipped buffalo-milk cream, and chapatis. We boiled all our drinking water and poured it into a terra-cotta container to keep it cold and clean.

We missionaries had to buy some supplies in Bombay. We left early in the morning by either train or Jeep, did our shopping, and made it home by nightfall. If any of us saw big tins of cheese, powdered milk, or peanut butter left from army-surplus supplies of World War II, we would buy and sell any that our families didn't need to other missionaries. It never entered our heads that the tinned food might be too outdated for us to eat.

Bananas were plentiful, tasty, cheap, and came in different varieties. We could buy four dozen bananas for the same price as one roll of toilet paper. The end of the hot season was a good time to arrive in India because mangoes, papayas, guavas, and custard apples were in season.

One of our favorite foods was *corunjis*. This was a mixture of cream of wheat, raisins, poppy seeds, freshly ground cloves, cinnamon, white cardamom, and sugar. It was enclosed in a thin wheat crust and deep-fried. Although our diet was adequate, parcels from home with cake mixes, Jell-O®, tuna fish, and Spam® were special treats.

Along with other new missionaries in Nasik, we studied Marathi, the official language of Bombay State and one of the fourteen official languages listed in the newly constructed Indian constitution. India has over sixteen hundred languages and dialects. Since India had only been independent from England for three years, most educated people spoke English—the official language during the British rule of India. The Indian National Congress, which had led the fight for independence, made Hindi the official language, but most people in western India didn't speak Hindi. In the various states, the official language of the state was used.

We began our Marathi language studies the week after we arrived. We learned to speak phonetically using English characters, and after a six-month examination in February, we learned the Marathi script. Then we went to a hill station called Mahableshwar, where we attended the Marathi Language School during March, April, and May. We entered into a concentrated, intensive study, with exams at the end of May. Most of us stayed there for an additional two weeks until the monsoon rains came and cooled the plains, since hot season on the plains was unbearable.

We each had two private lessons every day for five days a week with our *pandit* ("teacher"), who gave us lots of homework. We often took blankets or comfortable chairs into our garden and studied under the shade of trees. We hired Gracebai, a fine Christian Indian girl, to watch our little girls while I studied. When Gracebai tired of walking around with Miriam, our active child, she would brush her blond curly hair to keep her quiet. Mary Ellen quietly played with dolls or looked at her books for hours. Because Gracebai was so good with the children, I was able to study the language and not worry about them.

Ashuk Tilock, my pandit, came from an outstanding Christian family, but he was neither a Christian nor a Hindu. Elcho's pandit, Choudari, was a strong Hindu. As the culture of India is largely Hindu, Elcho learned much more than the language. One day when Elcho was having a lesson in our living room, the pandit asked him where we kept our gods. He was

Gracebai took care of Miriam and Mary Ellen while we were in Marathi language classes.

convinced that we hid them in the fireplace. Elcho took him all around the house, explaining that we didn't worship idols but the true God in heaven.

Although Gracebai didn't speak English, the girls communicated with her quickly. I also learned to give her simple requests: "Don't let them drink anything but boiled drinking water or tea." "Please wash their hands and yours often." "They can eat this or that," or "Please don't do anything except to watch them at all times." I don't know if it was because I'm a woman or because I needed to communicate with Gracebai about the girls, but I learned the language faster than Elcho. He waited until he could speak it perfectly. I just talked and made mistakes.

A few weeks after I'd been studying with my pandit, I ventured, "Sib bah teen het." ("My husband has three brothers.") He laughed and said that I had told him that Elcho had three arms. The word for brothers is *bhau*, and the word for arm is *bahu*. The accent is still on the *a*. Another time, I thought I'd asked another teacher if he wanted fresh corn on the cob (*mukern*). I was perplexed by his embarrassment until I was informed that I'd asked him for a kiss (*mukka*). Many words are pronounced almost the same but have different meanings.

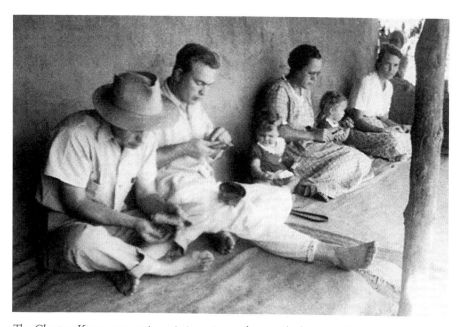

The Clayton Kents, our senior missionaries, took us with them to a home where we were introduced to rural Indian hospitality.

Both Mary Ellen and Miriam learned to speak Marathi faster than we did. They enjoyed visiting Gracebai's living quarters on our compound. She sometimes made them chapatis hot from her stove. They thought she made the best Indian tea. After we got a gas refrigerator, they took her some ice cream. It was so cold that she put it on the stove to warm it up.

Like everyone else in India, we rested after lunch. We spent this quiet time with the girls, often playing Chinese checkers or chess. If the children were sleeping, we had our quiet time with the Lord or studied for our afternoon Marathi lesson. About three o'clock, we enjoyed a traditional afternoon tea, a leftover from the colonial rule.

We had been encouraged to take pictures and write down our thoughts soon after we arrived to record things that seemed strange to us because soon enough everything would seem quite natural. This proved to be good advice. Although we were happy, we did get homesick for family, friends, and Western culture. We sometimes talked about how we would enjoy sitting in a tub of hot water or to have a refreshing shower, rather than to pour water over us, cup by cup. A flush toilet, electric lights, a telephone, a sofa, and overstuffed furniture would have been nice too. Nevertheless, we were glad to be learning the language and culture of India.

6

Beginning Missionary Work

Nasik, the city where we lived in western India, is on the Godavari River. It is the legendary home of Rama, a hero in Hinduism. Hindus believe the "holy" waters of the Godavari River cleanse a person who bathes in them from sin. During certain religious festivals, thousands of people flocked there to wash, to be cleansed from sin, and to gain merit with the gods. The river is lined with idols and temples containing many kinds of images that are worshipped. These idols can be images of men, animals, or just painted orange stones. Nasik has Hindu, Buddhist, and Jain temples. During our stay in 1950–51, there were no evangelical Christian churches in Nasik, but soon after we left, a young pastor named Lazarus Padali founded the Evangelical Alliance Christian Church with the help of our fellow TEAM missionary and close friend, Les Buhler. It continues to be a light in the Nasik area to this day.

We often went to the Godavari River and watched people washing clothes, bathing, and drinking the water. There were often as many cows as people. Cows are considered holy by many in India, so the animals can usually eat whatever they want and go wherever they want to go.

Followers of the Jain religion surprised us. With short brooms, they swept the road before them as they walked so as not to step on ants or any other creatures. They wore white robes and surgical masks over their mouths so they wouldn't accidentally swallow insects. We heard about a

Jain follower who committed suicide after seeing all the living organisms in a drop of water under a microscope.

Nasik was a fairly literate city. Many people spoke fluent English because they had been educated in English-speaking private schools. The city was important politically too. Many were turning to Communism, and the Indian Congress Party wanted to win over the people of Nasik. Pandit Jawaharlal Nehru became the first prime minister when India obtained its independence from Britain. Soon after our first Christmas in India, the Congress session of India met in Nasik. Some twenty thousand people passed by the road in front of our home on their way to meetings. We put up a big Marathi sign above the green hedge bordering our compound with this Scripture verse: "For the wages of sin is death, but the gift of God is eternal life in Christ Jesus our Lord" (Romans 6:23).

While these meetings were going on, an Indian pastor took Elcho, other missionary men, and some Indian Christians to town every day. They sang, preached, gave out tracts, sold Gospels, and took care of the loudspeaker equipment.

One afternoon while Elcho was in town, Pandit Jawaharlal Nehru rode slowly by in his elegant chauffeur-driven convertible. He waved and smiled at Elcho. My husband came home excited that he had seen this leading Indian statesman. Nehru was reelected when the Congress Party won India's first election in 1952.

A couple of months after we arrived in Nasik, Phillip Johnson and Mary Ellen both became very sick. At first, our fine English doctor thought they had malaria but later diagnosed it as polio. Apparently, a live virus was in the vaccine of their recent polio shots. Thankfully, they had light cases, and after about three weeks, they felt better. Mary Ellen had complications in her feet, but corrective surgeries when she was seven and eleven years old were successful.

Several months before we had arrived in India, Lois, the eight-year-old daughter of missionaries, had died in Nasik. With the insurance money, her parents arranged for a mission building to be built in Dindori, a city about twenty miles away. On Saturdays, Elcho and other missionary men helped construct the building. When it was completed, a dedication service was held, and Indian leaders and missionaries came from each of our twenty mission stations. That day, we not only dedicated the building but also our families and ourselves afresh to the Lord.

None of us knew how long we'd be able to work in the vast land of India. Mission leaders told us to work and plan like we had a lifetime to do so but to keep our suitcases packed. Although today no missionaries live in Dindori, it has a church with a fine Indian pastor. The building we dedicated now houses a Christian boys' hostel where village boys live and go to school. God is faithful.

Soon after we arrived, Elcho had to go to Bombay on mission business. He stayed in a cheap hotel there. As he checked in, the man at the desk told him that if he needed anything to just stick his head out and call, "Boy!" When he got to his room, he needed a restroom and couldn't find one. So he stuck his head out and called, "Boy!"

A toothless old man with a turban loosely tied around his head shuffled down the hall.

Elcho asked, "Boy?"

The old man said, "Me, boy."

Then Elcho told him in English that he needed to use the lavatory.

Obviously, the "boy" didn't understand. Finally, he grinned and motioned Elcho to follow him. They arrived at the elevator, and the man said, "Americans call it 'lavatory.' British call it 'lift.'"

We tried to put our Marathi to use as soon as we could. After a few lessons, we went to the Nasik bazaar to buy supplies. We asked the shopkeeper, "Hey kidna peyse ahae?" ("How much is this?")

The shopkeeper answered, "Engrege semzet nahi." ("I don't speak English.") That didn't do much for our self-confidence. When people did understand us, we were encouraged.

The best thing we had brought from home was a battery-operated phonograph and Marathi and English records from Gospel Recordings. We had brought our favorite long-play records too and especially enjoyed listening to George Beverly Shea sing.

Every Thursday evening, about twenty-five Christian Indian young people came to our home early so they could listen to records. Either they or their parents worked in the English mission hospital of the Balapur Children's Orphanage near our home.

The students liked learning English songs and teaching us simple Marathi choruses. We let Mary Ellen and Miriam stay up on Thursday nights, as they enjoyed singing too. After a simple Bible lesson, we ended the evening with refreshments. When Elcho and I were first married, we agreed that we wanted our home to be open for entertaining, and that became our lifestyle.

Elcho and other male missionary language students often went with an Indian evangelist or senior missionary to witness in various villages. They traveled by open Jeep over dusty, rough, narrow roads. Upon arrival in a village, they'd visit with the people awhile and then would ask the headman for permission to have a meeting. Usually, someone would bring a rope cot for the men to sit on in the courtyard. Then others served them hot cups of Indian *chai* (tea with milk, sugar, and spices boiled together).

After setting up a loudspeaker and playing music to attract a crowd, one of the missionaries and the Indian evangelist spoke. Then the men passed out tracts and sold Gospels cheaply. If they took a wind-up phonograph, they played Marathi records. Often in the evenings, they ran a projector from the Jeep battery and showed slides on the life of Christ.

One day when Elcho and Les Buhler were in town, they met the principal of an exclusive English-speaking boys' school. He was very friendly and invited them and some of their friends to come to the school for an assembly. Elcho played his accordion and sang in a men's quartet. Using flannelgraph figures, they told the story of Nicodemus. After the meeting, the boys crowded around the young Americans to get their autographs, to see the flannelgraph scenes up close, to touch the accordion, and to get acquainted. From this beginning, the principal invited the men back on a regular basis. They taught the boys Scripture choruses and told Bible stories with the flannelgraph. They also showed Moody Institute of Science slides on *The God of Creation*.

Elcho and Les often passed out tracts at the bazaar. One day, armed with one thousand tracts, they started distributing them. But a mob of people ripped the tracts out of their hands in their eagerness to get them. The unruly crowd blocked traffic, and the police asked Elcho and Les to move to a quieter part of town. Within an hour, the thousand tracts were gone.

We in TEAM offered a free Bible-correspondence course on the life of Christ written by Don Hillis, Dick's twin brother. At first, it was just in English, Marathi, and Hindi, but later it was translated into other languages. Soon, over five thousand people enrolled. We understand that it is still popular in India today. Who knows how many have studied this Bible course over the years?

In the fall of 1950, Youth for Christ had a ten-day crusade in Bombay, and Elcho joined the team. Every night they held a big rally, and during the daytime, Indian Christians and missionaries canvassed the area to invite people.

During the rallies, Elcho stayed in the home of Sundaribai and her nephew, Sundar Singh Amalik. Along with the family, Elcho slept on a mat on the floor. They sat on the floor for meals and ate delicious Indian food with their fingers. Sundar Singh and Elcho went out on the streets each day to invite people to the rallies. One day, people threw stones at them, and they left that part of town in a hurry.

While Elcho stayed in the Amalik home, Sundar and his aunt, Sundaribai, told him stories of God's faithfulness to them. A few years earlier, Sundar's father was preaching Christ in a village during the Hindu *holi shimga* festival. People told him to stop preaching, or they would throw him on a big bonfire. He didn't stop preaching, so they caught him up to throw him on the fire, but one man insisted that they let him go. As Sundar's father's clothes were already burning, he ran away naked.

While at the Bombay Youth for Christ Crusade, Elcho met C. K. Kolady, a vibrant Indian Christian railway official. He invited us to visit him and his wife in their home. We became close friends, and our families spent many happy times together over the next few years.

Shortly after the meetings, we went to Amalner, our mission headquarters in western India, for our first TEAM conference with seventy-eight missionaries and twenty-five children. More than half of us were in language studies. We had good times of singing, Bible study, prayer, sharing meals, and talking about our experiences in our first months in India. We all stayed in tents, and Indians cooked food over big fires in the largest pans we had ever seen.

We also talked with the field committee about our adjustments, our language learning, and where we thought we'd fit into the work after we finished our language study. We enjoyed talking to Don Hillis, who had also been our teacher at Biola along with his twin brother, Dick, especially since he had encouraged us to come to India.

Because the TEAM mission was previously called the Scandinavian Alliance Mission, many senior missionaries were from Sweden, Norway, and Denmark. They loved to sing, especially such songs as, "He the Pearly Gates Will Open," and they enjoyed Elcho's accordion accompaniment.

The conference closed with a communion service. For wine, we used juice boiled from raisins, and for bread, we used broken pieces of chapatis.

We spent our first Christmas in India with missionaries in Pimpalner, the largest and oldest mission station. When we arrived on Christmas Eve, we were surprised to see about three hundred Indian people pouring into the compound on foot or riding bullock carts. That night, students from mission schools in various villages put on a program in the church, which lasted until midnight. Then at four thirty on Christmas morning, three different groups caroled for us with Indian tunes and words. Without Christmas trees or commercialism, we enjoyed celebrating the birth of our Savior with Indian Christians and missionaries.

Over the next five days, we traveled to four different mission stations by train, bus, Jeep, oxcart, rickshaw, foot, and taxi. Sometimes, it took us almost all day to go fifty miles.

7

Going to Mahableshwar

After passing our six-month Marathi examinations in February, we prepared to go to the hills at Mahableshwar with other missionary-language students. We stored personal belongings that we weren't taking in locked barrels. A watchman would guard the compound, but we didn't want to leave things out as temptations for thieves while we were gone for three months. The girls made sure that we took their favorite toys and books. They loved to have us read and pray with them every evening. Mary Ellen always prayed for her grandparents—right after her request for a little red wagon like Phillip's. We had requested one for the girls, so they were thrilled when our fellow missionary Carris arrived with their little red wagon.

During the three months of hot season, March through June, in cool Mahableshwar, we lived by ourselves in a small line of apartments. This was not only a time of intensive language study but also of Christian fellowship with hundreds of new missionaries from many different denominations and countries. Mahableshwar was known as the "hill station where dysentery reigns." Fortunately, many missionary doctors were in our classes.

On Sunday evenings, we had wonderful "singspirations," with Elcho playing the accordion. We sat on the ground of a spacious compound, gazing at the beautiful scenery thousands of feet below. Various missionary men led the meetings and brought devotionals. Others led special events for the children.

That year, thirty-five TEAM missionaries were in different stages of learning Marathi. Including ourselves, there were three married couples, three single men, and the rest were single ladies.

Among the students in our classes were three missionaries who had previously served in China. They told us that learning Chinese was easy compared to learning Marathi. One lady, who had received honors in Chinese, failed her six-months' Marathi exam. That was not good news to us. Passing our exams was important, so we studied harder than ever.

Twelve miles from the language school in Mahableshwar were two highly rated schools, especially designed to educate India's outstanding young men and women. In one school, two princes were from Nepal and one from Bhutan, as well as sons of India's highest-ranking government officials. The principals of both schools asked missionaries to take part in their joint church services every other Sunday. One night after showing the film, *The God of Creation*, we heard one boy remark, "This is a big dose. It'll take a long time to think this through."

Mahableshwar is in the hills south of Bombay. More than three hundred inches of rain can fall during the monsoons, a period of four months. For that reason, we didn't stay there year around. Yet, ironically, we needed to have water brought to us daily in leather bags attached to the sides of a bullock. Each leather bag held a bucket of water, for which we paid two cents.

Since the dirt in this area was red, our clothes often got red. The *dhobi* ("laundry person") boiled them in a lye solution, beat them on rocks, then laid them on the ground to dry in the hot sun. I washed our better clothes on a washboard in the bathroom. Then I ironed them with a heavy charcoal iron that opened up and contained pieces of burning charcoal. That was in the days before synthetic fabrics, so everything needed ironing.

When we left Mahableshwar, we piled onto an old bus laden with people, animals, and luggage. Two officials were on the bus—the driver and the ticket collector. They checked on each other to make sure that no one rode free and that the other official didn't pocket money. The bus traveled thirty-five hundred feet down the mountain to Poona along a steep and winding road. We thought the bus was going too fast to manage the curves.

In a loud voice, the driver boasted, "I've driven this road so many times, I can do it with my eyes closed!"

"Oh, you can, can you?" someone challenged. "Let's see you try!"

We didn't understand everything the men said back and forth, but that was the gist of it. So the driver turned off the headlights and drove only by the bright moonlight.

We were frightened, but thankfully we made it to the train okay.

We went back to our mission compound at Rasul Bagh, Nasik, and continued much as we had the first year. Since the Johnsons were now stationed in Dindori, three single men—Les, Henry, and Bill—lived in the adjoining rooms. We all studied hard. Elcho and the other men continued the outreach in Nasik City and had meetings at the exclusive boys' school. The Indian young people again came to our home on Thursday evenings.

One day I baked a cake from a cake mix that had come in a parcel from home for a special occasion. I was about to frost the cake when Elcho ate a few crumbs. He made a face and spit them out. I tried a bite too, and it tasted like shampoo! Someone had put the shampoo next to the cake mix, and in the two-month journey to India, the cake had taken on a soapy taste.

When I told friends in California about that, they put cake mixes in tins and added candy. Mary Ellen and Miriam were always excited when we opened one of those cans, as they knew they'd get treats from America.

After we passed our first-year examinations in October, we took a break to visit the Beals in central India, the Nazarene missionaries who had been on the ship with us. First, we went to Yeotmal, the only evangelical biblical seminary in India, where a large Bible conference was in progress. We were glad to visit with Sundar Singh Amalik, whom we personally sponsored in the seminary. We were refreshed to see missionaries of different organizations working together and to see young people diligently studying the Word of God.

After the conference, we visited Chikalda, a school for missionary children. That night the thirty-five missionary children put on a program. This was the school that we'd be sending our own girls to in a few short years, as all missionaries were required to do in those days.

Packages from home were always a treat, even though they often took three months to come and clear Indian customs. One senior Norwegian missionary always told us, "Now eat this intelligently. Someone bought this, packaged it, and mailed it to us. Eat it slowly and appreciate their efforts."

We left Chikalda at six thirty in the morning and arrived at the Nazarene mission fourteen hours later. We had come about two hundred miles—transferring back and forth from bus to train six different times. Mr. Beals met us with his car for the last fifty-two miles. Otherwise, we would have had to take two more buses and wouldn't have reached their home the same day.

After breakfast the next morning, we all piled into the Jeep to head for a church service in a nearby village. A mile away, we turned off the main road, and a bullock cart was waiting for us. Rev. Beals asked if anyone wanted to go the rest of the way by bullock cart. We said we did. The girls stayed in the Jeep, and Elcho and I climbed into the cart. It took us forty-five minutes to go a little over a mile, while the Jeep made it in less than ten minutes. That Sunday evening, more than five hundred Indian Christians sat in an outdoor service listening to Elcho play the accordion and give a message in Marathi.

Afterwards, Elcho said he wasn't feeling well and went to bed. He soon developed a fever of 102 degrees that lasted for a couple of days. However, on the third day, his temperature rose, and we could not get it below 103 degrees. The Indian doctor did everything he could and thought that Elcho had typhoid fever. Since he had only two doses of medicine, he said Elcho needed to get to the TEAM hospital immediately.

I had never had to depend so completely on the Lord before as I cared for Elcho. Scripture verses that I had memorized became very real to me—"I will never leave you nor forsake you," "The Lord is my helper," and, "I am with you always."

We sent a telegram to our mission doctor, and Rev. Beals drove us to the train station fifty-two miles away. We had a two-hour train ride to Bulsava, where we changed trains for Chinchpada. Three-year-old Mary Ellen and two-year-old Miriam were good travelers.

When we arrived in Bulsava, Elcho was weak and had a high fever. He had taken the last dose of the medicine and needed more right away. But it was seven thirty in the evening, and all the stores were closed. I made Elcho as comfortable as possible on a bench in the train station's waiting room. I gave him cold boiled water from our thermos and kept a cold washcloth on his head. Then we prayed for help.

Just then, a veteran Christian and Missionary Alliance missionary, Fred Shalander, walked into the waiting room. He had felt that someone at the train station needed him. When I told him our problem, he left quickly and obtained another bottle of medicine from a pharmacist in his church. After giving a dose to Elcho, he helped us get on the next train. At the mission hospital, Dr. Klokke told me that if Elcho hadn't received the medicine then, he probably wouldn't have lived.

Later, we received letters from three different people, saying that during those very days, they had prayed earnestly for us. They wondered if we were going through an especially difficult time. God does care, hear, and answer prayer.

A few weeks after his recovery, Elcho wrote a friend:

> I doubt that many of us actually praise God for bringing on an illness. I never had occasion to praise Him for such before. However, this past typhoid sickness has been such a "timed" event in my life. I am sure that God prearranged this wonderful experience. I was ripe for a genuine "burning out of impurities," and He surely did that by literally burning me up with fever.
>
> At our TEAM Chinchpada Hospital for three weeks, I read the Bible and many Christian books that I'd been wanting to read and thought that I didn't have time. Strange to say, one doesn't have any more time here in the Orient for reading Scripture than in fast-moving America, so it was a blessed time. Seeing how God worked out each small detail put His faithfulness in the spotlight. He has restored unto me the joy of my salvation. A wonderful verse was brought to my attention through this illness: "Be still, and know that I am God; I will be exalted among the nations" (Psalm 46:10). Millie and I are eager to get into permanent work—and we are claiming the latter part of this verse.

During our Easter season, Hindus celebrate *holi shimga*, one of the biggest festivals of the year. Like our Easter, the moon determines the time of this festival, but unlike our Easter, the occasion holds no hope for its adherents. With heathen festivals and customs surrounding us on every hand, we realized more than ever before the joy of serving our living Lord. As we walked to the church for Good Friday services, we saw huge bonfires burning and people worshipping false gods. These fires told the tragic story of a religion without our Savior.

During the festival, devout Hindus tossed colored powders on everyone. Children and young people used squirt guns to spray colored water. On the afternoon of the day of holi shimga, men placed huge tree branches in the Hindu temple compound. Then people brought offerings of "precious" cow dung to place at the base of the branches. Cow dung was precious because it served a variety of purposes: people mixed it with

Our Indian pandit Bubbin Yadof celebrated with us when we passed our two-year Marathi exams and would now be stationed on our own.

water and spread it evenly over floors as a kind of "linoleum," or they spread it on walls for wallpaper. Dried, they used it for fuel. Also offered during holi shimga is anything one can steal, for things left outside of one's home are supposed to be offerings to the gods.

Women came with water jugs on their heads, and they carried plates laden with yellow turmeric, cloves, cinnamon sticks and other spices, coconuts, and chapatis. Before setting the branches ablaze, the women circled the pile, sprinkling water. As the branches were lit, they crushed coconuts and, with the spices, sprinkled them over the fire. The fire burned brilliantly, and people put chapatis on the ground before it. Then worshippers dropped to their knees, praying to the fire gods.

How different from the women years ago, who brought fine spices to Jesus's tomb and found that He was risen. How different to bow in prayer to the God who went into heaven to make intercession for His people.

As part of our language study our second year, we studied the book of Mark, taking a chapter a day. In the first chapter, we found 148 new Marathi words we'd never heard before. We were required to tell stories, give devotions from Mark, and pray in Marathi as part of our assignments. After Mark, we studied Acts and John in Marathi and another book called *Smriti Chitra*, written by the mother of my pandit about her conversion to Christ. Sometimes we got weary of learning hundreds of new words, but we wanted to learn the language as well as possible to be ready for our assignment in a few months.

We enjoyed learning many Marathi sayings, and our family liked saying them: "Eikava jinatsa kerava minatsa." ("Get everyone's opinion, and do what you think is best.") "Natsta aiega ungern wakaerda." ("I can't dance because the dance floor is so crooked.") "Kan tushi mati." ("The dirt will be like the well that it comes from.") "Ikerda vard tickerda vaher." ("Here's the well; there's the river.")

During the next few months, we attended several weddings. Les Buhler's fiancée, Verna, arrived from Canada, and she asked Elcho to act as her "father." Mary Ellen was her flower girl. In fact, three of the original single missionaries got married, and Mary Ellen was the flower girl for all three.

Then, later in the year, we were invited to a Parsi wedding in Bombay. Elcho had become friends with the Kapadia family, and they asked him to play love songs and hymns on his accordion for the reception. Five hundred people attended the wedding, and we were the only foreigners.

8

The First Missionaries in a Former King State

At the close of the language school in May, Carol Terry, a fellow Biola graduate who was now the director of the Ramabai Mukti Mission, invited us to continue our language studies there. We gladly accepted her invitation. We knew something of the work of this mission, since Dr. Louis Talbot from Biola had visited it and had shown us pictures when we were students. We only had three months left before our final Marathi examination, and Desmuck, the best pandit in the language school, taught at Mukti.

The Ramabai Mukti Mission is an orphanage for hundreds of girls who have been abandoned by their families. Many baby girls had been left on the doorstep of the mission. Friends of family members who could not raise the girls for various reasons had brought others. Girls were not wanted because they cost families so much when they gave dowries for marriages. Brides also had to live with the husbands' families, so they were not able to care for their parents in their old age.

A big kindergarten on the compound had many little Indian girls to play with. Mary Ellen and Miriam loved going to school with them and playing on the nice play equipment. We were amazed at how fluent our girls were in both Marathi and English. They hadn't spent hours with the pandits as we had, but they could speak better than we could. They'd speak Marathi with the Indians then speak English with us. They could count to fifty in Marathi, sing Marathi songs, and repeat Bible verses in Marathi.

The first night we were at Mukti, we heard a loud thumping sound and someone calling out every hour on the hour. The next morning, we were told that the night watchman called out the hour and thumped his stick to keep thieves away.

Elcho wrote to his folks one day from Mukti:

> As I am typing this letter, I see five or six oxcarts running along the road as though they are in a race. Bells on the oxen and the wooden wheels on the rocky dirt road make quite a noise. As if this is not enough, the red-turbaned farmers sitting in front of their carts with upraised arms and whips yell at the tops of their voices to get their oxen to go faster. The dust is high and coming this way—ugh.
>
> No rain here, so there is lots of dust, even though this is the rainy season, and mud is supposed to be on the roads. Mukti usually gets sixteen inches of rain each year. The rains are nearly over, and we've barely had four inches. It is terrible to see these empty, newly ploughed fields with the seed already in and still waiting for rain. This is a dry and barren place.

We were glad to see the work of this mission founded by a fine Christian lady, Pandita Ramabai. Besides the orphanage with hundreds of girls, the mission had an outreach in adult literacy, village industry, dispensary work, and village evangelism. We learned much that would help us in our own work when we would be on our own. We were thrilled to hear hundreds of people, mostly ladies and girls, singing together for Sunday services.

Pandita Ramabai had died, but her niece, a lovely Indian lady about our age, was one of the administrators of the Mukti mission and became our good friend. She had attended college in the States, and she talked about her experiences in America. Her favorite food in America was pineapple upside-down cake. Several weeks later, we invited her to our apartment and told her in Marathi that I had made her favorite upside-down cake. She laughed and told me the Marathi word for "upside-down" also meant to "throw up!"

Three months at Mukti went by quickly, and we passed our two-year exams on schedule. We were able to buy a World War II Jeep in good condition. It had two big hunting spotlights and even a radio! So we drove to our annual TEAM conference in our own Jeep. The girls kept telling Elcho not to drive so fast, but we were only going thirty miles an hour on the main highway. At the conference, we would receive our new assignment. We wondered what the Lord had for us next.

In August 1947, when India gained independence from the British, 562 native-king states were absorbed into the Republic of India. These king states comprised two-fifths of India's land area and one-fifth of India's population. The newly formed constitution granted religious freedom to everyone, including people living in these former king states.

We heard about Dharampur, a former king state in western India, where for two hundred years the king had never permitted missionaries entrance. Now it was open to missions. Elcho, Les, and Salvi, an Indian Christian government official temporarily stationed in Dharampur, made a survey trip there. Salvi told Elcho about the only Christian, Ann Chumbolkar, an Anglo-Indian lady from Bombay who lived in Dharampur City with her nonpracticing Hindu husband, Chummy. They visited Ann and Chummy in their home, and Elcho was encouraged to work in Dharampur. It seems that Chummy's family had been friends of the former king, and the king had given them some farmland. Chummy and Ann promised to help us. Elcho liked them and wanted to be stationed in Dharampur.

On their way home, Elcho and Les drove over a rough road through the mountains, and the Jeep developed a flat tire. They realized that the inner tube was beyond repair, so they filled it with grass and drove slowly the rest of the way.

After two years of orientation and passing our Marathi examinations, we were ready at the annual TEAM conference to be stationed on our own. We hoped the field committee would station us in Dharampur. At first, the older missionaries were reluctant to send us so far from other missionaries. They may have thought we were too young and inexperienced for pioneer work. However, after five days at the conference, our fellow missionaries unanimously agreed to station us there. We felt honored when, in the fall of 1952, we became the first missionaries to live and work in the former king state of Dharampur.

The very first missionaries! We were going to live and work in Dharampur where people had never heard the message of Jesus. Dharampur borders Marathi-speaking Bombay State but is in Gujarati-speaking Sarashtra State. After independence, the official language of India became Hindi. However, the individual states of India still used their own languages for everything but official government business. The Dharampur district covered an area of 704 square miles of jungle-mountain forests of bamboo and teak and lowlands lush with rice paddy fields. Dharampur had 125,000 people in its 342 villages. In the city of Dharampur itself, nine thousand people spoke Gujarati, while the villagers spoke a mixture of Marathi and Gujarati.

The people in Dharampur City were mostly shopkeepers who lived with their families behind or above their shops. Their living conditions were much better than the mountain villagers. They could read and write and often took advantage of the primitive people who lived in the jungle-mountain villages. When we spent time in the villages, we couldn't find one person who could read. We discovered that the shopkeepers purposely kept these people illiterate. When the villagers borrowed money on the grain they brought in after harvest, the shopkeepers cheated them. Since the farmers could not read or write, the shopkeepers had them put X's and thumbprints on the invoices, saying that they had borrowed more money than the shopkeepers had actually given them.

While we looked for a suitable house to rent, we stayed with Ann and Chummy. Ann had a new servant girl from a mountain village helping her, and it was her first day working in their home. We were on the verandah having tea when she came running. Excitedly, she told us that someone was in the bedroom. She'd been asking this person questions and didn't get any answers. When we went into the bedroom, we were surprised to see this village girl looking at herself in a mirror. She had never seen herself in a mirror before!

The only place that we could find to live in was a typical Indian home in the heart of the city bazaar. Although it was a new house, it had been standing empty for a year. The floors were covered with cow dung, which we covered with bamboo matting. Our stove was a charcoal-burning,

Mary Ellen and Miriam with an Indian family that befriended us in Dharampur City

box-like affair built into the floor. Our lights were kerosene lanterns. A girl brought us water every morning from the village well, about three blocks away. After carrying it in a bright, shiny copper vessel on her head, she poured it into two barrels, one in the kitchen and one in the bathroom.

After we moved in, we asked our friends why it had never been rented. They told us that the neighbor next door was a worshipper of black magic, and he had cursed the house. He was angry with the landowner because the house blocked the sunlight to his house. He declared that anyone who lived there would get sick and die. The people believed him, but they knew we were Christians and wouldn't believe in his black magic.

The house was originally planned to accommodate two Indian families, but it actually had three separate housekeeping quarters. Elcho, Mary Ellen, Miriam, and I lived in the downstairs. Lazarus, our Indian evangelist, his wife, and two young sons lived over our living room. Sundaribai, the Bible woman, and my helper, Gracebai, lived over our two small bedrooms. It was not a convenient arrangement, and our lives were an open book for everyone to read.

The villagers had never seen white people before. When we were home, our front door was open, and we had many visitors. We often did not see them come inside and wouldn't know they were there if they didn't cough or talk. At any time, we could expect to find someone we had never seen before walking around inspecting things. We had been warned to watch them, but we never lost anything. Living in the heart of the city like we were, we had no privacy, and the girls had no place to play. Since we were on the main thoroughfare, many oxcarts and much foot traffic went by. An open sewer ran in front of our house, and sanitary conditions were impossible.

As the tropical sun beat down on us that first Christmas in Dharampur, only the calendar reminded us of the season. We had no decorations, no carols, no nativity scenes, and no snow. Christmas in Dharampur was just another day. The people worked in their fields, shops, or homes as usual. They were unaware that much of the world's population was, in some form, celebrating the birth of the Savior. In fact, they had never even heard of Jesus, who had been born to save them from their sins.

This was a difficult Christmas for our little family because I became very ill. It looked like our neighbor's prophecy was coming true. I stayed in bed, burning with a high fever, while Elcho led the first Christmas service in the history of Dharampur. However, our loving Lord was watching over us. Although we were in Satan's territory, God healed me after only three days. Elcho told me that our next-door neighbor, the black-magic priest, looked surprised when I walked onto our dirt verandah. Although weak, I was alive. Our Lord is all-powerful, and He cares for His own!

We asked the Lord to guide us as we visited villagers in their thatched-roof huts. We observed people cutting wood, making charcoal in the bamboo forests, and working in their rice paddies.

These village people were very primitive. The men wore only G-string loincloths. The women wore bright-colored material tied like short brassieres, with material draping over their hips. They drew up additional material between their legs from behind and tucked it below their bulging stomachs. Since they had no contact with the outside world, they had no idea who Mahatma Gandhi and Nehru were or even what the name of their country was.

Life is very hard for the villagers in rural India.

Because we did a lot of traveling, we were thankful for our Jeep. The so-called roads were worse than imaginable. The former king was an avid tiger hunter, so the roads he used were better than most.

When Elcho was on a survey trip by Jeep, he and his Indian guide drove three hours to their destination. Elcho asked, "How long would it take us to come this far by oxcart?"

The guide thought and finally said, "It would take two days to get here."

The first week after our arrival in Dharampur City, we began midweek and Sunday services in our home. The Indian Christian helpers and some folks from town joined us. Usually, we were about twenty in our small living room. People took their shoes off at the door, and we all sat cross-legged on the floor. Others watched from our dirt verandah. Mary Ellen and Miriam enjoyed singing in Marathi along with us.

We visited six mountain villages the week we moved in. At first, the people were frightened of us, and the children ran away. As Lazarus, the Indian evangelist, and Elcho talked to the men and Sundaribai and I talked with the women, the people gradually became friendly. Gracebai, Mary Ellen, and Miriam often went with us to visit the village huts. Even though their language was a mixture of Gujarati and Marathi, they understood our Marathi well, and we tried to learn Gujarati words as quickly as we could. Their simple thatched-roof huts were more scattered than in the Nasik-area villages. In the first village that we visited, we counted 120 huts. About twelve people, plus goats, lived in each hut. That made about fifteen hundred people in the village.

The children were as curious about the Jeep as they were about us. When we asked them if they wanted to touch the Jeep, they giggled. But soon several boys were brave enough to touch it. Eventually, Elcho took them for a ride. That was a big adventure!

Of all the people that we visited, no one had heard of Jesus Christ or had even heard His name. Our hearts were sick, and to each new group, we asked, "Have you ever heard of Jesus Christ?" Again and again, we would always get the same answer: "No, never!" We found that they could not remember His name, and we couldn't leave tracts for them because they couldn't read. However, we did leave a few here and there, in case someone who could read should come to the village. We simply told them the good news of Jesus. Many times, they would ask us what was written on the tracts. Of course, we were glad to tell them.

9

Establishing Village Schools

On our first Easter Sunday in Dharampur, we were surrounded by idolatry and darkness. Thankfully, our Indian Christian friends, the Koladys, came to visit us from Bombay. We enthusiastically sang songs about our risen Lord until late into the evening.

We told the Koladys about the curse that the worshipper of black magic had placed on our home. In the afternoon, that same neighbor gave our girls Indian sweets while they were playing outside. They brought the candy to us, as we had taught them to do, and I threw it outside in the backyard. Two black crows flew down and ate the sweets. Our guests thought I was overreacting.

Later, the same neighbor sent over curries for our dinner. Mr. Kolady wanted to eat it, but I discouraged him from doing so. Instead of throwing it out, I gave it to our water girl and told her where the food had come from. She took it home and ate it. The next morning, two crows lay dead in our backyard, and our servant girl got sick and vomited several times.

As we continued visiting the villages, we often took Mary Ellen and Miriam with us. The people enjoyed seeing them, and the girls liked singing duets together in English, Marathi, and Gujarati. When we returned the second and third time, the people were much more friendly. However, we knew we must teach these villagers to read if we ever expected abiding fruit. So we needed to spend time with them.

One of our village camps in Dharampur

With this in mind, we made plans to camp in a jungle village for two weeks at a time during the winter months. With so many wild animals prowling around, no one slept outside. We borrowed two tents from Ann and Chummy, and Elcho went to Bombay to buy camping supplies. We bought wheat, cleaned it, and took it to a mill to be ground. It was ground extra-fine for cakes and cookies, medium-ground for bread and chapatis, and coarsely ground for cereal. We took all the basics—rice, lentils, spices for curry, onions, potatoes, cabbage, or any other vegetable we could find in the bazaar. For our camping days, we had been saving special food from home—Prem® (similar to Spam®), instant soup, and dried fruit. I also took basic medical supplies, not only for our family and the Indian Christian workers but also for sick villagers.

We sent letters to our friends in the United States, asking them to pray for us. We knew we needed the prayers of God's people and the Lord's strength and wisdom to do this pioneer work.

The villagers were glad to have us come. They were hardworking, friendly, and curious about everything we did. Even though the king demanded taxes from them, no one had ever provided them with medical clinics or schools.

For our first camp, we chose the village of Pangerbardi. As we set up the tents, the villagers were curious. Some men even volunteered to help us—a good sign. We had a small meeting that evening then Elcho and Lazarus left before dawn the next morning and drove to the surrounding villages to invite people to the evening meetings.

Gracebai had come to help me take care of Mary Ellen and Miriam. Sundaribai had come from Bombay to be our Bible woman. As a mature Christian and a paid staff member, she supported me in my ministry to the women. She translated, taught, and made the ladies feel comfortable. Sundaribai helped me tell the flannelgraph stories about Jesus, taught simple choruses, and helped with sewing classes several afternoons a week.

I usually wore a simple cotton sari in the villages rather than my Western-style dresses. When I wore Western dresses, women and children often stroked my legs to see if the white color of my skin would rub off. I didn't mind the children doing it, but I certainly didn't want the men trying it!

If we thought that our home in the city was an open book, it was nothing compared to living in a tent in a mountain village. When we put the flap door down for privacy, the villagers would look through the cracks to see what we were doing.

When we brushed our teeth in the bushes outside the tent, villagers would gather around and ask us what the white stuff was when we spit. They also asked why we used colored "sticks" (toothbrushes). To clean their teeth, they chewed twigs from certain trees and then threw the sticks away. They also wondered why we blew our noses in little pieces of cloth and put them in our pockets. Why did we want to save them? They simply blew mucus into their hands and then rubbed them on trees or posts.

In the evenings, we showed Bible stories by using the "magic lantern." As no electricity was available, Elcho ran the projector off the car battery. The village people were curious, but in those first meetings, they didn't comprehend much. Their attention spans were short, but they liked hearing the "talking box" (phonograph) speak their own language. Gospel Recordings provided us with records in English, Marathi, and Gujarati. We always got a crowd when we played records over the loudspeaker.

The more we spent time in the villages, the more we saw the need for schools. When people in two villages seemed interested, we gathered the men together and asked them for a commitment to send their boys. Although they wanted a school, they would not make commitments. "Who is going to help in the fields?" they asked. Sending the girls was out of the question because they thought girls could never learn to read and write.

Just when we were beginning to lose hope, a headman asked us if we would open a school in his nearby village. He would commit to forty boys, which probably meant about twenty-five. He also invited us to hold our next camp meeting there. This truly was the Lord's doing since this village was more centrally located. Pindval (pronounced "pinned wall") had many more huts and a strategic location. Years before, it had been the capital of Dharampur and still had ruins of old stone buildings.

After we broke up our ten-day camp in Pangerbardi, we returned to our home in Dharampur, had baths (of sorts), and got fresh supplies for a ten-day camp in Pindval. We sent word to a missionary friend to ask several Indian Christian teachers we knew if they wanted to work with us. Since most educated people didn't like to live in primitive mountain villages, we prayed for an Indian teacher who desired to serve the Lord in this out-of-the-way place.

After our first camp, Sundaribai told us that she found living in villages too difficult. She not only feared tigers, scorpions, and cobras, but the lack of electricity, the dust, and water problems were too much for her. Reluctantly, we let her return to her home near Bombay. We didn't blame her. Sometimes we felt like packing up and going home too.

The men of Pindval eagerly built the schoolhouse with bamboo poles and a thatched roof. They also built a thatched-roof hut for the schoolteacher and his family.

When we came home from Pindval, our teacher, John Pardvi, his wife, and little baby girl were waiting for us. We oriented them and moved them to Pindval to open the first mission school in Dharampur. Within the month, another village was asking for a school. So our second teacher, Shivaji Gavit, and his wife came to teach in that village. A few weeks later, the villagers of Pangerbardi, where we initially wanted to open a school, requested one for their village. We hired our third teacher, an older Indian named Moses McWan, and his wife, Padmabai, for that one.

Now three villages had Christian witnesses. We thanked the Lord for what He had done in our first nine months in Dharampur.

10

An Unusual Christmas

"Would you like to move into the Rani's guesthouse?" Ann and Chummy asked us one day in May. The Rani's father had been the last king of Dharampur from 1923 to 1947 (*rani* means "queen"). Before that, her grandfather had been king. The house was in a mango grove on the same compound as the palace. It had stone floors, electricity, a water faucet, and privacy. Did we want it? We certainly did! The rent was even less than the house where we were living in the heart of town.

Nearby were dwellings for Indian Christian helpers and teachers when they came to town. That very morning we had been puzzled about the daily reading that we read in our devotions: "The glory of this latter house shall be greater than of the former, said the Lord of hosts; and in this place will I give peace" (Haggai 2:9 KJV). Now we rejoiced.

The Rani was about our age, and we became friends. She enjoyed Mary Ellen and Miriam and brought them gifts. She invited us for tea many times and often sent us delicious Gujarati dishes. We invited her to our home also, and she liked to play table games with us. I remember playing Pick-Up-Sticks with her. She didn't like to be corrected, and she and Elcho would often disagree as to whether her stick had moved.

Many friends in America sent us used Christmas cards. We put Marathi verses on them and gave them to youngsters who came to the children's meetings. They liked the flannelgraph stories and were delighted

One of our seven Indian village schools and the teacher's home next door, in the village of Pindval, Dharampur District, Gujarat State

to take the pretty cards home. Mary Ellen and Miriam enjoyed helping with stories and singing Marathi songs.

The positive influence of the schools and our Christian schoolteachers encouraged us. When Elcho and the evangelist went to the villages for meetings, they could stay in the schoolhouses and did not have to set up tents.

Winter and spring were the best times to work in the villages because summers were unbearably hot. Heavy monsoons poured down rain in the middle of July. After the intense heat of summer, everyone was glad to have rain. They ran outside with outstretched arms to feel the refreshing water. We were no exceptions—we did it too!

We continued to sleep under nets, not only for protection from mosquitoes but also to keep out lizards, centipedes, scorpions, bats, and rats that came out of the rain. Our dog Tippy loved to kill rats. When we saw a rat in a room, we would close the doors and window shutters. Within minutes, Tippy captured it and wanted to take it outside. We often did this several times a night.

During the monsoon season, the heavy rains made the roads into the mountain villages impassable, so Elcho and Lazarus walked miles to the schools. When they came to a village on the way up, Lazarus took Elcho's load for him, but as soon as they got away from the village, he gave it back to him. We discovered later that Lazarus was embarrassed to have people see him letting the "sahib" carry a load, but he was glad to let Elcho carry the load if no one was watching. Although we didn't have meetings during the heavy rains, Elcho visited the schools, paid the teachers, took them fresh food supplies, and saw how they were doing.

One day, we received a telegram from a fellow missionary: "I have a fine Christian teacher who has just finished Bible school. He and his wife are newlyweds who want to serve the Lord. I think they'd fit into a village setting very well. Are you interested in having Luther as a teacher in one of your villages?"

"Send them!" Elcho telegraphed in reply.

Although we didn't have the money to pay a new teacher, we both knew that we should open another school, the sooner the better. In the mail the next day, we received a letter from a friend in Altadena, California, telling us that she wanted to sponsor another village teacher and had already sent the money to TEAM headquarters for his support. We were reminded of the Scripture verse, "It shall come to pass that before they call, I will answer; and while they are still speaking, I will hear" (Isaiah 65:24). By the end of the first year, we had seven schools and seven Christian homes established in seven mountain villages.

Although we spent much of our time in mountain villages, we did not want to neglect the educated people in the city of Dharampur. The United States Information Service offered us the loan of a movie projector and films on health care, agriculture, and nature. They said we could use the projector for our own films too, so we showed *The God of Creation* in Marathi and Gujarati for ten nights. Hundreds of people came for every showing at our home, where we had electricity. They sat on the grounds of the dead king who had never allowed missionaries into his kingdom. The Rani came every night.

In September 1953, Elcho wrote to his folks:

> We recently learned that two teachers had called together the whole village of Pangerbardi two different evenings and preached to them. This was without our prompting. We were thrilled when we heard of it because it is an indication that these teachers have real zeal and a true burden to reach their own people for the Lord. We feel we have invested in these Indian Christian young men wisely. Teachers rarely ever do this type of preaching.

> We'll be soon able to get the Jeep up in the mountains, as the rains are almost over, and the ground is beginning to dry up. Millie is now at a women's Bible-training conference where she is helping with the teaching.

Christmas was enjoyable that year. All seven teachers and their families came to Dharampur City for the holidays, and we had a potluck Christmas dinner together. We were glad that Ann, Chummy, and the Rani joined us too. After dinner, we sang Christmas carols in Marathi, and Lazarus read the Christmas story. A number of us told how God had shown His faithfulness to us in the past year. It was different from our Christmas the year before. Hundreds in the Dharampur district had heard the story of Jesus and His love for the very first time.

After Christmas, we again put up our tents for evangelistic outreach in the village of Wagh, which means "tiger." How differently the people responded to us that year, for they came running to us. We held meetings outside in a large open space like a town square in the center of the village. The meetings started at seven in the evenings with the phonograph records playing over the public-address system, run off the Jeep battery. This was to attract people and to signal that the meetings were ready to begin.

The people sang enthusiastically. With *tar*, tambourine, *tabla*, and *dohki*—all clanging Indian instruments—we had music with a real jungle flavor. Someone also played the *baja*. This instrument is something like an organ. It sits on the floor and has a keyboard like a piano. The musician pushes bellows back and forth with one hand and plays with the other hand. Elcho often played Indian choruses on the accordion as we sang.

We showed pictures on the "magic lantern"—a projector also run off the Jeep battery. We had filmstrips of creation, the fall of man, Noah, and the life of Christ. The pictures attracted the crowds, and the salvation story was always told. The schoolboys were helpful, as they knew the songs and had heard many of the stories in school. We averaged about four hundred men, women, and children nightly for a total of over one thousand people during the ten days we were there.

When we camped in the villages, we set up a small dispensary just outside our tent. We treated infected eyes, worms, stomach problems, and coughs. We also applied disinfectants and cleaned and bandaged sores. Sometimes we took the very sick in our Jeep down the mountain to the hospital in Dharampur City.

I was amazed how hard the village women worked. Up at four in the morning, they fetched water from the well, made breakfast, and ground grain for *bakher*, a thick pancake-like bread, for lunch. By eight or nine o'clock in the morning, they were working in the rice fields or in the jungle gathering wood.

While we were in the village of Zamrlya, I heard that the village chief's wife had given birth to a baby three days earlier. I went to visit her, only to find her ten-year-old daughter minding the newborn. The mother was already in the jungle cutting wood!

Several times, I was called to help deliver a baby. One village lady had complications, and we decided to take her to the hospital, twenty-five miles down the mountain. So many men climbed into the Jeep that there was no room for the woman. We made them all get out except her husband and young son.

Since the children wore practically no clothing, we held sewing classes. Some women stayed home for a couple of days to make clothes for their little ones. Most had never held needles before. Naturally, we used simple patterns. These sewing classes helped me make friends with the women.

When the time came to return home, we had a frightening experience on our journey down the mountain. Elcho noticed something wrong with the brakes on the Jeep. Before going down a steep incline, he stopped the Jeep and asked us all to get out and walk down the hill. He realized the brakes had gone out completely. Somehow, with many prayers, and by shifting gears, he got down the hill.

At the bottom of the hill, still deep in the jungle forest, the Jeep stopped on a flat area next to a stream. Our helper, Chegin, started walking to Ann and Chummy's home about five miles away to get help. Fortunately, a lorry picked him up and took him into Dharampur. Since it was beginning to get dark and we were hungry, we made a couple of campfires. We got water from the stream and found tea, sugar, and powdered milk in our supplies to make tea. From the few potatoes and onions left from camp, we made vegetable curry over one of the fires. We kept the bigger fire burning not only for warmth but also to scare away any tigers that might come to drink.

After several hours, Chummy and Chegin came in a bullock cart to rescue us. They had tried with no avail to get a lorry. Chummy said he was glad that we had kept a big fire burning, as this was the king's favorite place to hunt tigers. He showed us a distant tree house where the king had a good hunting position for killing them. The bumpy bullock cart ride was quite an experience. Finally, we arrived home safely and were glad to climb into our own beds that night.

11

Off to Boarding School

In May 1954, the Koladys, our Indian Christian friends from Bombay, invited us to visit their relatives and friends in South India. Although the Koladys were evangelical Christians, they had been raised in the Mar Thoma Church of South India. Today, for the most part, the Mar Thoma Church is considered quite liberal and legalistic. With the Koladys, we had a rare opportunity to visit several of these churches. We were shown special robes that priests wear for different ceremonies. Only priests in special robes can go into the "holy place" to pray.

These churches are named for the apostle Thomas ("Doubting Thomas"). Tradition says that he brought Christianity to India and died there. More Christians are in South India than in any other part of the country. Now, many independent churches are growing rapidly and are sending their own Indian missionaries to Nepal, North India, and Thailand.

The Koladys took us to Cochin (modern-day Kochi) in the southern tip of India, where we toured the backwaters of Malabar. I couldn't sightsee as much as I wished because my stomach was constantly upset. After ten days with our friends, we relaxed in a missionary rest house in the Nilgeris. As a number of missionary children were also on vacation in the hills, we had a birthday party for Mary Ellen's sixth birthday and Miriam's fifth.

A Nazarene-mission doctor was also a guest in this boardinghouse, and she confirmed my suspicions. We were going to have a baby! During our three-week vacation, we had a restful and refreshing time with our girls and fellow missionaries. We went back to Dharampur knowing that changes were ahead.

Sunrise School, located in the small community of Chikalda, was in the middle of India. We had visited this boarding school for missionary children during our first year in India. Now we had to decide whether or not we should send our six-year-old Mary Ellen many miles away to that school.

Even though missionaries did not homeschool their children in those days in India, I wanted to teach the girls at home and had even ordered the Calvert course for them. However, the mission discouraged us from doing this. Other missionaries told us that children needed peer relationships with other American children. The school had trained teachers, and if I taught them, I could not go to the villages with Elcho, so we decided to send Mary Ellen away to school. If we had it to do again, we would make a different decision. At the time, we thought we were doing the best thing for her, but a little six-year-old girl needs her parents.

During our vacation, I had taught the girls with school materials, and Mary Ellen wanted to learn. When we returned home from vacation, a letter waiting for us from the school said they were expecting Mary Ellen in the boarding school that would open in two weeks.

Reluctantly, we prepared her for this new adventure. The school had sent us a long list of things she needed to bring. Everything had to be marked with her name on it. I had ordered some name tags from home in case we needed them. We also had brought extra clothes when we came to India, but I hadn't realized how much my little girls would grow in four years.

For boarding school, Mary Ellen needed eight dresses and three pairs of sturdy shoes. She had play clothes, but she needed to wear dresses at school. During the rains, it often took two or three weeks to get clothes washed and dried. We were able to get suitable material for dresses in Bulsar, the larger town twenty miles away. The Rani asked her *shimpi* (tailor) to make the school dresses for us. I showed him pictures from our Sears catalog, and it was amazing how he could sew them from just the pictures.

Our girls usually went barefoot or wore sandals like their Indian playmates. Mary Ellen had lost the right shoe of her only good pair

through the hole in the floor of the bathroom on a train. As her feet were chubby and wide, we couldn't get shoes for her. We had a pair made in town and hoped that Elcho could find another pair in Bombay on their way to the boarding school.

Mary Ellen loved to play with her big doll. My heart broke as I heard her tell her doll, "I'm a big girl now, and I have to go away to school. You stay with Grandma, and I'll be back for Christmas to see you." The night before Mary Ellen left, she said, "Mommy, I am very sad about leaving you, but I know Jesus wants me to be happy, so I'm trying to be!"

Dharampur was still and dark at four o'clock in the morning as Gracebai, Miriam, and I walked Elcho and Mary Ellen, with her small doll, to the bus station. My heart was heavy, and tears streamed down my face as we walked back home. This was much more difficult than leaving the shores of California.

Elcho told us later that as the bus left Dharampur for the train in Bulsar, Mary Ellen didn't cry but entertained the busload of people with her singing. She sang all kinds of songs—songs in Marathi, Gujarati,

English Christmas songs, children's songs, and songs she even made up herself. They boarded the train at six thirty in the morning and arrived in Bombay at ten thirty in the morning. Elcho bought Mary Ellen a raincoat, barrettes, shoes, socks, and a flashlight for school. Mary Ellen was glad to be with her daddy but was missing Miriam, so she asked him to buy a toy to take home to her.

After dinner in the first-class dining room in Victoria Station in Bombay, Elcho and Mary Ellen boarded the afternoon train to go to the missionary boarding school, where she would spend most of the next nine months. It was a long night. They each had a bench in a second-class compartment. Mary Ellen slept. In order to keep the sheet over her as she tossed and turned, Elcho didn't sleep a wink. He had a magazine and read articles twice. He could only think that he was taking his daughter to the center of India to leave her there, and he started to worry about her. Then a Scripture verse kept going through his mind: "Be anxious for nothing" (Philippians 4:6). He thought of how Mary Ellen had sung on the bus to Bulsar. He decided that he would at least hum, and these words came:

Why should I care? Why should I care? You're in His care!

He feeds the cattle on a thousand hills,
Gives to you His word and all fulfills.

Why should I care? You're in His care.

He numbers each hair of your head, He tells.
Have no anxiety, but all fears dispel.

He clothes the lilies in garments so rare.
No earthly father with Him can compare.

He who notes the smallest sparrow fall
Loves you His child far dearer than all.

Why should I care? You're in His care!

Elcho was surprised that the words came easily, and the tune was pretty. He jotted down the words on an old scrap of paper. His worry turned to thanksgiving that our little girl was in God's loving care. When he returned home, he played the tune on the accordion and sang the words to me. It calmed my anxious heart… a little bit.

12

LeRoy Is Born

Since I was almost nine months pregnant, riding in an old Army Jeep over a rough, bumpy road was difficult, to say the least. Elcho drove Gracebai, Miriam, and me to the Brethren Mission Hospital in Bulsar, twenty miles away. The mission doctor and his wife let us stay in their guest room.

Elcho had to get Mary Ellen, bring her to us for Christmas vacation, and then go to our TEAM annual conference in Poona.

How happy we were to be reunited with Mary Ellen! Since I felt fine, the girls and I took long walks on the compound, visiting doctors, nurses, and patients. The hospitals in India are different from hospitals in the States. Family members stay in the same hospital room as the patient and do the cooking and laundry in the outside courtyard. More than once, we saw a family member sleeping on the hospital bed and the patient on the floor. Again, we heard the familiar thumping of the bamboo stick and the night watchman calling out the hours to let people know he was on watch.

On December 16, 1954, Elcho LeRoy Redding was born. I sent a telegram to Elcho at the mission conference, "Our nine-pound son born on the sixteenth." I also sent a cablegram to my mother in Yakima, Washington, at the same time. She, in turn, called Elcho's folks in Medford, Oregon. As soon as they got the phone call, his mother called the local newspaper. Elcho's brother read about the birth in the newspaper before Elcho got the news less than two hundred miles away. Elcho let out a big yell when he got the telegram. He sent a return telegram, "Wildly happy. Coming. Everyone sends greetings." When he shared the news at a meeting, everyone clapped, and the chairman prayed for our entire family. Elcho was then excused for the rest of the conference so he could drive to us right away and take us home.

We had been calling our new son "Baby Elcho," but when Elcho saw him, he said, "He's too cute to be called by my name. Let's call him LeRoy." LeRoy means "the king." He was the first white baby in the long history of Dharampur, so he was big news! Everyone was curious to see him, and Mary Ellen and Miriam were proud to show him off. People came from the town and villages to see this child.

Ever since we had moved to the former guesthouse of the royal family, people from mountain villages often stayed in our yard when they came to the city. If it rained, they slept on our big verandah, which extended across the front of our home. When the weather was nice, they slept under the mango trees. We had a running water tap in the front yard from which we got our water, and they enjoyed this convenience as well. We often saw them bathing or cooking dinner in our front yard.

One day we woke up to find more than one hundred villagers in our yard. They were mostly men dressed in new G-strings and open vests.

When we greeted them, we discovered they had walked ten to twenty miles from their homes just to see our new baby. We brought LeRoy's cradle out on the verandah and told them not to touch him or put their hands in his cradle. They agreed to just look and filed past, admiring LeRoy and giggling in amazement.

The Indian Christian teachers in the seven villages did more than teach the schoolboys. In the evenings, they also taught the men to read. The teachers took their jobs seriously, and the students learned quickly. Better yet, the teachers showed the villagers what Christians were by their godly lives. Seven boys in one school confessed Christ, and the teacher gave them special Bible lessons.

The field chairman visited our schools and afterwards reported in his annual report to TEAM's United States headquarters: "We firmly believe that the village schools, which are being carried on successfully, are a forceful factor in breaking down prejudice, giving Christian workers a point of contact and an opportunity to sow the Word."

When Elcho visited the schools, the boys were excited to show him what they had learned. They proudly recited new Bible verses for him, and he rewarded their efforts with special sweets. In all the schools, only one family enrolled their daughter. The villagers told us that it was a waste of time for girls to learn.

Hevtya was a teenage, uneducated boy who wanted to serve the Lord. We hired him as a helper to do many things that relieved Elcho. He was such a big help in the work that we thought he should get Bible training. The next year, we helped put him through Bible school. Many years later, our former missionary coworkers Les and Margaret Buhler told us that Hevtya had been a faithful pastor and was responsible for eighty churches in western India until his death in 2010.

The townspeople and villagers continued to be friendly. Many gave us cucumbers, peanuts, chilies, or invitations to their homes for tea. At the same time, certain Hindus opposed our village schools. Since 270 villages in our area still had no schools or schoolteachers, the government could establish their own schools without bothering ours. We could only conclude that Satan wanted to stop the work.

When LeRoy was two months old, Elcho took Miriam, LeRoy, and me to the village where he and Lazarus were camping. The delighted villagers

Mary Ellen and Miriam went camping in the villages with us when they were home from boarding school. They saw that the Indian girls their age did not go to school but worked very hard in village life.

crowded around Miriam and LeRoy. We stayed in a small hut with five goats on the other side of a four-foot mud divider. Since I couldn't tolerate the smell, I took LeRoy with me to sleep outside in the open doorway. A villager told us to get inside, as a tiger had taken a goat from that very spot a few days earlier, so we went back inside the dark, smelly hut.

The next night, Elcho and the evangelist had a big meeting with approximately one thousand people in attendance. They were preaching and showing slides on the life of Christ. Suddenly, LeRoy started to cry, and I realized it was past time to feed him and put him to bed. Since I wanted to hear the message, I sat in the Jeep and nursed my baby.

About a hundred people got up, disturbing the meeting as they crowded around LeRoy and me in the Jeep. They said they wanted to see how I fed him. I asked the men to return to their seats, and I would show the women. As soon as I started to nurse him, our baby stopped crying, and the women went back to the meeting. Apparently, someone had told them that white people didn't nurse their babies but used bottles filled with cow's milk. The women were satisfied that I wasn't so different after all.

After several days, Lazarus, LeRoy, Miriam, and I climbed into the Jeep, and Elcho began driving us the fourteen miles down the mountain to our home. As we started down the steep grade and made a turn, we saw a huge tiger sitting on a rock. Lazarus said it was the largest one he had ever seen. He guessed it to be about eleven feet long, but Elcho thought it was nearer nine or ten. Elcho sped up, quickly passed it, and hoped the Jeep wouldn't stall. We continued down the grade a few turns and then remembered two men at the mountaintop who were going to walk down. We knew the tiger would certainly get them. We hadn't picked them up there, as the Jeep was crowded, but after dropping off some passengers, we turned around and drove back to get them.

Since the muffler was off the Jeep, it sounded like an airplane when we turned around, but the tiger didn't seem afraid. On our way back down, we saw the tiger again. The men were certainly grateful to have been picked up.

Elcho and Lazarus had often walked by that spot in the rainy season when the road was impassable by Jeep. They told us about a cave in the mountain behind a bamboo thicket. They jokingly used to tell each other that a tiger lived there. They now realized this was no joking matter, and tigers did live there. They learned later that during the rainy season, villagers always traveled in groups and carried weapons.

We felt it best not to take baby LeRoy to the villages until he was older, so Elcho went camping without us. On February 1955, he wrote to his folks from the next village.

> Greetings from a small jungle village in the heart of Dharampur State. This village has about twenty huts. Multiply this by eight, and you have the approximate population of the village. I'm sitting in the cool shade of a roof made of freshly threshed *nagli* grass—a grain villagers use for making flat bread. Split bamboo poles support the grass, and heavy teak logs, in turn, support them. The walls of the hut provided for me by the village are made of branches of a newly cut *zamarn* tree and are interwoven to support each other. The floor is made of dirt. The cot upon which I am sitting is made of *sis* fiber woven together and strung

on a teakwood frame. The "better" families of the village own cots—two cots in this village. Apart from these cots, there is not another stick of furniture in the village, not even a lowly stool.

Just in front of me, the *parteel's* (head villager's) wife is mixing water with cow dung to make a smooth paste. She uses both hands to mix the paste and wipes her nose on her arm. Now she spreads the mixture over the floor.

To one side, the parteel's son, dressed in a short vest and G-string, squats. Excitement is in the air because a dozen young women, all dressed in bright-red prints, file by. Rupee pieces hang on silver chains about their necks. The ornaments slap their stomachs as they march by—hips swinging. Upon some hips are small boys and girls, each dressed in a bright-colored shirt (nothing more). The women all have the same hairdo, parted in the exact middle and pulled tightly to form buns at the nape of their necks. Silver chains, which pierce the upper part of the ears, are fixed into the back of their hair on opposite sides. Each girl wears a dozen or so brass, silver, and glass bangles on each arm. Above both elbows are large silver bracelets. The parteel's son told me they are going to a bazaar four miles down to the bottom of the mountain. The elevation is about two thousand feet here. They will walk down to sea level and, of course, back up too.

I see young men in front of several huts tying up grain into "sacks." There is no sewing on the sacks, but they roll the tops so cleverly that they merely need to be tied on both ends to keep the grain in. Quite a few sacks are being piled against the hut here; so quite a few must be going. There is a festival—a disgusting, immoral one—coming soon: the holi shimga. They must be preparing for it. Now the sacks are all being picked up, one by one. The men, all dressed up with *dhotis* (long white cloths) tied turban fashion on their heads, short vests, and G-strings— are going to town. They'll sell the grain and get money.

The boys in the schoolhouse two huts over are shouting out their lessons. "Sahib is here. Shout louder!" I can almost hear my teacher encouraging the boys to whoop it up. They evidently think the louder they yell, the harder they are studying, and I should really be pleased.

To encourage them, I went to the school, stooped low to get under the roof and door, and found thirty grinning boys giving me a handsome salute and a hearty, "Salaam, Sahib!" (greeting of utmost respect). They were pleased to do arithmetic, reading, and singing for me. Again, I heard their memory verse for the week. They are progressing well, and this makes me glad. After a few "shahbashses" of encouragement, I came back here to sit down.

Now, I smell my own dinner. The cook is pounding the spices and frying onions for my curry. The smell from the room behind me and the smell of the fresh "linoleum" being spread before me seem to be waging a war. The woman gives me a toothy grin and wants my approval of her work. I nod and tell her in her own language, "How beautifully you have done it!" She seems pleased.

But I was going to tell you about our meeting last night. Lazarus, the Indian evangelist, and Chugin, my cook, and I came here yesterday. The schoolteacher and his wife invited me to a chicken-curry dinner. A very kind gesture, and the curry was good in spite of the fact that the chicken's head, beak, eyes, feet, as well as most of the entrails, were cooked right along with my favorite pieces, the thigh and wishbone. This teacher is very hospitable, and I thrill at his hospitality! The chicken must have set him back a day's pay.

It was exactly eight o'clock when I lit my hurricane lantern of 400 candle-power. Seeing the brilliant light, the people know it is time to come to the meeting. The lights are a great attraction, since the boys and girls have never seen anything brighter than a candle in their lives! The evangelist played the baja, and we sang hymns. The teacher gave Indian percussion instruments to the schoolboys, and they all started making noise and singing the Marathi hymns and choruses as we led them. Of course, children in the huts became more excited and yelled for mothers to hurry with the last-minute chores so they could get seats as near to the baja as possible.

The stories last night were about the Samaritan woman (interesting that these people never draw water in midday—a woman who would do it is automatically considered a bad woman), choosing the twelve disciples, sermon of the "lilies of the field and fowls of the air," and the nobleman's son. The Word went forth, and Lazarus closed with good applications. I counted one hundred and sixty men and boys and about seventy women and girls. This was a much smaller group than usual, but there was good attention. Many are still threshing grain and sleep on the threshing floors so cannot come to the meetings unless their floors are near the village. We must start as late as eight, as the people don't finish evening meals until then at this time of the year. The people were quiet last night, and most of them took part in the singing. There seems to be a much better grasping of the Word this time than the last time when we stayed here. The school has broken down many barriers. We closed the meeting at 9:45 in the evening. There was only about 45 minutes of solid preaching. The teacher announced that the meeting would be longer tonight, and the people beamed with pleasure.

I sometimes went with LeRoy and Miriam downtown in the city of Dharampur for shopping, mailing letters, or visiting new friends. One very hot day when we went to town together, I had dressed baby LeRoy in a blue sunsuit with two straps crossing his back. I was surprised to hear a stranger, carrying a baby with a bare bottom, say to her companion, "Rich people let their babies go naked." Gracebai told me that the important thing to cover was one's back. Nothing else matters.

We were happy to have Mary Ellen with us for the hot-season vacation. We decided to go to Kodaikanal, a popular hill station in South India, for our vacation during the summer of 1955. Dr. Klokke, the TEAM mission doctor who had helped Elcho when he had typhoid, had returned to the States and was successful in his medical practice. He donated money so our mission could buy property in Kodaikanal for our missionaries to use for rest, relaxation, and restoration. We were assigned a cute little cottage called Rose Cottage. The Koladys accepted our invitation to share it with us. Hot-season vacation was always a great time of Christian fellowship,

LeRoy and Mary Ellen with Mr. C.K. Kolady, an Indian Christian railway official. He was our dear friend for many years.

as people from all over India usually leave the hot tropical plains for a few weeks and go to one of the resorts in the hills. Miriam would be going back with Mary Ellen to the boarding school, so I was busy getting her things ready. We had a happy time together that month in Kodaikanal.

13

Scarlet Fever in Parola

While we were on our vacation in Kodaikanal, a scarlet-fever epidemic broke out at one of our TEAM stations in Parola, and staff members at the dispensary were overworked. Since we couldn't do much in the villages of Dharampur during the monsoon rains, mission leaders asked us to help at this station for a couple of months until the rains were over. The sixty-mile "road" to Parola was more of a mountain path than a road and was impassable during the rainy season. As soon as we got back to Dharampur, we packed a few things and drove by open Jeep the longer way around to Parola.

Before we got too involved in the work there, we had to once again do the hardest thing that I have ever had to do—taking our little girls a day's journey away to boarding school and leaving them there for five months. We could not make the trip there and back in one day, so we stayed the night in a guest room at the school. As we drove away the next morning, our little girls stood with their friends and waved good-bye. I cried much of the way home, and our daughters told us later that they both went to their rooms and cried. I am glad that today most missions now let parents homeschool their young children.

When we returned to Parola, we did what we could to help the overworked missionaries. I worked in the dispensary and taught a Marathi women's Bible class, mostly for the workers' wives. Gracebai babysat LeRoy and did our laundry when I was busy. Elcho did many things, including driving nurses in our Jeep to the villages or driving Pastor Jardov, the church leader, into villages for evangelistic meetings. Elcho went once to Dharampur to pay the teachers and check on the seven village schools. As the shortcut through the mountains was impassable during the rains, he took the train to Bombay, another train to Bulsar, and then the bus to Dharampur. He often bought supplies in Bombay on his return to Parola.

On July 29, 1955, Elcho wrote to his folks in Oregon:

> I am now in Bombay on my way to Dharampur to pay the teachers and to see how things are going there. Since we've been in India over five years now, we're beginning to think about furlough plans. Thanks for letting us stay with you part of the time. I was surprised to hear you have a television. The girls are going to have a surprise in store for them. They don't know anything about a thing like that. Actually, neither do we. We saw a television once just before we sailed for India.
>
> We have been enjoying the work in Parola very much. There seems to be more interest here than in Dharampur City. Of course, these people have been exposed to the gospel for nearly fifty years. A nice stone church stands on the mission compound next to the dispensary. Many higher-caste people are becoming interested and are asking intelligent questions, buying Gospels, New Testaments, and Bibles, as well as taking correspondence courses on the life of Christ.
>
> Higher-caste people find it difficult to become Christians because of their families. Marriage is the greatest factor involved, and parents arrange all marriages. If a boy should become a Christian, then in all probability the girls of the family would either not be able to marry or would have to marry "beneath" themselves. Then the whole family would suffer terrible disgrace and would be shunned by relatives. The whole social structure of India is around the family and relatives.
>
> The special festivals are times when relatives visit one another. Lower-caste people are knit together just as much as the higher castes. The outcasts have nothing to lose by becoming Christians, so most of India's Christian converts

these past 150 years are of that category. Their standard has been raised to such an extent that the government has taken notice. Many of these people have become educators or doctors, etc. I saw a piece in the newspaper a few days ago praising the work of Christian missionaries to this effect.

Some dispensary cases are pathetic. We stare at them, not believing what we see. The very worst are burn cases among women. In the villages, if a husband is tired of his wife, the common practice is to set her on fire and tell people that her sari caught fire when she was squatting on the floor cooking the evening meal. Most of the time she just dies, but several have been brought to the dispensary. Often infections have already set in, and we can't do much to save them.

Elcho taking care of a village school student's infected hand

A good majority of cases are men with venereal diseases. As soon as a man finds out something is drastically wrong with his sex organs, he comes in. He doesn't usually bring his wife, so it's a never-ending process. Even if he is cured, he is sure to contract it again.

If a patient has a headache, he wants an injection in the head. Wherever his ache is, that is the place he wants the injection. There's lots of tuberculosis and very little being done to cure it. Some babies have huge brand marks all over their stomachs. We see many cases of eyes gone, running ears, and troubles with digestive tracts. Insufficient diets and poor hygiene accounts for a good share of the ills. We give most patients glasses of prepared powdered milk daily. Statistics show that India has more cattle than any other nation, yet has the lowest milk supply.

While writing this letter, I got a splitting headache. Just took two aspirin and lay down for two hours and feel better now. Millie and I usually take Camoquin when we feel malaria coming on. I hope I'm not getting sick, as when I leave here by train in the morning, I must go up into the mountains on a six-day jaunt. Thirty-five miles in the mountains during the monsoon rains is quite a walk. I do it in three days, stop at all the schools, and visit with the teachers, students, and villagers in seven different villages. I have the schools strung out in a line to the furthest one. Then I walk back down the mountain to our home in Dharampur.

We'll be going by Jeep to the boarding school to visit the girls next month. We need to get them inoculated for furlough. We have to go sixty miles to the nearest government doctor, so going there and back will be a day's journey. Mary Ellen writes in every letter to us how glad she is to have her sister with her this year. How good it will be to live in a normal family again. Will let you know when we're coming. We can make definite plans when we know for sure that the family replacing us has their visas and sailing date. I'll apply for our "no objection to return to India" then. We will definitely not be returning to India if we do not obtain it. Our wedding gifts have stood us in good stead these past eight years, but the linens are mostly rags by now.

When Elcho visited one of the schools, the rain witch doctor of the village came running to him. He was obviously frightened, and he pled with Elcho to tell the people that he was not a god and couldn't stop the rain. Elcho did as he requested. The next hot season, the same witch doctor came again to Elcho when the people wanted rain. He admitted that he couldn't bring rain. This was an opening for Elcho to tell them again about the God of creation.

Elcho returned to us in Parola, and we helped there for six more weeks. When the rains let up in the latter part of September, we moved back to our home in Dharampur. Before returning there, we visited the girls in Chikalda. Mary Ellen and Miriam especially enjoyed seeing their nine-month-old baby brother. It was so good being with them and extremely hard to say good-bye. Fortunately, there were only two months before furlough, and then we would be together for a year. We had requested tickets on a ship leaving Bombay the first week in December.

On October 22, 1955, Elcho wrote his folks:

> You can be sure we're going to enjoy our stay with you like we haven't enjoyed anything for a long time. We often wonder what it will be like to turn on a faucet instead of dipping a can into a barrel for water. And won't it be nice to not have to put a pan on the stove and wait for the water to heat for a shave but to just turn on a faucet? I think it'll be fun to sit in a tub of water, stand under a shower, and to sit on a toilet that flushes. But, most of all, together with you, we'll enjoy Mary Ellen, Miriam, and LeRoy. Oh, you don't know the blessings that we're going to enjoy to the nth degree! We can hardly wait.

The next months went by quickly, and the couple assigned to replace us arrived in Dharampur. Before we could get our "no objection to return to India" stamped in our passports, we had to get clearance from the Indian IRS. This was to prove that we'd paid our income taxes. Elcho went to Surat City to get income-tax clearance and the coveted "no objection to return." Although all our funds came from America and he had all the needed papers, the officers would not believe that we lived and worked in India for such a small amount of money. They kept telling Elcho to "come back the next day." He came back for a quick farewell, went back to Surat, and told us to go on to Bombay, and he would meet us there. Our future was dependent on that stamp in our passports. We had booked passage on a ship leaving Bombay the next week, and all this unnecessary red tape was disappointing. The man that could give us clearance was holding out for a bribe that Elcho refused to give him. The local police inspector came to our home and thanked us for all that we had done for the people. We were surprised that he was so friendly and full of praise.

The children and I left Dharampur without Elcho, and he finally met us at our small hotel in Bombay. The officers in the district IRS had refused to give him the needed papers.

The next day, we went to the government IRS office. The man in charge had gone to a Catholic high school and knew missionaries. He kept calling Elcho "Father" and was friendly with the children. He gave each of them a little Air India gift as a memento. He looked at our records and pointed out that the

When the girls came home from boarding school before our first furlough, we went up to Pangerbardi village to say good-bye. The villagers played a farewell song for us.

"friendly" police inspector had given us a bad report and recommended that we not return. We should not have been surprised, but we were. Within minutes, the top man in Bombay gave us all the needed forms, and "No objection to return to India" was stamped on our passports.

By this time, all we wanted to do was to get on the ship headed for America. Some of our time in India had been frustrating and lonely, but we both had peace and joy in our ministry. It had been five-and-a-half years since we had arrived in Bombay, and we were anxious to see our family and friends again.

14

Our First Furlough

Our Indian friends Chummy, Gracebai, and the Koladys came to the ship to bid us bon voyage. We said good-bye with mixed emotions. We took an Italian liner, the *Victoria*, from Bombay to Italy, and from Italy traveled to New York City. It was nice being together as a family again. We had missed the girls so much while they had been at Sunrise boarding school in Chikalda. Now we enjoyed watching the girls and LeRoy interacting with each other. The girls had missed him so much while they had been far away. We jubilantly celebrated LeRoy's first birthday on the ship.

As we came into the New York City harbor, the Statue of Liberty was a beautiful sight. Elcho said, "The first thing I'm going to do is to eat a whole head of lettuce." A retired TEAM couple met our ship and took us to the mission apartment in New York. I was busy getting things settled in the apartment and hadn't missed Elcho. After ten minutes, he arrived with treats for the children and two heads of lettuce. He washed them and ate an entire head in one sitting. It was the first lettuce we'd had in almost six years.

We flew to be with my mother in Yakima, Washington, for a few weeks and enjoyed going to the supermarkets with her. They seemed to be so much bigger than when we had left for India. One day when we were with her, she told the girls they could have anything they wanted. At the checkout counter, Mother was surprised to see several cans of beer being rung up.

Going to America on our first furlough. LeRoy had his first birthday on the ship home.

"Those aren't mine," she told the clerk.

"Yes, they are, Grandma," six-year-old Miriam explained. "I put them in." She had no idea what was in those shiny tins with pretty mountain scenes printed on them.

My grandmothers and sisters have always been special to me. I was glad that during the first few weeks we were with Mother, her mother, my grandma Clithero, was staying with her. We later drove to Everett, Washington, to see my grandma Kooistra. My grandmothers and our children enjoyed interacting with one another. My sister Sadie and her family were in Africa as missionaries with the Sudan Interior Mission (SIM), so we didn't see them, but I was glad to spend time with my sisters Jeane and Polly and their families.

From Washington State, we drove to Medford, Oregon, to be with Elcho's folks. They, his grandma Fowle, and his siblings were all living in the southern part of the state. While in Washington and Oregon, we also visited friends and supporting churches to thank them and give reports of our work.

Oysters were a specialty in the Redding household. The girls had never tasted them before. Grandma Fowle fixed them for dinner one evening. As Miriam was chewing, she asked, "Ugh, who made these things anyway? What are they?"

Television was new to us. Every home we visited had one or more. We had briefly seen TV the night before we left for India, but the children had never seen it before.

In the summer of 1956, we drove to Southern California to thank and give an update to friends and supporting churches in the area. We also wanted to put the girls in school for one semester, so we had written friends that we needed a place to stay for six months. Douglas and Mary Marshburn kindly offered us their comfortably furnished guest quarters above their garage, which they called their "prophet's chamber" (guest quarters for missionary families). The term "prophet's chamber" comes from the story of a woman who kept a furnished room ready for the prophet Elisha in his travels (2 Kings 4:10).

The Marshburn family home was cozily settled in their large orange grove. Riding the school bus was a happy experience for Mary Ellen and Miriam. When we moved in, we were grateful that our friends in Calvary Church had already filled the cupboards and refrigerator with food.

We enjoyed our time with the Marshburn family, and Mrs. Marshburn became our beloved "Aunt Mary." Throughout the next thirty-two years until her death in 1987, we had a loving relationship with her. Before we returned to India, Aunt Mary sewed five shirts for Elcho and three twin dresses for the girls. She also purchased clothes for LeRoy and me and many things for our home overseas.

A new theme park, Disneyland, had recently opened up. Our pastor gave us money to spend a day there. His gift got all four of us into the park and enough tickets to enjoy various rides and attractions. A lady in the church watched LeRoy, since we thought it would be too hard for him.

In December 1956, our friends Bob and Bitsy Welch said, "We're going away for three weeks. Would you like to stay in our home while we're away?"

"We surely would! That would be great," we answered. So we enjoyed a wonderful Christmas in their beautiful home. Elcho's folks spent ten days with us, and my mom came for a few days.

While visiting friends and supporting churches, we were grateful that many were also faithfully remembering us in prayer and were genuinely interested in our ministry. One Sunday after church, a little lady talked to me. We had met her before going to India, and she occasionally had written to us. We knew she was a school nurse who had spent several years in India as a missionary in the 1930s. I was moved when she said she had prayed for our family every day for the last six years. She became our "Grandma Dunn" and a dear friend until the Lord took her home.

All too soon, it was time to say our good-byes again. The weekend before we left Southern California, Calvary Church had their missionary conference. On the last night, the church was filled to capacity. As it was our farewell service, the pastor asked us to speak briefly. It was an emotional time for me. Our friend, Marvin Francine, sang one of our favorite songs, "Follow Me." For the closing song, the congregation sang, "Have Thine Own Way, Lord."

"Does that mean going back to boarding school?" Mary Ellen whispered.

"I'm afraid it does, honey," I answered.

"Then I'm not going to sing it," she said.

Later, as we drove to the Marshburn's, Mary Ellen asked, "Did you notice that I sang the last verse?"

"Yes, I did. I was glad to see you sing."

"I told the Lord I really don't want to go back to boarding school, but I'm willing to go if that's what He wants."

How proud we were of our little seven-year-old girl. However, if we had realized the trauma that our little girls were going through, we would have made a different decision. Sending our children away to be raised by others was a mistake. In boarding school, the rules were too strict, and punishment sometimes was not given wisely or in love. Many missionary children have been scarred for life. Thankfully, our girls learned to lean on the Lord and on each other.

We are thankful that our three children accepted Jesus Christ as their personal Savior when they were about five, six, or seven years old. When children grow up listening to Bible stories and praying, they may not remember for sure when they accepted Jesus as Savior. Mary Ellen believes she was five when she was in a Sunday-school class taught by Carris, a fellow missionary. The teacher asked how many wanted to be sure they were going to heaven, and Mary Ellen raised her hand. Carris told them that they needed to ask Jesus to come into their hearts, and Mary Ellen did so.

Miriam's not sure when she received the Lord. "I raised my hand and prayed many times," she says. "I wanted to make sure that I really had. But I think I accepted Him when we were camping in a village of Dharampur. You were telling the ladies in Marathi about Jesus."

One day when LeRoy was six or seven, he and I were walking along a path in Landour, Mussoorie, India. I was surprised when he asked, "Am I a Christian?"

"That depends on whether you've asked Jesus to come into your heart."

He didn't think that he had done that, so we sat down on some steps and talked about how we are born in sin and need a Savior. Then he asked Jesus to come into his heart. I am convinced that our children were just as much missionaries as we were.

After six months in California, we went back to the Pacific Northwest to say good-bye to our family and friends and to make final preparations for our return to India. Although we had many joys in sharing the gospel during our first term, we found it difficult to go the second time. We knew what to expect—the language, the customs, the frustrations, the hardships, and the heartache of sending Mary Ellen and Miriam to boarding school. Still, we had peace about returning to India and believed this was God's will for us.

15

Expired Visas!

We again sailed to India by way of the Pacific Ocean and were due to arrive in Bombay five days before our visas expired. We thought that gave us enough time and were not overly concerned. However, the rains came earlier than usual, and the seas were rough, causing the ship to run behind schedule. We could do nothing about that.

We arrived in Colombo, Ceylon (now Sri Lanka), on the day before our visas expired. Fortunately, our friends and fellow TEAM missionaries Don and Frieda Rubesh, who worked with the *Back to the Bible* radio broadcast, lived there. They met our ship and invited us to stay with them until we could get a plane to Bombay. Because it was a Friday evening, no planes were going until Monday, and all government offices were closed. Our barrels in the ship's hold went on to Bombay and would wait for us there. We sat in Colombo while our visas to India expired. We were so close and yet so far from Bombay.

All we could do was to apply for new visas. Elcho went every day to the Indian visa office in Colombo to see if our new visas had arrived. Every day he got the same response. They could not issue the visas until they heard from the district police in Bombay. After a week, our friends' house seemed too crowded with our two families, including seven children. We were told that we could rent a Dutch Reformed mission bungalow by the week, so we did.

An Indian evangelist, Bakht Singh Chabra, a Sikh who had become a Christian while studying in Canada, was holding meetings in Colombo. A powerful speaker, he was used by God in Asia. We were able to be a small part of his tent meetings and to help distribute fliers throughout the city.

One day LeRoy, our two-year-old toddler, woke up with a high fever. Before we could get him to the hospital, he went into convulsions. Frightened, we held cold compresses on him and rushed him to the hospital. When Bakht Singh learned about LeRoy, he prayed for him in a meeting. The next day, LeRoy was fine and had no complications.

We enjoyed our little cottage by the sea, surrounded by palm trees, and we had happy times playing on the beach. We were privileged to see the work of *Back to the Bible* that our friends were carrying on.

Fortunately, after three weeks, our visas for India finally came. We quickly packed and booked the next plane for Bombay. Our cargo from the ship's hold was waiting for us in Bombay. We cleared customs and went up country to Parola, our next assignment with our mission.

TEAM had asked us to take over the work of the Parola station, where we had helped for a few weeks before furlough. Parola was one of the first cities where TEAM had established work in India nearly fifty years before. On the mission compound were two bungalows, a church building, and a dispensary with a clinic that had six rooms for patients to stay in for long-term care, and a pharmacy. We lived in the larger bungalow. We had electricity, but the only "running water" was when our Indian helper ran with it. He carried the water from the well to our kitchen and bathrooms in two big kerosene tins with a heavy rope over his shoulder. The well on the compound had plenty of water during the rains but often went dry in the hot summer months. Zaida, a single Canadian nurse, was a dedicated, hardworking missionary in charge of the dispensary. She lived up the hill from us in the smaller bungalow.

We bought a green Jeep station wagon from a missionary going on furlough. This was a big help in getting to the villages. Thousands of people in this district had been helped with medicines and seemed open to the gospel.

In our living room, we had a large fish aquarium with lights, aerators, and tropical fish. It not only gave us pleasure, but it also was a big attraction to Indians and other missionaries. We often sat and watched the fish as we relaxed in the evenings.

Mary Ellen and Miriam went directly to school. Although this was difficult for all of us, we tried to put on happy faces. We heard that a circus was coming to Bombay, so we promised to take the girls to see it during the Christmas holidays. We always tried to give them something to look forward to when they came home. Of course, their greatest joy was just being with LeRoy and us.

Soon after we were settled into our new home, Babu Kelkar, an Indian Brahmin gentleman, came to visit Zaida. We invited Zaida and Babu to our home for dinner before he went on his way.

"How did you two meet?" Elcho asked them at the table.

"Several years ago, I was at Bombay's Victoria train station waiting in a long line to buy a ticket," Babu said. "In front of me was a good-looking, tall, heavyset white man. In those days even after the British had left, white people were still given preferential treatment in Bombay. The stationmaster walked over and told the gentleman that he didn't have to wait in line, but he could go to the front to get his ticket. The white man said he didn't want to do that and he'd wait like everyone else. As a young Indian, I was surprised at his response and began a conversation with him.

"I discovered that he was an American missionary living in Parola," Babu continued. "Since my family has a chemical company, I often drove through Parola on business trips. Bill, the American, invited me to visit him and his family here. I visited them several times and met Zaida. I became interested in the compassionate work she is doing to help the poor sick village people in the dispensary here. Although Bill left India a couple of years ago, I've continued to stop for a visit whenever I'm driving for business in this part of India."

We liked Babu immediately. He invited us to his home in Bombay to meet his family, and when the girls came home for their Christmas break, we took him up on his offer. We saw the circus, visited the Koladys, and went to see Babu and meet his wife, Shaila, and their three well-mannered little boys. Shaila was an excellent cook, and we all enjoyed her hospitality. We went with them to see the new movie, *The Sound of Music*. We remained friends until Babu's death in 2006, and I still keep in touch with Shaila. A friendship began because one American refused to go to the head of a line.

The girls remained with us a few more days at home, and then they had to go to boarding school again. One of the other missionary families drove them with their children.

For us, it was camping time again. LeRoy and I went with Elcho for the first time since our return. On January 21, 1958, I wrote to Elcho's folks:

> We are now camping in the villages as we tour our district. I had almost forgotten what village life was like in India. Since I started typing this letter, I've gathered a crowd of no less than twelve people, and they're laughing at this funny machine. When I told them what I was doing, they said they'd never seen such a machine before. LeRoy is playing nicely under the shade tree with his cars.
>
> Our Parola dispensary is famous. People know we're from there, and although we've just finished setting up camp, they're asking me when I'll open the clinic. I'll plan to have it in the mornings. Every evening, we will show pictures on the life of Christ. Elcho and Daniel, the Indian evangelist who works with us, visit surrounding villages for preaching and gospel-tract distribution. We plan to get a tract in every hut.
>
> This little tent is quite a contrast to our bungalow. The sides of the tent are two feet tall, and the only place we can stand up is in the very middle. I'm sitting at a table that has four chairs, and everything folds up into a suitcase-like box. We do everything outside the tent, except sleep and change clothes. Gracebai is cleaning the lamps now. She came along this time to be my moral support and help wherever I need her. The village women are friendly, but I enjoy talking with them more when I have an Indian lady with me. We're only going to use the picture rolls in the ladies' meetings this week, as I didn't have time to get the flannelgraph ready before we came.
>
> Elcho and the evangelists will be here soon, so I'd better stop and get supper on the table. It has been cooking in the pressure

cooker on the open fire beside me. We have to eat and get ready for the night meeting as soon as the men get here.

Six days later:

I had thirty-six patients this morning at the dispensary under a big tree twenty yards from our tent. Women brought a lot of sick babies and malnourished children, some with bad eyes. I gave medicine and powdered milk to the mothers and babies, but it is such a little help. Last night I visited a sick two-year-old boy. I couldn't find a place on his little body to give an injection, as he was literally skin and bones.

LeRoy is fine and a joy to us. He has gone with Elcho and the evangelists, Daniel and Moses, to a village three miles away for meetings this morning. Sometimes he comes up with the cutest sayings. Sunday evening, when we came back from Parola and he saw the tiny tent, he exclaimed, "Here we are! Home again!" Sunday afternoon in Parola, he toddled up the hill to visit Zaida, the missionary nurse. She always gives him treats. However, we have told him never to ask for anything. After visiting with her awhile, he said, "I smell candy." When he came home with candy, he said, "I didn't ask for it. She just gave it to me when I told her I smelled it."

I haven't had many patients this morning. They usually come from ten in the morning to two in the afternoon. I guess I spoke too soon, as I see people coming from four different directions now. It has been cold here—fifty degrees last night and ninety degrees yesterday afternoon. That's a big span for the human body in twenty-four hours, and our tent offers little protection. The people of Parola City were more educated than those in Dharampur. So Elcho opened a reading room in town with secular and Christian books and magazines in Marathi and English. We also had a lending library and a bookstore where people could borrow or buy literature. Moses and Padmabai came from Dharampur to work with us. Moses ran the bookstore, and Padmabai was a Bible woman in the dispensary.

We discovered that about thirty-five young men from Parola were studying in different colleges in Bombay. When they came home for the holidays, they often came to the library. Many visited us in our home and joined classes we had with Christian young people. They loved to look through our set of encyclopedias.

Elcho and I both seemed to relate better with more educated young people than with illiterate villagers. We were glad to tell the gospel story to the poor, but we felt that the future of India and the church depended on educated people.

Elcho continued to go to the villages with Daniel, the Indian pastor. They worked well together. During the years that LeRoy was four and five, he frequently went with them to the villages for evangelistic meetings. Elcho always enjoyed having LeRoy with him.

As these villages were easier to get to, we didn't camp in them as much as we did in Dharampur. Because the dispensary was so busy, I spent much of my time helping there. One day after the rains, I decided to go with the men to take pictures. I wanted to show how the Jeep was a big help in taking the gospel to the villages. About five miles out of Parola City, I climbed out to take a picture of the Jeep crossing a river. The Jeep became stuck, and we had to call villagers to come with a bullock cart to pull us out!

LeRoy loved to go with his dad and Daniel, the Indian pastor, to the villages. He didn't mind waiting for the Jeep to get pulled out of the mud at all. He enjoyed playing in it. I can't believe we let him play in such dirty water!

Even though we had peace that we were where the Lord wanted us to be, we occasionally got frustrated. One big problem was our mail. Unless we had a trusted helper, we had to put the stamps on and mail the packages and letters ourselves. The postage for one letter was a day's wages for many people, so stamps often were taken off and sold. Our packages were held up for months in customs. One time we received a package with most of the contents removed. A note in English said the candy had been "eaten by rats" in customs.

Another frustration was getting supplies for the villagers sent to us by world relief organizations. We did get cans of powdered milk, but grains were a problem. The people in many villages were dying of starvation. Even though we knew that relief supplies were in customs, we couldn't get the food to distribute to the people. Yet, we read in the English newspaper that it had been held up in customs and that tons of wheat had been eaten by rats or damaged by the rains. It was all moldy and had to be destroyed. We had been trying to get this food for months to give to their own people who were starving to death!

In March 1958, I wrote to Mother:

We had lots of cucumbers in our garden, so I canned thirty
pints of pickles. It is already getting hot, and summer
hasn't even started yet. Every day the thermometer
goes to 108 degrees. They tell us that the temperature
in May will be about 120 degrees every day.

The Koladys are coming again for Easter. He doesn't speak
Marathi, but he communicates. He'll speak in English for the
church service, and Elcho will translate into Marathi. Isn't that
something—a missionary translating for an Indian in India?

This weekend is the medical seminar here. We're expecting at
least twenty medical personnel here. Our mission doctor will be
leading the seminar, and all nurses working in dispensaries or
any others working in medicine are encouraged to be here. Guess
what? I'm in charge of hospitality. That means finding places for
everyone to sleep and making sure they have enough to eat. But I
enjoy doing this. Hospitality is so much easier now that we have
a refrigerator and electricity. We also remodeled the kitchen.

Ten days later, Elcho wrote to his folks:

We tried to send you cable greetings, but the postmaster
here didn't understand how to send it, and we finally gave
up. That's why we didn't tell you about Millie's surgery.

Millie has been having health problems, so we went to
Chinchpada, our mission hospital, to see Dr. Holt. It was
time for our required annual checkups, anyway. LeRoy went
with us for his checkup too. The girls had theirs at Chikalda.
Nothing seriously wrong with LeRoy and me, except a few
amoeba bugs and pinworms in the anatomy where they don't
belong. The doctor felt that Millie needed a hysterectomy,
so he operated on her in that small village hospital. During
the surgery, the generator stopped working, and the only
one who knew how to start it again was the doctor that
was operating on her. So he had to go outside and then
scrub again. I'm not sure how they kept her alive while the

doctor started the electricity. She had a hard time for a few days but is doing fine now. It's hard to keep her down.

We're back home, and it is hot. It's almost six o'clock at night, and the thermometer still says 106 degrees. It cools off by morning a little bit, though never enough to want a sheet over us.

Both wells are dry and have been for nearly three weeks, so we have been buying water. We don't require much, though. We have known how to take a bath in a quart of water since 1950. Sixteen different households use the two wells, and we are responsible for supplying everyone with water. I went to Jalgaon, about thirty-eight miles away, and searched fruitlessly for dynamiting gangs to deepen our wells. I finally located a gang in a village twenty miles from here that will come tomorrow to give us an estimate for digging. If we do find enough water, I'm going to ask friends at home to help us get an electric pump. It's difficult to drag all that water up bucket by bucket.

I have been waiting for permission to purchase cement for about a month now. I put in the request so long ago I'd have forgotten about it if it weren't for the fact that we need it so badly. Cement is government-controlled. We have a family living in a room ten by ten, which includes all their household goods. A sister is here for the hot season, which makes ten, and another sister is to come next week, making eleven living together. We got rid of the horses that were here when we came and are trying to convert that shed into additional quarters for this family. I've had to take all the tiles off one roof and insert a new main beam, as the other was broken and was supported by four smaller beams.

We've been bargaining for bricks with no results, but I'm determined not to give up. I was told that first I could have them for rupees thirty five a thousand, then rupees thirty seven a thousand, and then rupees forty a thousand. Now I'm dickering in Amalner, which is twelve miles from us, and have found bricks for rupees twenty a thousand. My problem now is to bargain with a lorry to bring them over. Then I'll dicker for sand. I figure I'll need about thirty-two oxcart loads of sand for six thousand bricks and twenty-two bags of cement.

LeRoy and I have to go to Dhulia, about twenty-three miles from here, to have a wheel on the Jeep welded. I've been running it without a spare for over a month now, and that's not wise, as it's so easy to pick up an ox shoe. It's like a horseshoe, only much smaller. When they are worn, they become sharp and play havoc with tires. Roads are lined with oxcarts, so there are plenty of shoes around.

LeRoy is growing up so fast. He just isn't a little boy anymore. The girls have changed considerably in one year too. Mary Ellen will be ten in June and Miriam nine in July.

A tragic accident occurred in Chikalda a couple of weeks ago. Our girls' classmate, Janie Grubbs, was killed while riding her bicycle down a hill. She ran into a Jeep being driven up the hill by her Conservative Baptist housemother. It's especially sad, as her daddy died here on the field nine months ago. Her mother has four other daughters. The Baptist church in Medford supports them.

By May the weather was almost unbearable. We went to Chikalda to bring the girls home. As we were driving on a narrow road, a village boy, holding a long stick in his hand, walked beside the road with some cattle. Just as we got near, a calf ran in front of our Jeep. We hit it and climbed out to see the damage. The calf got up and limped away. We stopped at the next police station and reported it. When we returned home, the Indians told us that a policeman had been there and said we had hit a foreigner. The word for cow is *gora*, and the word for foreigner is *ghora*. Later, the police said the calf had died, so the cow didn't give milk, and the owner wanted a big sum of money. Elcho had to go back to that village to the local police court. Fortunately, a missionary in that town was our friend and went with Elcho to the police court. Finally, Elcho was exonerated, but it was quite an ordeal.

16

The Taj Mahal

The girls were home for a few days, and then, as planned, we drove our Jeep north to see the Taj Mahal and visit New Delhi. We left Parola about ten o'clock in the evening. For makeshift "air-conditioning" in our Jeep, we soaked big towels in a bucket of water, wrung them out, and used them to cover our heads and most of our bodies.

We drove the nearly three hundred miles on the Bombay-Agra road to the home of our missionary friends Carl and Marie. When we arrived at their home the next evening, it was very hot. So we spent time on their flat roof where the night air was cooler. By lamplight, we adults played Rook, and the children played games. Later, while still up on the roof, we all slept on—not in—our sleeping bags.

The next day, we drove another fifty miles to Agra to visit the historic Taj Mahal several times. By sunlight or moonlight, it is a sight to behold. The Magul emperor, Shah Jahan, built the Taj Mahal as a tomb for his queen in 1611.

It was a long 125 miles to New Delhi. The tar road was not only very hot, but it also had lots of sharp shoes left by oxcarts. We had three flat tires in those few miles. It was a hot and tiring job for Elcho to patch them beside the road. The third time we had a flat, we saw a big sign that said, "Good Year tires sold here." The children and I stayed with the Jeep while Elcho bought new tires. We were glad to finally get to the YMCA in New Delhi, where we had reserved a room.

The Taj Mahal, built in 1611 by Shah Jahan, is a wonder of India. We enjoyed a stop there on our way to Mussoorie.

While there, we visited many forts and learned a great deal about the history of India. New Delhi is a modern city with wide streets and beautiful homes. We visited India's capitol buildings and the United States embassy. Even though we stayed in a simple room at the YMCA, we were able to swim in the pool and enjoy a meal at a five-star, air-conditioned hotel for tourists.

For this vacation, we rented a 16-millimeter movie camera. Film was expensive and difficult to find, but we wanted to keep this memory. We went boating in the shadow of the capitol buildings, and the children and I climbed 328 steps to the top of the Qutub Minar, the gigantic twelfth-century tower of victory. We waved to Elcho standing far below at the base of the tower and then walked back down those same steps.

"How many feet of film did you take?" I asked him.

"I took lots of good pictures, but I forgot to put the film in!" he replied. So we did it all again.

We saw a very different India than the one we knew in Parola and Dharampur. Unfortunately, the majority of Indians do not live in the modern cities of New Delhi and Bombay. The majority of the people of India live in villages.

We also saw a striking difference between Old Delhi and New Delhi. Old Delhi is more like the majority of India, with its narrow, crowded streets jammed with people browsing at small shops in bazaars.

From New Delhi, we drove to Chikalda to have a few weeks in a rented bungalow with our friends Les, Verna, and their family. The girls knew the area well and enjoyed showing us around. All too soon, it was time for them to move into the boarding school again and for Elcho, LeRoy, and me to return to Parola.

Back home in Parola, we became busy in the work again. In June 1958, Elcho wrote his folks:

> We had a wonderful vacation with the girls. Now they are back in boarding school, and we are busy in the work here in Parola. I must leave soon for Amalner, twelve miles away on the railway line, to pick up merchandise. LeRoy is anxious to go. He is always with me. He's certainly a joy to us and is a nice companion when he rides beside me with his hand on my shoulder.
>
> Wish you could see the screened-in verandah in this house. We have four different types of philodendron and various plants out here. The desk is here as well as the Formica kitchen table that we brought from home. Two light-blue parakeets keep up a steady chatter, and a light breeze is refreshing. We have a neon light out here for the nights when the high school and college students study with me. We have given them another room where they can study and visit with lots of light, comfortable chairs, and a table.
>
> We put in two toilets that flush when a bucket of water is poured into them. Making a septic tank was quite a job but worth the effort. The sweeper lady that had been emptying the commodes told us we had dug her grave. But we will still give her a job of sweeping around the compound.

Every Sunday we attended the little stone church on the mission compound. The majority of the worshippers were mission workers and their families. We sat cross-legged on the floor with the women sitting on one side and the men on the other. One lady alternately nursed her one-year-old son and her three-year-old daughter. After she finished, she gave each of them an ear of corn to chew on.

Accompanied by the baja, drums, tablas, and other Indian instruments, we enjoyed singing hymns and choruses. We sang every verse of a hymn, even if there were seven. Daniel, the pastor, always preached for more than an hour, but no one seemed to mind the long sermons.

That year our life on the Parola station was routine. Young people's Bible studies and retreats, women's conferences, dispensary work, and village evangelism outreach kept us busy. LeRoy was a happy, well-adjusted little boy. He enjoyed driving to the villages in the green Jeep with his dad and the Indian evangelist.

We missed the girls in boarding school so much. We wrote them often and sent them parcels of goodies. They always sounded happy in their letters, but we didn't know the houseparents were censoring their letters. They told the children that they must sound happy in their letters or their parents would have to return to the United States. Then they could no longer tell the Indians about Jesus, and Indians would go to hell because of the children's discontent.

While our girls' early years in boarding school were difficult for them, they did get a good education, memorized lots of Scripture, and the Lord was very real to them.

17

The Himalayan Foothills

In May 1959, our hot season break was a special time for us. We accepted the invitation of our missionary friend, Carl Flickner, to share a rented bungalow with his family in the hill station of Mussoorie. We drove to their home in Shivpuri, nearly three hundred miles north of Parola. Again, we started at night and used a bucket of water to keep the towels wet. Together with the Flickner family, they in their Jeep and we in ours, we drove to New Delhi. Then we drove six hours on a busy two-way road 150 miles to the historic army town of Dehra Dun.

From the sea-level town of Dehra Dun, we drove twenty-two miles up the side of the mountain on a zigzag road to an elevation of 7,500 feet in Landour, Mussoorie. Scotsburn, the bungalow we had rented sight unseen, was an old army place, badly in need of repairs.

We loved the scenery, the climate, our fellow missionaries, and almost everything about the place. One problem was the hills, as Landour is a very hilly place.

Landour is part of Mussoorie, a famous hill station in North India, situated on the first ridge of the Himalayan Mountains. Mussoorie is a resort town for Westerners and wealthy Indians who want to escape the intense heat of the plains. The Hindi Language School, for missionaries and others who studied Hindi, held classes in Mussoorie. Several private schools were there, including Woodstock School, an American school, mostly attended by missionary children. There were two Catholic schools in Mussoorie, one for girls and one for boys. There was also a Christian school, Wynberg-Allen, where all of the classes were taught in English. The students were Indian (including many Sikhs and Anglo-Indians), Bhutanese, Nepalese, Sikkimese, and Tibetans.

In the heyday of the British rule, many English people, the Nehru family, and a few maharajas used to come to Mussoorie to get out of the furnace of Delhi. They built summer homes on the hillsides. Many mainstream denominations had already purchased bungalows, but when the British left India, many Indian nationals and several more mission organizations bought bungalows perched on the hillsides. Perhaps the most spectacular things about Mussoorie are its magnificent panoramic views of snow-capped mountains and its fresh mountain air.

Indira Gandhi, former prime minister of India, once said, "No statement about India is wholly true." When we compared Mussoorie and New Delhi to Dharampur and Parola, we knew what she said was true. Missionaries from all over India went to Mussoorie for the hot season. Dr. Zerne Chapman, our fellow TEAM missionary, was in charge of the Landour Community Hospital. Fine American missionary doctors spent part of their vacation time working in the hospital.

Dr. Chapman arranged for a visiting orthopedic surgeon from Ludhiana Medical Center to examine Mary Ellen's twisted foot. The doctor thought that an operation would repair the damage done by polio. In June 1959, on her eleventh birthday, Mary Ellen had successful surgery. Zerne's wife, Carolyn, made her a birthday cake.

We enjoyed meeting other missionaries from all over India, especially our fellow TEAM missionaries on the Tibetan frontier field and to see the work they were doing. A spiritual retreat had several outstanding speakers from India and England, including Allan Redpath, Major W. Ian Thomas, Sam Camalesent, and E. Stanley Jones.

We had been reading about the tragic events that led to the Dalai Lama's difficult escape from Tibet, but we hadn't realized that he was going to live in Mussoorie. We talked with our fellow missionaries to see what help might be given to the Tibetan people at this crucial time in their history. Gordon Van Rooy, the field chairman at the time, knew that we wanted to serve in the North India field when we first applied to the mission. Since missionaries serving there were now busy with

In July 1959, we had a farewell in Parola. Per our request, we were transferred to the North India field of TEAM mission and moved to Mussoorie.

other ministries, they suggested that Elcho could help in the Landour Bible Institute until something opened up for him to work directly with Tibetans. So we formally requested a change in status from the western India field. Little did we know how much our lives were going to change because of that vacation in Mussoorie.

We went back to Parola and prepared to turn the work over to Annie Goertz, who would be replacing us. The girls went back to Sunrise School, and we arranged for them to transfer to Woodstock School in Mussoorie.

In her book *Miss Annie*, Annie wrote, "On July 27, 1959, a wire came from our field chairman (western India field), Roy Martens. He asked if I would move to Parola to work in the dispensary with Zaida. I had been training a young Indian Christian man to do the work that I was doing, so I was free to make the move. Two days later, I moved bag and baggage to Parola. Elcho and Millie Redding had been working there but now were leaving."

Yes, we were transferred to the Tibetan frontier field as we had requested. The Indians and missionaries gave us a farewell. It had been a good, although sometimes lonely and difficult nine years working in the villages of India. We went to Sunrise School to pick up our girls, moved to Mussoorie, and enrolled them in Woodstock School.

We knew we were beginning a new chapter in our missionary work. We didn't know what was ahead of us, but we claimed the Lord's promises: "I will instruct you and teach you in the way you should go; I will guide you with My eye" (Psalm 32:8). "Trust in the Lord with all your heart, and lean not on your own understanding. In all your ways acknowledge Him, and He shall direct your paths" (Proverbs 3:5–6). "Behold, I will do a new thing" (Isaiah 43:19). That is exactly what He did.

Part 3
Tibetan Border

18

The Path to the Tibetan Border

We had originally become interested in TEAM because of its work in India near the borders of Tibet and Nepal. In 1927 a missionary couple, Mr. and Mrs. E. B. Steiner, was working in central India when they felt the Lord leading them to establish a new work on the borders of Tibet and Nepal. They established the Tibetan Frontier Mission. With the encouragement of their daughter, Anita Warren, and their son, Dr. Brad Steiner, this successful work was turned over to TEAM in 1947.

Ten years later, government restrictions forced the dozen TEAM missionaries to leave the border areas where they had planted churches and move to Mussoorie. When we arrived in Mussoorie, they were involved in various ministries: radio programming, the Landour Community Hospital, the Woodstock and Wynberg-Allen Schools, the Kellogg and Union churches, the Hill Village Missions, and the Landour Bible Institute.

Living in Mussoorie provided us a chance to show hospitality. That summer Dr. Vernon Mortensen, the international director of TEAM, visited us. It was good to see him again and to have all the TEAM missionaries for an Indian dinner in our front yard.

Three Christian Anglo-Indian young ladies, Elcho's former students from Calcutta Bible College, stayed ten days with us. At their request, we sang for hours around the piano. Their favorite song was one that Elcho had taught them, "I Will Sing of the Mercies of the Lord."

Elcho helped in the Landour Bible Institute and met Tibetans who had either come with the Dalai Lama or had followed him there.

In the late 1800s, a wealthy English lady built a hotel made up of two big buildings and a cottage in Happy Valley, Mussoorie. She later was converted to Christ, and the dance hall became a conference room for Christian meetings. Upon her death in the mid-1950s, the hotel, consisting of Deodars and Firland Hall, was willed to the National Council of Churches to be run as a Christian conference center and a Bible training center. The hotel became a dilemma for the NCC, as no mission in the organization could fulfill the requirements of the will. TEAM was asked if they were interested, and we were very interested. The buildings were run-down but well constructed. It was decided that TEAM could fulfill the requirements of the will, and we were given the trusteeship of both Deodars and Firland Hall.

The entire second story of Firland Hall became the follow-up center for the rapidly developing correspondence ministry of the Landour Bible Institute. The Landour Bible Institute is a Bible correspondence school that offers twelve different courses in seventeen languages. Deodars became a Christian conference center. Today Indian Christians are still running the conference center and the correspondence courses there. The two sections downstairs of Firland Hall were designated for missionary families. When TEAM took control of the property, the leaders asked us if we would like to move into Firland Hall, which we did. It was almost

Our family in 1959, when we moved to Mussoorie

next door to the Tibetan school and hostel and a stone's throw away from Bir House, the compound the Indian government had given to the Dalai Lama for his refuge. We had a beautiful view, a garden, and tall, majestic Deodar (cedar) trees surrounding our home. It was a wonderful place for entertaining, and we had many guests.

Now that we were in Firland Hall and five miles away from the school, the girls stayed in boarding school in Woodstock but usually came home on the weekends. LeRoy started classes at Woodstock, but with Ed Dubland, another first-grade boy, he went in a rickshaw the ten miles there and back every school day. The Dublands and we bought the rickshaw and each hired a *chawkidar*. These men were really gardeners, but they pulled the rickshaw to and from the school and then worked in the garden for a couple of hours when they got home. It worked out well.

19

Jigme and Mary Taring

The Dalai Lama concerned himself with the welfare of his people. Soon after he arrived in Mussoorie, he opened a class to teach English to thirty of his bodyguards. These young men had been willing to give their lives in escorting him to India. Many of their companions had died in the flight. We were told that more bodyguards died in the flight than those who made it to India.

The Dalai Lama asked a Tibetan couple, Jigme and Mary "Amala" Taring, to be responsible for the English classes. Ruth Stam, niece of John and Betty Stam, who were martyred in China, had been living in Mussoorie and had met the Tarings. She introduced us to this remarkable couple. When they requested our help, we were glad to do whatever we could. We gave our full time to work with the Tibetans. Elcho taught English classes to the bodyguards and some Tibetan teenagers and also helped Mr. Taring write letters to relief organizations around the world.

We had been hoping for a way to get to the Tibetan people, never dreaming that they would come to us. When news spread that the Dalai Lama had escaped, thousands of Tibetans fled to India. The Dalai Lama established a boarding school, the Tibetan Refugee Educational Institute, for hundreds of refugee children who came to Mussoorie from the hot plains of India. Ragged, diseased, lice-infected refugee children poured into school. Our hearts ached for them. Many had been orphaned in the

Left to right: George Taring, Mary "Amala" Taring, Millie, Elcho, LeRoy, Betty, and Jigme Taring. Jigme and Mary Taring became our very good friends almost right away.

flight to freedom. Others had parents sick in hospitals or breaking rocks and carrying dirt on roads, who could not take care of them.

When the Tibetan Refugee Educational Institute was established, Mr. Taring was asked to be the first principal. The Tibetans needed our help not only in teaching and in writing letters to many organizations but also in entertaining representatives of relief organizations who came to visit. This was the beginning of the Tibetan schools in India. It was also the beginning of the happy relationship with Tibetans that our family has enjoyed through the years.

That first year, more than fifty thousand people followed their leader to India. In the fall of 1960, the Indian government asked the Dalai Lama to move to Dharamsala, where there was more room for the ever-increasing number of refugees. At that time, Dharamsala was almost a ghost town and difficult to get to. We thought he was transferred to this out-of-the-way, abandoned place so he would not be so visible. It didn't take the Tibetans long to transform the town.

Many Tibetans arrived in Mussoorie sick. In India they were exposed to many diseases that they didn't have in Tibet. Malaria, tuberculosis, and stomach disorders were common among children. When medical missionaries came to Mussoorie during their hot-season vacations, they helped the sick Tibetans, especially as they arrived from Tibet. We assisted them in arranging medical clinics at the Tibetan school. Dr. Zerne Chapman and Dr. Maynard Seamons, both TEAM doctors, worked long hours to relieve the health problems of the Tibetan refugee children.

Early in the 1920s, Mrs. Taring was the first Tibetan girl to come to India for schooling. Fortunately, she came to Mt. Hermon in Kalimpong, a good Christian school where she developed close friendships with children of missionaries named Schoonamaker and Smith. She saw the other girls celebrating their birthdays. As she had never celebrated her own birthday, she didn't even know when it was. She chose a day, and forty years later, we started celebrating her birthday. It was a privilege having the Tarings, the Dalai Lama's older sister, and many others to our home for afternoon teas, meals, table games, and singing.

I helped Mrs. Taring with the hundreds of children that poured into the Tibetan boarding school. We frequently enjoyed tasty Tibetan lunches with the Tarings. We especially enjoyed the *momos*—delicious steamed dumplings filled with minced onions and ground meat.

One day Mrs. Taring and I went to town and bought bolts of cotton drapery material. The Tibetan tailors made several hundred shirts of various sizes for the young boys. The cute little ragamuffins looked

Mrs. Taring asked me to hold a class for these Tibetan refugee girls in Mussoorie.

quite different, all bathed and dressed alike, in their new shirts. One relief organization sent five hundred pairs of shoes. Lowell Thomas's representative was visiting the school and wondering what he could do. I suggested that the children should have sandals for the summer weather and save the shoes for the cold winter months. He liked the idea, and we went to town, where he purchased five hundred pairs of sandals in different sizes.

Elcho's older teenage students liked to come to our home in the evenings for games, singing around the piano, practicing English, telling us about their escape from Tibet, and eating refreshments. I felt this was an important part of my work. This gave us a chance to live the Christian life in front of them and say a word for our Lord from time to time.

20

Mother Redding's Visit

We were excited that Elcho's mother and his former accordion teacher visited us during the winter of 1960. On December 23 at three in the morning, we met them at the New Delhi airport and then drove them in our Jeep station wagon to our home seven thousand feet up in the foothills of the Himalayas. Mary Ellen, Miriam, and LeRoy were happy, not only to have Grandma visiting but also to have lots of snow. Whoever thought to bring a sled to India?

Christmas Day 1960 was a Sunday, and we all went to the little church for our Christmas service. The Tarings joined us for church and for dinner afterwards. Mary Ellen and Miriam sang a duet, accompanied by Elcho, in the church service. Our hearts were full of praise.

When we were working on the hot plains, we took our vacation in the blistering summer months. When we moved to Mussoorie, we took a break during the cold, snowy days of January.

Elcho's mother had always been interested in our work. Many of our fellow missionaries had been guests in her Oregon home during their furloughs. So she wanted to visit them and see more of India. We liked the idea, so the seven of us packed our things into our green Jeep station wagon and had a great three weeks traveling and visiting friends and places from Mussoorie to Bombay, with lots of side trips.

On January 30, 1961, she wrote a letter to Elcho's dad back in Oregon.

> I guess I have seen nearly every temple, cave, and palace of importance in India. We went to the Sunrise School, where the girls used to go. We visited Parola, where the kids worked for a number of years. We stayed with several missionary families—three Indian families and one Tibetan family.
>
> We went to a circus in Bombay, which was very good. The tiger, lion, and elephant acts were the best I have ever seen.
>
> We saw as many as eight peacocks in one flock, monkeys by the dozen, green parrots, and as many sparrows as at home. Also met a herd of fifty camels in one place. The trees in bloom are beautiful—some purple, pink, white, and red. Another tree is a flame color.

Mother Redding sent reports of our trip to the *Mail Tribune* in Medford. This letter from Bombay was printed in the February 14, 1961, issue:

> After visiting my son and his wife, Elcho and Millie Redding, who are serving in India as missionaries with The Evangelical Alliance Mission, we, along with their three children, began our tour of India by Jeep station wagon. We left their home in Mussoorie in the foothills of the Himalayas (7,500 feet) on New Year's Day. The next night we saw the beautiful Taj Mahal in the light of the full moon. There it was, in all of its breathtaking beauty and splendor—so delicate. It looked like an eggshell, which would turn to powder if one touched it. But it is far from that, for it is solid white marble and has stood 350 years already. Going closer, we saw flowers, which jewelers had formed into wreaths and scrolls, inlaid into the white marble. One flower alone would have as many as sixty-four pieces in its design. I counted ten varieties of flowers, including columbines, lilies, marigolds, and roses. The Shah Jahan built the world-famous Taj Mahal in loving memory of his wife. Twenty thousand men took twenty-two years building it.
>
> The next morning in Agra, my two granddaughters, Mary Ellen (12), Miriam (11), and I went for a walk down the

Miriam with the vegetable and fruit wallah

street. We hadn't gone very far when a Brahma bull with long horns came after Mary Ellen. She grabbed him by the horns. All I could do was stand there and scream. The Indians nearby rescued her. The street seemed alive with cows!

In one store that morning, we saw a jeweled carpet worth over a million dollars. The motif of this carpet was taken from the Taj Mahal. On the ground of peacock-blue velvet, fringed with an ivory white-velvet border, thousands of pearls, emeralds, rubies, sapphires, and diamonds glittered with striking brilliance. The shopkeeper told us that it had been on display in California last year.

The trees that lined the narrow paved highway on both sides as we left Agra the next morning amazed me. Some were large shade trees, like the banyan, which may have dozens of trunks. Others were flame of the forest, sweet-scented *neem*, and tamarind with its edible, sour beans. As we drove throughout India, brilliant red-and-purple bougainvillea was a common sight here and there. The trees were all the leafy type, no evergreens. On either side of the roadway were fields of yellow *dal,* a lentil variety, and also acres and acres of yellow mustard and peas in white blossom.

The road itself was literally alive with bicycles. Within seven miles, we counted three hundred! There were many people walking, and their bright-colored clothing was certainly eye-catching. So were the handsome Sikhs, men with turbans of white, pink, red, and yellow. These turbans were plain muslin cloth, about forty feet long.

The women in their gorgeous saris, sometimes trimmed with gold, walked along the highway. Many others in more plain attire carry on their heads loads of wood, grass, or water pots. Then there were the oxcarts, hundreds of them. They seem to chug along in groups. We passed one string of thirty, all loaded with sugar cane.

We stopped at a village bazaar. Elcho, my son, bought a sack of Indian sweets. I selected one and was engaged in unwrapping the thin paper when he said, "No, Mama, you eat that too. It is good for the digestion." Being curious and accepting his enthusism, I downed it all and had no indigestion.

Back on the road again, we saw few cars. The buses moved politely over. However, the lorries—big, bright-colored trucks— went very fast and could not see cars behind them, having no rearview mirrors and carrying heavy loads. Each carrier had a man riding on top of the load, and each truck was equipped with a buzzer to let the driver know that a car wanted to pass. We passed by most of the cows with little difficulty, but the water buffalo is queen-of-the-road, and all the traffic moves around it.

The cyclist swerved out of one's way only when a car was a few feet away, and the pedestrian would only jump at the sound of the horn when he was almost run down. The oxcarts were unpredictable. Sometimes they would move to the left and sometimes to the right and more likely not move to either side but take the whole narrow road. The oxen horns were gaily painted in bright colors.

While traveling through one desert area, we met herds of camels, both tan and black. Once, while stopping for a train, we were held up for twenty minutes. The crossing was so fixed that an accident was impossible. At this crossing, three snake charmers took advantage of the wait to give us a demonstration. Out came their pipes, and out of the baskets came cobras swaying this way and that, truly charmed!

The Gwalior maharaja's summer palace in Shivpuri the next day was a noteworthy sight. The building itself, although built in 1926–1932, was beautifully painted. A patio floor of checkered black-and-white marble was two hundred feet by four hundred feet. Fifty living-room suites were covered with expensive Persian carpets. This same day, we visited a temple where the maharaja had made a statue of his mother. She was made of white marble, sitting in the center of the temple. She was dressed and fed three times a day by women of the Hindu faith. An electric fan cooled her in the hot weather, and a heater kept her warm in the winter.

Going on, we noted the rivers near the villages were always scenes of much activity—men giving drink to oxen, cows, goats, and water buffalo; people bathing, washing clothes, fishing, and drawing water to carry to their homes. The washing of clothes made loud plops as people whacked them on large stones to get them clean. All along the banks were spread shirts and pants, dhotis (a long, five-yard cloth men used for trousers), and saris of every color drying in the sun. In the nearly dry river bottoms, watermelon plants grew that would produce fruit before the monsoon filled up the river.

At one place, we came upon three men prostrating themselves on the road, rising, and lying down again. As we passed by, Elcho said, "They are Hindu pilgrims trying to earn salvation by karma in doing good works. They measure their length like inchworms as they go from shrine to shrine." We later met four white-masked Jain men walking and brushing insects out of their way because they believe it a terrible sin to take the life of anything.

Millie, my daughter-in-law, had planned our trip so we would stop for meals and a night's lodging either at missionary friends' or in *dak* bungalows. India is blessed the length and breadth of the country with these government bungalows, which were built for government officials and travelers. In Chalisgaon, what a pleasant surprise to see Ethel coming to greet us. She treated us to an American fried-chicken dinner. Only six months previously, she had visited me in Medford, Oregon. That evening, we were all invited to an Indian home for a typical Indian meal. We ladies, all five of us, dressed in saris to make the Indian atmosphere seem more real. The daughter of our host presented us with *bangerdis*, glass bangles, which she ceremoniously put on our arms.

Our friend, Ethel, had made two cakes for the Farmers World Affairs, Inc. group—twelve Americans who were scheduled for Chalisgaon that evening. When we heard they had arrived, we hurried to meet them. Their tightly timed itinerary didn't allow for dinner, only cake and coffee or tea. They had to hurry back to the station for the train. The Indian official gave us permits to go into the station. As the train was pulling out with all the windows open, we serenaded them with, "Home on the Range." They heartily joined in the singing. The Indians seemed to enjoy it too. Afterwards, the Indian official asked us, "Is that your national anthem?"

After we got home to Mussoorie, Elcho's mother sent another article to the Medford *Mail Tribune*, printed on February 28, 1961:

The Ajunta and Ellora caves were breathtaking sights! Some ancient architectures were excavated on a scarp of a large rock plateau. Huge temples carved out of solid rock were over two thousand years old. One hand-carved temple stands 259 feet high. One set of chiseled caves extends in a circle along a riverbed for one-third of a mile. It has Hindu, Buddhist, and Jain influence. We were told that it took about one hundred years to carve.

The beautiful Taj Mahal Hotel in Bombay the next day was a welcome stop. From our balcony, we could see the picturesque harbor studded with hilly islands. The boats and ships that filled the harbor made a refreshing view and deserve its name, "The Gateway of India." We shopped in exotic bazaars and purchased gifts for family and friends. We picnicked and went swimming at Juhu Beach, a palm-fringed resort on the Arabian Sea. Our Brahmin host, Babu, and his charming wife and children, treated us to their delicious food, and their hospitality was unmatched.

On our return north, we visited friends of Elcho, my son, in Gwalior. They took us to the Gwalior king's palace. Although it is 150 years old, it appeared new and was fascinating. One room had the largest chandelier in the world with 1,250 lights. In this room was also the largest Persian rug ever made, measuring foty-eight feet by ninety feet. It took sixty men to roll it.

The palace displayed gold and ivory everywhere. The nine-feet-high draperies were brocaded in pure gold. Everywhere we turned, we saw something of pure gold.

A portrait of an English lord being received by the maharajah hung on the wall in a wide gold frame. The guide momentarily forgot the lord's name. "Lord Redding," Elcho quickly supplied. "Yes," he said, "that's Lord Wedding." Chuckling, we went on.

Gwalior, as can be said of all India, was becoming industrialized. We visited the Gwalior Pottery Factory and Gwalior Silk Mill. That evening we were guests of the owner of the factory, Shri Birla, for a delicious eleven-course Indian dinner, which our host insisted had to be eaten with our fingers.

On our way to Jaipur, we visited Fatepur Sikri, the ancient capital of India. Here the king used to play the Indian game of Parcheesi with his queen. The board, still there, was made of solid marble in an open courtyard. The king and queen used slave girls as pawns.

Many welcome signs and beautifully decorated streets greeted us as we rolled into the enchanted rose-pink city of Jaipur.

Queen Elizabeth and Prince Philip had just been there. That morning, they had left for a tiger hunt in a nearby forest. This magnificent fairy-book like city, built in the 1700s, was well planned and looked quite modern. Most buildings were made of rose-colored stone. It was noted for its skilled craftsmen in the art of cutting precious stones, especially garnets. We took rides on the superbly decorated elephants. The elephants knelt as we mounted up tiny ladders.

Between Jaipur and New Delhi, we saw many wild peacocks. One time we counted an even dozen beside the road. Parrots darted in and out among the trees, making lively splashes of vivid green here and there. Monkeys by the dozens played and jumped from tree to tree. The highways were narrow with bright-colored lorries (trucks) going far too fast. When we were near a town, cows, bullock carts, and people were in the road.

Tibetan friends were our hosts during our four-day stay in Delhi. Their customs and manners bubbled with hospitality, and we were comfortable with them. Their food was Tibetan, of course, and very tasty—a cross between Chinese and Indian dishes. We always ate with chopsticks.

We were awakened at five thirty the next morning, January 26, Republic Day in India, with delicious hot Indian tea, made with milk, sugar, tea, and spices all boiled together. We made our way to the parade site, where we had especially reserved seats. Thus, we could see the parade well as it passed directly in front of us.

Before the parade started, Prime Minister Jawaharlal Nehru walked by us, greeting the people and occasionally kissing a child. Helicopters overhead dropped load after load of roses and marigolds for a carpet for the queen and duke as they rode by in their elegant carriage to begin the parade. The colorful parade lasted for two hours. I liked the Sixty-first Cavalry Lancers as they pranced by on spirited Arabian horses, the Thirteenth Camel Grenadiers Corps, and troops of elephants, which trumpeted salutes with raised trunks as they passed by.

The conclusion of the parade was topped with various military aircraft flying in formation directly over the parade route between the Secretariat and India Gate. Hundreds of white, orange, and green balloons, India's national colors, were released into the air to float in the sunshine. India knows pageantry, color, pomp, and ceremony. I felt especially fortunate to have seen this particular extravaganza, which will probably not be duplicated in a long time.

Now we are back in Mussoorie. A heavy snow has fallen this morning—over twenty-four inches. A leopard took our closest neighbor's cow last night.

For me, the highlight of the parade was sitting next to Corrie ten Boom. She was in India speaking at the Evangelical Fellowship of India conference and just happened to have a seat next to us. I don't really know how much we knew about her life at that time, but she was a sweet old lady who radiated the love of Jesus. Fortunately, ten years later, our lives crossed again, and I found out how special she was.

We had the pleasure of meeting Corrie ten Boom at the Indian Independence Day celebrations in New Delhi. We would meet again years later in Orange County.

21

Mission Schools

We wondered what more we could do to be positive Christian witnesses. With our fellow TEAM missionaries Ruth Stam and Irma Jeane Wessels, we considered putting a few of the brightest Tibetan students in Woodstock and Wynberg-Allen, two fine Christian schools. The Tarings and TEAM both liked the idea. The Tibetan Children's Fund was established at TEAM headquarters in the United States, and friends helped sponsor the students. Three Tibetan children went to Woodstock and eight to Wynberg-Allen, an Anglo-Christian school. The selection was made through aptitude tests. Eleven Tibetan refugee children began new lives.

The students did very well in these English-medium schools. Since Irma Jeane was teaching in Woodstock, she was responsible for Nurdi, Dachin, and Tsultrum, the three in Woodstock. We took responsibility for Thubten, Dawa, Tashi, Achi, Rapgay, Jamyang, Kalsang, Sonam, Renchin, and Dolma, the eight going to Wynberg-Allen. They were all about seven years old and in the first grade. On holidays and weekends, they often came home to us. If there was a problem, the principal called us.

We met ten-year-old Ngwang Tender, who wanted to go to Wynberg-Allen. He had been refused because he knew very little English and was too big to go into first grade. I talked with the principal, Mr. Kid, and he said that if we helped Ngwang with English and if he could pass a

TEAM Mission sponsored ten Tibetan young people in Wynberg-Allen. We encouraged other mission organizations to take Tibetan children in their schools and they did. LeRoy is pictured here with the students we sponsored.

test, they would accept him. We let him live with us awhile. We gave him special help, and he passed the test and went into third grade.

I was particularly fond of a handsome seven-year-old little boy, Tenzin Dhargyal. He had rosy cheeks and a sweet smile. When IQ tests were given at the Tibetan school, he had come in ninth for the Wynberg-Allen selection. We had taken only the top eight, so that meant that he was next in line to go to Wynberg-Allen. All we needed was another sponsor.

One day, when I was showing our good friends, Dexter and Lenore Lutz, around the Tibetan school, they met Tenzin Dhargyal. I told them his story. They asked what he needed to attend the private English Christian school. I told them twenty dollars a month. They agreed to pay this. Therefore, Tenzin joined his friends at Wynberg-Allen, and for the next ten years, Mr. and Mrs. Lutz paid his expenses. As an adult, Tenzin sent his own daughter to the school and paid her fees himself. Wherever we have lived in various parts of the world, we have received nice Christmas cards and a handwritten letters from Tenzin in Dharamsala, India, and we keep up with each other these days on Facebook.

Often Mrs. Taring asked me to help her sort used clothing from relief organizations. Much of the bigger clothing was made smaller for the children, and big skirts were made into long pants for the little boys. We went through each child's clothes to see what he or she had. We wanted each one to have one good change of clothes for school and a pair of shoes that fit. They also had older clothes for work and play.

One day when we were working together, Mrs. Taring told me how glad she was that our family lived so near and helped her with the children.

"Yes, the Lord gave us a nice home near you," I said. "I am glad to be living here and to be a help to Tibetans in this hour of need."

"And God gave me you, such a good friend," she replied.

I felt humbled as I heard that. Even though she was a strong Buddhist, her early education was in a Christian school. She had heard about the Lord there and was now hearing about Him again.

My mother came with her husband for a few days in May 1961. She liked seeing the work we were doing and meeting many of our friends. Our children were happy to have both their grandmothers visit within a few months. Mother didn't have much time, as she was going on to Africa to see my sister Sadie and her husband Pete Ackley, missionaries with the Sudan Interior Mission.

During the hot season vacation in 1961, Ruth Stam and I invited a number of vacationing principals and representatives of various mission schools in India to an English tea party. We wanted them to recognize the challenge of helping Tibetan children in their various schools. They all seemed interested and promised to see what they could do to help.

In June, I went with three other missionaries to Dharamsala to have my first audience with the Dalai Lama. He's a very gracious man and, at that time, knew very little English. I was honored to give him a Gospel Recordings special gift set of Bible portions, read in clear, simple English. I wrapped it in silver foil. He thanked me and asked how the Tibetan children were doing at Wynberg-Allen School in Mussoorie. I assured him they were doing extremely well.

On a hill near us was the National Indian Academy. We could see it clearly from our home in Firland Hall. India's highest-ranking military have special training there. One year Kunsang Wangchuk, the younger brother of the king of Bhutan, was studying at the academy. Tessla,

Mrs. Taring's niece and our friend, introduced us to him. After that, he spent much time with us in our home. Before he went back to Bhutan after his studies, he gave Elcho (or possibly LeRoy) a big Bhutanese bow and each of the girls a woolen Bhutanese jacket. The crown was passed to his older brother's son, so now he is uncle of the present king of Bhutan.

Elcho, Tashi Wangdu, Tenzin, Millie, Tsering, Ngawang, Rapgay, Thubten, and Achi. These students often came to our home. Tashi later became the Dalai Lama's representative in the U.S., Tenzin worked with Tibetans in the U.K., and Ngawang, Thubten, and Ashi worked in the U.S.

22

Meeting the Needs of the Tibetans

That summer, Ruth Stam wrote an article, "Meeting the Needs of Tibetan Refugees in India." It was published in the November/December 1960 issue of the TEAM *Missionary Broadcaster*. Here are some excerpts:

> Before you begin to read this, stop and think, "What would it be like if I were a refugee from Tibet?"
>
> Suppose you are a young mother with four small children. Somehow you crossed those mountain passes in the deep snow of winter. Your husband is either in hiding or waiting once more to harass the Communist columns—or he may be dead.
>
> Or you are a young man who had been taken to China for Communist indoctrination. Because you seemed cooperative, you were sent back to indoctrinate your people. Instead, you joined the Freedom Fighters, for death seemed closer to freedom than did these fetters. Now you are a refugee in India. For a time, you thought you had lost your mind.
>
> Or maybe you are a teenage girl with three small brothers. Your father died in the fighting, and your mother became insane—and died after she had helped you get to India.
>
> Small child, wounded soldier, disillusioned monk—whoever you are—you had to face the bitter cold of the mountain

pass, carrying all you possessed on your back. The heavy coat was threadbare against the howling winds and the boots in tatters. You trudged and hid and begged for over a month.

Imagine coming down into the steaming heat of India, still wearing the heavy, soiled, sweaty, homespun coat. Your feet are bare and bleeding. And then in the moist, humid forest: leeches. First, one found on your leg. Then many more insidiously attach themselves to your body and gradually swell from the size of an eyelash to that of a finger—with your blood. You finally manage to pull off the leech, but the wound continues to bleed. It gets inflamed and full of pus. And food—you haven't had much for a long time!

Multiply this by eighty thousand—a conservative count for Tibetan refugees in India and the neighboring countries of Nepal, Sikkim, and Bhutan.

When the children of Tibetan refugees were dying on the hot plains of India, the Dalai Lama's sister opened an orphanage in the hills. She now cares for more than three hundred preschool children. Many of them are complete orphans. Others have parents trying to eke out a living in a strange, new, and already overpopulated land.

The Dalai Lama's sister-in-law opened a center for training in crafts and weaving. Over two hundred refugees are cared for at the center, where some are learning, some teaching, and some already earning.

The Dalai Lama concerns himself constantly and exclusively with the welfare of his people. Although he has been urged by some to content himself with spiritual leadership as head of all Buddhist Tibetans, he has gone out of his way to show favor to Tibetan Muslims and Christians—because they are Tibetan.

Although he is considered a god by Buddhist Tibetans, the Dalai Lama spends the major portion of his time on temporal or nonreligious matters, keeps in constant contact with refugees scattered all over India, and knows their needs.

It has been with the encouragement of the Dalai Lama and his officials that TEAM and other mission societies have had an opportunity to work with the Tibetan refugees and help them.

In 1959, the world breathlessly watched the escape of the ruler of Tibet from the clutches of Communism and the sad wave of refugees who followed him out of the country. We missionaries watched the Dalai Lama's arrival in Mussoorie, where the Indian government had prepared a residence for him—just across the way from TEAM's newly acquired properties.

We watched and wept for a broken country and all that caused that calamity. When the Tibetans asked for help, we were in God's appointed time to do His will.

Some of those who fled from the closed land of Tibet now live as our neighbors in Mussoorie. While in Tibet the silent war continues, in India there is opportunity to bind up the physical and mental wounds of eighty thousand Tibetans in exile. Opportunities to help are growing, for the flow of refugees has not diminished. TEAM medical personnel continue to give increasing aid to refugees. In Mussoorie, TEAM has concentrated its help on the four hundred Tibetan children, plus the school staff.

Mr. and Mrs. Elcho Redding and Miss Wessels now assist at the Tibetan Refugee Educational Institute where I was first asked to help with producing modern Tibetan primers and readers. Tibetans opened the school themselves, and the Dalai Lama is the honorary director.

Eleven refugee children have been sent under TEAM sponsorship to Wynberg-Allen and Woodstock, nearby Christian schools with high spiritual standards. It is planned to send at least forty more to evangelical schools as soon as possible.

If the sorrow of eighty thousand be too great a burden, could you pray for one Tibetan child that he or she might enter the kingdom of God?

Miriam, the Dalai Lama's sister, Tsering Dolma, LeRoy, Millie, and Mrs. Taring.

At Christmas 1961, we sent this letter to family and friends in the States. At the top of the letter, we had a picture of Tibetan children.

> Greetings from the Himalayas! These children are only a few of the four hundred students we see every day. We continue to teach English and help otherwise at the Tibetan school, which is a few minutes' walk from our home. Various educators have remarked about the astounding progress the students are making in English, and we truly thank God for this.
>
> At the request of the Tarings, Elcho has been teaching three young men privately. The eighteen-year-old son of Tibet's last prime minister has been progressing in his English studies.
>
> Another young man has been especially selected to be a personal servant of the Dalai Lama, and Millie has been teaching him how to bake chocolate cake and other goodies.

Need we be reminded that Nehemiah, the cupbearer of King Xerxes, was instrumental in God's program for His people?

Another student, a private bodyguard of the Dalai Lama, spent many hours learning to type and now, after eighteen months learning English, is off to Nepal as an English interpreter.

We bade a sad farewell to twelve others of Elcho's older Tibetan students, many of them former bodyguards of the Dalai Lama, as they went to various places in India for specialized training. It was comforting to us to present each one with a beautifully bound Tibetan New Testament, as well as a Phillips' version of the New Testament in English.

Elcho confesses that it was a thrill to present the Dalai Lama with a leather-bound Phillips' New Testament, along with four pounds of homemade almond cookies. This month, he had a forty-five-minute interview with this great man, who is considered a god by millions of Tibetans. While at Dharamsala, Elcho helped our TEAM doctor and his wife give physical examinations to three hundred and fifty small Tibetan children in our friend Tsering Dolma's nursery. Over one hundred others, from the lowest to the highest rank in the Kashang, came for medical examinations.

Our home has been much used this year. God brought many different nationalities to our table. Had you been a guest, you might have sat with the prince of Bhutan on one side and an Indian Brahmin on the other, with an American missionary and a Tibetan of highest nobility across from you.

The Dalai Lama's charming sister, Tsering Dolma, and her husband, were our guests for ten days. We celebrated their lovely daughter Khando's birthday in our home.

Then, we had the supreme joy of entertaining both of our mothers in our home in this faraway land.

Mary Ellen and Miriam are in boarding school. We enjoy their weekends at home. LeRoy, our six-year-old, has been going back and forth the ten miles in a rickshaw, but now with the cold weather, Millie is teaching him at home.

Speaking of weather—we're sure to have another white Christmas here in the Himalayas. We love this time of year when we are reminded of His condescending love for us.

Pray for us and the dear friends brought into our home that "the savor of His knowledge" will always be made manifest by us in this place. Thank you for your encouragement to us through your letters, prayers, and support this past year.

We wish you a very Merry Christmas! And if 1962 is for you only a small portion of the blessing we had in 1961, you'll truly have a wonderful year!

23

Pearl S. Buck

In the spring of 1962, author Pearl S. Buck, Nobel Prize in Literature recipient, came to Mussoorie to visit the Tibetan school for three days. The Tarings asked Elcho and me to help entertain her. We were honored to do this. As we visited with her, she was surprised to see the close relationship that we had with the Tibetans. She had been raised in China by missionary parents, but she lived behind the walls of a mission compound and hadn't enjoyed the close relationship with the Chinese that our family had with the Tibetans. She was a friendly person, and we enjoyed being with her for several days.

The principal of Woodstock wanted me to ask her to speak to the American students. At first, she said she was here to see Tibetans, not Americans. The Tarings told her how much the Americans in Mussoorie had helped Tibetans. Finally, on the third day, just hours before she was to leave, she told me she would.

Pearl Buck had a fancy limousine with a driver that Khando and I rode in through the bazaar. Elcho rode in our green Jeep station wagon behind us. When we got near Landour, the driver stopped and refused to go any further. Actually, his limousine would never have made it over the mountain road, so Mrs. Buck, her male secretary, the Dalai Lama's niece Khando and I joined Elcho in the Jeep. She kept telling Elcho to stop and turn back. I told her that when I read about her mountain roads in China in the book *My Several Worlds*, I pictured this road to Woodstock School.

She told us that our road was much worse, but Elcho could not turn back. She kept saying, "Mr. Redding, stop!" and he kept on going. Finally, we were at the school.

The principal had called a special assembly, and all the students were excited to hear her speak to them. She encouraged them to have goals, to try to achieve them, and not to get discouraged. She had always wanted to be a writer. Many publishers rejected her first stories, but she succeeded in the end.

After she autographed books, we again took the Jeep over that terrible road to her limousine. It had been an interesting and enjoyable experience.

Many administrators from Christian schools provided scholarships for Tibetan children. Miss Yelland from the Panchagani Girls' School, where we had helped during our Marathi language study, invited twenty girls to come there to study. Missionary and author Amy Carmichael's school, the Dohnavur Fellowship, took twenty girls, and so it went. By 1963, when we left for our furlough, several hundred Tibetan children were enrolled in various mission schools throughout India. Most were on full scholarships. It was more than we had anticipated!

24

The Dalai Lama

Jetsun Pema, the youngest sister of the Dalai Lama, invited our family to Dharamsala as her guests before we went to America on our second furlough. She arranged for us to have another visit with the Dalai Lama. It would be the first time that our children would meet him personally.

Therefore, in December 1962, just before LeRoy's eighth birthday, we made a trip to Dharamsala to be guests of Jetsun Pema and to see the Dalai Lama and many other Tibetan friends there.

We had all been given beautiful Tibetan clothing, and we wore it for our audience with the Dalai Lama. We had to walk a distance from the guesthouse, where we were staying, to his home. We were almost ready for furlough, and LeRoy's favorite shoes were tattered and torn. We had bought him new shoes, but they hurt his feet. So we let him wear his old shoes to walk to the place where we would meet the Dalai Lama. A Tibetan boy wanted to carry the bag with his shoes. When it was time to see the Dalai Lama, the boy had not shown up. We had to go in, and LeRoy was embarrassed.

We presented the Dalai Lama with silk scarves, and he presented some to us. He beckoned us to sit down. We all sat cross-legged on Tibetan rugs, and he was sitting a little higher than we were. LeRoy kept pulling his Tibetan dress down to cover up his shoes. The Dalai Lama, through his interpreter, asked us a number of questions. He especially seemed to like LeRoy and asked him how old he was. Then, the next question was,

Mary Ellen, LeRoy, and Miriam with the Dalai Lama in 1962

"How old are your shoes?" I guess he had seen LeRoy's toes sticking out from the old tennis shoes.

We had a nice audience with the Dalai Lama. He thanked us again for our help to his people. We assured him that it had been our privilege. He asked what we would do after we had gone home to the United States. We told him we hoped to come back to India and asked him about having a tutorial school for older boys. He liked the idea and assured us of his help in getting students. All too soon, it was time to leave. He agreed to pose with us for pictures. He found a stub of a pencil in LeRoy's *chubba* (Tibetan dress) pocket. "What's this?" the Dalai Lama asked LeRoy, and they both smiled.

We had lunch with Jetsun Pema at the home of the Dalai Lama's tutor. The Tibetan food was delicious. We also were guests in the home of Lukhang, the last prime minister of Tibet. His children and grandchildren had all stayed with us in our home in Mussoorie. That time in Dharamsala is a happy memory for our family.

LeRoy with the Dalai Lama in Dharamsala, India, in 1962

Ruth Stam returned from furlough in America. In her Christmas letter of 1962, she wrote:

> My first week back in Mussoorie, I was caught in the whirl of fun, which the Redding household provides for the children you are praying for. School holidays can be dreary affairs when there is no home to go to. Elcho and Millie Redding have taken it as a privilege to open theirs to the sixteen Tibetan children in the Wynberg-Allen School, plus two Bhutanese girls, plus three Tibetan children in Woodstock, plus their own three children—just to add up the total! That means fixing lunch and supper for thirty plus people.
>
> We all eat at the Reddings'. The boys sleep at the Reddings', and the girls sleep at my place, a cottage next door.
>
> The children often come "home" to the Reddings'. This was a four-day holiday at the end of October. What amazed me was how smoothly everything went—even to getting the dishes done by children who are just learning our queer ideas about hot water and soap. Lunch was always in the yard to keep warm in the sun. Supper was in the Reddings' living room in front of the fireplace.
>
> What did the children do? They just amused themselves. Tibetan children are very good at that. They'd play hopscotch and ball with LeRoy and other missionary children or neighboring Indian children or go over and visit friends, and sometimes brothers or sisters, at the Tibetan school—just a ten-minute walk around the hill. The piano is used overtime when any Tibetan children are around, and I suddenly find my fingers need to be limbered up because there is a constant request, "Auntie, play for us so we can sing!" And sing we do, morning, noon, and night, before and after every meal. In the evening, there is sometimes a movie. The most popular movie is *Something to Die For*.
>
> Millie Redding and the children, Mary Ellen, Miriam, and LeRoy, will be going home on furlough soon. Elcho will stay a couple of months longer to finish some projects

that he is doing. With the Reddings gone for a year, this
will leave a big hole for the rest of us to try to fill.

Many Tibetan students who once sat around our dining table or in our
classes are now in places of leadership, scattered throughout the world.
Since the time that we moved to Mussoorie in 1959, we have taught and had
in our home hundreds of Tibetans. One of those students, the son of the last
prime minister of Tibet, Gelden Lhukhang, studied English privately with
Elcho. We helped him immigrate to the United States in 1964.

Elcho wanted to have a tutorial school for young Tibetan men when we
returned from furlough. Until students were sixteen, there were schools
for them, but after sixteen, no higher education was available. Miss
Wessels wanted to have the same kind of school for young women. Both
Elcho and Irma Jeane had a genuine vision to see these young people have a
chance at higher education and to let them meet Christians that cared for
their situations. Although the Tibetan young people were intelligent and
motivated, without an education their options were limited to working on
the roads and weaving carpets. The Tarings and TEAM were supportive
of the tentative plans for providing higher education for them.

25

A Fabulous Trip Home

When Mary Ellen, Miriam, and LeRoy had their winter vacation from Woodstock School in 1963, I wanted to go home on our regular furlough. Because Elcho was helping the Tarings with several projects, he wanted to stay awhile longer in Mussoorie, but he agreed that we should go on ahead to the States and get the children ready for their new schools. We both felt confident that we would return to the Tibetan border to continue working with Tibetans.

After almost six years in India, Mary Ellen, Miriam, LeRoy, and I boarded a plane in New Delhi and began our journey back to America. In those days, no commercial airlines flew directly to the States, but they always stopped in various countries. Mr. Chugh, our Indian Sikh travel agent, arranged for us to stop in places that we wanted to visit. The price of air tickets was the same if we broke our journey or flew directly. We thought that this was too great an opportunity to pass up. We flew to Tehran, Iran, where we had a refueling stop for a couple of hours. Even though it was the middle of the night, we disembarked for a while. We wanted to say we had been in Iran.

Then we flew to Beirut, Lebanon, en route to Jerusalem. Mr. Chugh had arranged for us to stay free in a nice hotel in Beirut not far from the airport. The children were delighted that our hotel had a swimming pool and an ice-skating rink, and we enjoyed both of these attractions. On a tour of the city before we boarded the small plane for Jerusalem, we were surprised to see many armed soldiers and armored vehicles.

In Jerusalem, Mrs. Lambie, aunt to our dear friend Anita Warren, had invited us to stay with her. She met us with her car and driver and took us to her lovely home in Bethlehem. Mrs. Lambie and her medical doctor husband were Presbyterian missionaries who had lived in Bethlehem for many years. They had established a thriving hospital in the city. After his death, she remained in Bethlehem.

We had a wonderful few days, walking where Jesus walked. In Bethlehem, we visited several places that "could have been the inn." In Jerusalem, we stood on the Mount of Olives, looked down on the city, and saw the magnificent Dome of the Rock. Visiting the garden tomb was a highlight for us. Even though it seemed to us that it could be the real tomb, we liked what the guide said, "The most important thing is that the tomb is empty!" Yes, we have a risen Lord!

I can't say that we swam in the Dead Sea, but we liked falling backwards in the water and not sinking. LeRoy and the girls went boating on the Jordan River. What a thrill to be where John the Baptist baptized our Lord (Mark 1:9). While we missed Elcho, still in India, the children and I enjoyed seeing these historic places.

After excursions in Switzerland and France, we flew to Los Angeles, where my mother met us and took us to the house in Orange, California, she had arranged for us to rent. The children settled into school, and we visited friends and relatives. Three months later, Mother stayed with the children, and a friend bought me a ticket to fly to New York to meet Elcho and then for us to go to the TEAM conference in Wheaton, Illinois.

We were delighted to spend the day in New York with Norbu, the Dalai Lama's older brother. Anthropologist Dr. Margaret Mead's office was next to his, and he introduced us to her. During lunch, Norbu put a pat of butter, a tea bag, a pinch of salt, and a little half-and-half in his cup before he added hot water. He asked us to do the same, and we did. He asked us how we liked his version of Tibetan tea. Elcho laughed and told him that he had been in the States long enough to forget what real Tibetan tea tasted like.

We also visited Ilia Tolstoy in his office. We had met him in Mussoorie when he visited the Tarings. They had befriended him in Tibet when President Franklin D. Roosevelt chose him to fly the shorter route to Russia over Tibet. Mr. Tolstoy had many rare pictures taken in the early 1940s of Lhasa and gave us some.

From New York, we flew to Minneapolis, Minnesota, where we were the guests of Ruth Stam's loving parents. Her father had a radio program and was teaching at Bethel College in St. Paul. He arranged several meetings for us to show slides and tell about our ministry with Tibetans.

Elcho's first meeting was for the chapel service at Bethel College. Dr. Stam gave him a flattering introduction then Elcho spoke briefly and started to show slides. After the first slide, he hit the reverse button on the remote control instead of the forward button, and all fifty slides spilled all over the floor. We sang a few hymns while we frantically tried to get the slides back into some kind of order. Our furlough had begun!

At our TEAM conference in Wheaton, Illinois, we enjoyed fellowship with missionaries from all over the world. Elcho spoke to an adult Sunday-school class at Wheaton Bible Church, and I spoke to several hundred young people in the college group. My friend from Yakima, Washington, and a former missionary in China, Winifred Crapushetts, was their teacher. I told the young people what God was doing among the Tibetan people in India and challenged them to give their lives for His service.

Then we flew on to Orange, California, to be with Mary Ellen, Miriam, and LeRoy. One of the hardest things about living overseas was not getting to know our nieces and nephews and not seeing our families for years on end. My sister Sadie and her husband Pete Ackley and their five children, visited us in Orange. They had been in Africa during the years we were in India, so we had not seen each other for fifteen years.

We enjoyed our furlough more than the children did. We were seeing old friends, while everyone and everything was different for them. Their classmates at school sometimes talked about things they didn't understand, and many didn't understand them. One day LeRoy came home from school very upset. When I asked him what the matter was, he showed me his paper with the multiple-choice sentence: "Camels are found in the open field, the zoo, or a city street." LeRoy, of course, chose the open field, as that was the only place he had seen camels. It had been marked wrong, and he didn't know why. He had never been to a zoo but had seen many camels in the fields of India. Fortunately, his teacher was in our church and asked us about it the next Sunday. She agreed to give him full credit for a correct answer.

We had good slides and bought a projector on which we learned how to push the right buttons at the right time. We often presented the ministry to churches and friends. During the summer months, we went to Oregon and Washington State to visit family, friends, and supporting churches. My mother arranged a reunion for us sisters in Yakima. My three sisters Sadie, Jeane, and Polly and their families were there. It was the only time we were ever all together with our families.

My sister Jeane and Bill were living in Seattle. They knew we wanted to spend time with Tibetans who were at the University of Washington. So they gave a delicious barbecue picnic for us, and we invited many of our Tibetan friends, including Geleg's mother, Lhadun, and eight others.

While in Seattle, Elcho visited the University of Washington and met several Tibetans teaching and studying there. He was accepted for the summer session of Tibetan language and studies.

26

Our Second Furlough

In the fall, we returned to our rented home in Orange County, California. The children went back to school, and we presented our work in various churches, often giving an Indian dinner before the slides. We were almost like a normal American family for a few months.

When we spoke about our ministry with Tibetan refugees, we asked for warm, used clothing for the children. We sewed two hundred bundles into strong burlap sacks and sent them to the Tibetans in Mussoorie. Friends in churches helped us sew the bundles, and some even helped pay the postage.

Jetsun Pema, our friend and the Dalai Lama's younger sister, visited us for ten days. She especially enjoyed visiting with "Aunt Mary" Marshburn and picking fresh oranges. While she was there, we put on an Indian dinner for two hundred people in a church where we told of our opportunities to help and witness to the Tibetans. Jetsun Pema helped us cook the dinner, and her tears flowed as she peeled onions. On her return to India, she played a major part in the education of Tibetan refugee children and was the first woman minister ever to be part of the Tibetan government in exile.

We showed Jetsun Pema and her friend Legin Tsering, who had accompanied her to California, some of the attractions of Southern California: Disneyland, Knott's Berry Farm, Forest Lawn (including the stained-glass window of Leonardo da Vinci's *The Last Supper*), the beach, and several nice restaurants.

One day, we took Jetsun Pema for a buffet lunch. Although she had been schooled in England and Switzerland, she had never eaten mashed potatoes before. "What is that?" Pema asked the lady behind the counter in the buffet line.

"What does it look like?" the woman snapped back.

I was embarrassed and explained to Jetsun Pema about mashed potatoes. The rude woman would have asked the same question if she had been in Tibet eating Tibetan food, I'm sure.

Aunt Mary and I drove Jetsun Pema to Visalia and Three Rivers to visit Aunt Mary's brother and his wife. They had a comfortable home on the river. We enjoyed walking along the river in the evenings and going to sleep with the sound of the roaring water. In her book, *Tibet, My Story*, published in 1987, Jetsun Pema mentions her visit with us.

As soon as school was out, we vacated the house in Orange County and drove to Seattle, Washington. Along the way, we stopped and said good-bye to family and friends as we made plans to return to India.

We decided that the children and I would return to India first to get Mary Ellen, Miriam, and LeRoy settled for the beginning term in Woodstock School, and Elcho would stay in Seattle to study the Tibetan language for the summer quarter at the University of Washington.

While in Seattle, we stayed with former TEAM missionaries Dr. and Mrs. Zerne and Carolyn Chapman. The night before we were to return to India, I had a fever and wasn't feeling well. Zerne called the airlines and changed my ticket for three days later. He also called people who were meeting us along the journey back to India. I recuperated while Carolyn took the children shopping for more school clothes and prepared delicious meals. Zerne's parents invited Elcho to live with them while he studied at the university. Three days later, I felt fine, and we left for Tokyo, Japan— the first leg of our return journey to Mussoorie, India.

In the 1950s, we enjoyed leisurely ship travel to India, but flying in the early 1960s had many advantages. Our Indian travel agent, Mr. Chugh, got us flights where the airlines paid for our stay in luxury hotels. When the children and I flew back to India in 1964, Japan Airlines put us up in two adjoining rooms in the Tokyo Hilton. They also gave us meal vouchers in their beautiful dining room for dinner and breakfast. Our missionary friend, Betty Lyons, spent the night with us. Mary Ellen and

Miriam enjoyed the big-screen TV in their private room with two full-sized beds. LeRoy and I both had two big beds in our room too. He slept, but Betty and I talked all night. Betty was homesick, and we talked about our mutual friends and the joys and hardships of being missionaries.

The next morning, we enjoyed a tour of Tokyo, then boarded the hotel's shuttle to the airport and flew to Bangkok, Thailand. We stayed in a missionary guesthouse in downtown Bangkok, which was managed by the parents of Miriam's classmates at Woodstock. We went to church with another missionary family whose daughter was in Woodstock and to their home for a Thai dinner. Afterwards, we went sightseeing around the city. The children and I didn't enjoy seeing the many temples, but we did enjoy the boat cruise and seeing the floating gardens.

Two days later, we flew to New Delhi, India, where we arrived at two o'clock in the morning. As we got off the plane, an Indian official sprayed us with disinfectant. We surmised he did this so we wouldn't bring germs into the country. We took an airport bus to the YWCA, where we had a room waiting for us. We had a good night's sleep and left on the noon train for Dehra Dun, en route to Landour, Mussoorie. Our missionary friend Charles Warren, met us in his Jeep in Dehra Dun and drove us up the winding road to Landour. We were glad to be back in Mussoorie.

I was asked to be the supervisor of Ridgewood, the little boys' hostel at Woodstock School, until Elcho returned and got the Tibetan Tutorial School established. LeRoy and I stayed in the supervisor's quarters, and Mary Ellen and Miriam went into the high-school girls' dormitory a few yards further down the hillside from Ridgewood.

27

Back in Mussoorie

Ridgewood was the boarding hostel for boys who were in the first through eighth grades. We frequently had about one hundred boys in residence. At the time, most of the boys were missionary children.

Joan Fitzroy, an Anglo-Sinhalese single mother of three girls, was the matron of the first- and second-grade boys. Her husband had been killed four years earlier in a Jeep accident. One day, I went to her home and found her crying and obviously upset. When I asked her what was wrong, she told me that singer Jim Reeves had just been killed in a plane crash. I had never heard of him, but she lent us some of his records. Our family grew to like his singing, and we often played his records in the evenings. Joan had two teenage daughters, Kathy and Janet, in the Wynberg-Allen boarding school, and six-year-old Judy lived with her.

One weekend an Indian lady came to Ridgewood, dressed elegantly in a beautiful silk sari and wearing long, dangling earrings. She said that she was there to leave Suneil Anand, her third-grade boy, in our boarding school. I had not been notified of this, and I could not get hold of Canon Burgoyne, the principal, but I decided to admit the handsome little boy. His mother told me she had been raised in a Christian family and wanted her son in a Christian school. After Suneil said good-bye to his mother, I helped him unpack in the primary boys' dorm. Everything in his suitcase was brand-new and of excellent quality. I found out the next day that his mother, Kalpana Kartik, was a movie star, and his father was Dev Anand,

Tenzin Dhargyal (to the left of LeRoy) keeps in contact with us. He's in Dharamsala, India. Next to him is Tenzin Chodak, one of the students we helped to come to the U.S. He was in charge of the Tibet office in New York for many years and presented us with a brocade tapestry of the Potala when he visited us before Elcho's death.

the "Clark Gable" of India. When the father came to visit, I understood why he was such a popular movie star, as he was quite good-looking. Later, Suneil's three younger sisters joined him in Woodstock, and they all graduated from there.

While we were on furlough, Ruth Stam tried to decide how we could best help the Tibetans in Mussoorie. In the TEAM *Missionary Broadcaster* (June 1964), Ruth wrote an article entitled, "Old House Becomes New Home for Tibetan Refugee Children."

> For three years, TEAM has sponsored several Tibetan refugee children at the Wynberg-Allen School in Mussoorie, the northern part of India. They are part of the vast company of Tibetans who fled with their leader, the Dalai Lama, when Communist Chinese took control of their country. Within the first two years, fifty thousand Tibetans fled to India, many of them settling in camps in the Landour-Mussoorie area.

Because of more recent conflicts on the Indo-Tibetan border, seven schools and several thousand children located near the border had to flee a second time from the Communists.

When this happened, the question for us as TEAM missionaries was no longer, "Can we raise funds for half-a-dozen children?" but rather, "What can we do about caring for half a hundred?"

The few children we were already sponsoring at the Wynberg-Allen School had been carefully chosen, and they were doing well. We rejoiced to see their development in such a splendid Christian institution.

Although dormitory space at the school was already overcrowded, we were faced with the urgent need for the care and education of more Tibetan children. When everything seemed impossible, a solution was found: a special hostel where children could live while attending the Wynberg-Allen School. This would enable the school to take in forty new Tibetan refugee children in a year.

By the time the Dalai Lama visited Mussoorie in April, a large but empty old house had been found. It was bought for the school by one of the relief agencies, and I was asked to organize the hostel and get it started.

Within ten days from the date of purchase, thirty-five children had been selected, and we moved in. We hardly had time to clean out the six-year accumulation of dirt and cobwebs.

We had mattresses but no beds. We had cooking utensils but no tables. Relief rations of milk, wheat, and beans arrived twelve hours before the children. We had a roof, food, and bedding and, thank God, a staff to help. When the children arrived, we also had chicken pox, mumps, sore eyes, and various intestinal parasites, not to mention lice. Later, more children came until we had fifty-six in the house. A Christian Tibetan from Dharchula, a former TEAM station near the Tibetan border, came to help with the cooking, washing, and mending. The children learned Hindi and English in school. In the hostel, we had evening Bible reading in

Tibetan. Several other missionaries helped me, and after two months, we got a full-time matron who also spoke Tibetan.

The last few months have given us much reason for thanksgiving for beds, tables, chairs, and equipment provided by CARE and other organizations; for proper sanitary facilities completed and repairs begun; for donations of used clothing and funds to buy new things; and for those who have helped us add vegetables, fruit, and a little meat to our relief rations.

For the provision of all these material blessings, we give thanks to God and to His children who have had a part in it.

We thank God, too, for bringing us several Tibetan teenagers whose lives had already been touched by His servants and whose hearts longed to know Him.

It is no light task for workers at the hostel and teachers in the school to be responsible for these children from strong Buddhist backgrounds who have suffered so much.

LeRoy with Jigme and "Amala" in our front yard in Landour, Mussoorie. We had a majestic view of the Himalayan mountain range and enjoyed entertaining in our yard.

But here is tremendous potential. These keen, alert children can, in time, be leaders among their own people in education, economic progress, and, we trust, in spiritual counsel. Every day there are needs to be met in these young lives—mental, social, and spiritual. Only the Spirit of God can give us the wisdom we need.

We were never able to enter Tibet, but God, in sovereign wisdom, has permitted the Tibetans to be brought to us. This is our day of opportunity!

In the spring of 1964, Jigme Dorji, the prime minister of Bhutan, was assassinated. We were sorry to hear this, as his wife, Tessla, Mrs. Taring's niece, was a good friend of ours. She helped a great deal with the Tibetan refugees in Mussoorie. In the next few years, we got to know her even better. Later, she married another friend of ours, Shamchok, who was a few years older than she was but had never married. We were delighted to have them as our guests in our Orange, California, home when they visited America in 1978.

28

Tibetan Tutorial School

Two young men, Gedun Phunsok and Kalsang Wangden, had been waiting several weeks for Elcho to open his school. They had come to me earlier at Woodstock.

Gedun spent time with us while he waited. He and ten-year-old LeRoy became good friends. When LeRoy got the measles and couldn't stay in the dorm, he didn't want to go to the hospital to recuperate. Ruth Stam was in South India for a conference and had given us permission to use her cottage in Happy Valley any time we wanted to do so. I decided that LeRoy was better off staying in Ruth Stam's cottage with Gedun for several days.

At the end of the summer, Elcho joined us in Mussoorie. He had studied hard and done well in his Tibetan studies at the University of Washington. Soon after his return, we moved to a bungalow, Seaforth Lodge, on the back of the hill above Woodstock School.

Since Elcho had given our well-used green Jeep station wagon to TEAM for their use before we went on furlough, we bought a used Jeep. Elcho rented an empty, run-down bungalow, The Firs, for the new school. When the news spread that Elcho had returned and that the school was opening, other young men joined Gedun and Wangden. Before long, thirty young Tibetan men came, ages sixteen to thirty. The students painted the inside of their new home and made it comfortable. Elcho hired an older Tibetan man to organize the kitchen and do the cooking, and the students divided

Elcho taught the Dalai Lama's bodyguard, classes in the Tibetan school, as well as his own Tibetan Tutorial classes (pictured here)

up the chores. They ate lots of cabbage (it was cheap) and bulgar wheat (free from CARE). We charged the students about six dollars per month for everything.

Not only did the students live in The Firs bungalow, but classes were also held there. Before long, Elcho realized that he needed two levels of English and more help in the teaching responsibilities. Fellow TEAM missionary Ralph Seefeldt joined Elcho in teaching English as a Second Language (ESL), as well as geography, mathematics, biology, history, Bible, and current events.

Elcho seldom turned any young Tibetan man away for lack of funds. He did decide not to enroll Lobsang Tashi because he knew absolutely no English and didn't seem to have the ability to learn it. When he came back one day, he begged Elcho to let him just audit. If he didn't pass the first exams, he promised to leave. Tashi studied hard in the lower class, passed the first examinations, and stayed on at the school. But he had one problem: He had already used his limited resources the first month.

An older student in the lower class, Lobsang Thupten, wanted to stay but didn't have any money. We wanted both Tashi and Thupten to study with us, so we found a happy solution. They helped us in our home and yard a couple of times a week, and we paid them for their work. Both these young men were good workers but not very academic.

In the second year of their studies in the Tibetan Tutorial School, we got requests from American diplomats and various company workers for household helpers. Indian servants usually did just one thing. For example, an *ayah* took care of the children, a cook did only the cooking and kitchen cleanup, the gardener did the outside work, and another servant did the inside cleanup. Tibetans would do all these things and made loyal servants. Both Tashi and Thupten went to New Delhi to work for government employers who eventually sponsored them to come to America. In the States they worked hard, became American citizens, and did well.

One day when we were working at the Tibetan school, Mrs. Taring asked us if we'd like to buy an eight-foot by ten-foot Tibetan carpet that had been handmade for the Dalai Lama. We did. The Dalai Lama's advisors did not like the blue color in the carpet, so they decided to raffle it. Hundreds of Tibetans paid one rupee each for the chance to get it. Our friend Tessla the widow of Jigme Dorji, the assassinated prime minister of Bhutan, was in charge of the drawing. The man who bought the winning ticket worked on roads breaking rocks and had no home. She asked him if he'd like her to sell it for him. He did, and we bought it. That beautiful carpet is a treasured remembrance in LeRoy's home today.

The Tibetan Tutorial young men often came to our home. The young people we sponsored in the Wynberg-Allen School also came to our home for the holidays, and some came on weekends.

During the next three years, more than sixty young men studied in the Tibetan Tutorial School. Now they had a chance to do something besides work on the roads in India. Various missionaries who came to the hillside for vacations helped Elcho by teaching different subjects. I taught a few classes, but my main job was hospitality, caring for our family and our many guests.

Geleg Kyarsip, the little Tibetan boy we first met in Kalimpong when he was four years old, came to live with us. Geleg's father had been guarding the Potala, the Dalai Lama's palace in Lhasa, when the Dalai Lama escaped to India in 1959. He encouraged Lhadun, Geleg's nineteen-year-old mother, to flee with their nine-month-old son to India. We knew Lhadun, who was teaching at the University of Washington and helping to write a Tibetan textbook. Geleg and LeRoy shared a bedroom. Geleg went to the Wynberg-Allen School and many days walked three miles down the hill to school and then back up the hill after school. He was a good little boy, and we have always considered him a part of our own family.

We enjoyed having the girls and LeRoy living at home and having their friends visit. We went to activities at both Woodstock, where our own children were in programs, and Wynberg-Allen, where the Tibetan children studied. We especially enjoyed watching sports days when both schools took part. Our children received a good education at Woodstock School. Miriam enjoyed acting, and one year she received the first-prize trophy as the best performer in an English language play in the entire Dehra Dun district. Both Mary Ellen and Miriam sang in the choir and were in several musicals at Woodstock.

The Wynberg-Allen students, our Tibetan Tutorial young men, and Irma Jeane's Tibetan girls often joined the church services of the Union Church in Mussoorie, where Charles Warren was the pastor. If Charles knew that Mary Ellen and Miriam were going to be there, he would ask them to sing a duet or two for the service.

The young men in the Tibetan Tutorial School studied hard and progressed rapidly in English and other subjects. Some of them came to our home to cook meals with us, play carrom, sing around the piano, or just visit over cups of tea. Irma Jeane Wessels had a similar school for girls. Sometimes our young men had dinners and other socials with her girls. The Tibetan young adults seemed to especially like those evenings.

Sometimes they would trek into the hills, away from the busy life of Mussoorie. Walking up and down those hills gave us lots of exercise, but a trek away from civilization was different. LeRoy remembers one weekend when he walked thirty miles with his dad and some students.

29

Kashmir and Tibetan Carpets

During our vacation, our family drove in our open army Jeep to Srinagar, Kashmir. We stayed two weeks in a houseboat called the *Mona Lisa*. We enjoyed riding in little covered rowboats on the lake to the Shalimar Gardens. As we rowed, we passed vendors selling their wares, such as flowers, fruits, vegetables, as well as handmade tablecloths, woodcarvings, lamps, and music boxes. Sometimes these little boats came right to our houseboat, and we invited the vendors in so we could have a better look at their wares. We each chose a souvenir to remember that happy family time.

We decided to drive home a different way, but we took a wrong turn and the road kept going further into the foothills of the Himalayas. There were no signs or places to turn around. We were glad that we had brought food and water along with us as we kept going higher into the mountains and saw less civilization. Finally, we came to a border patrol, and the guards angrily stopped us. They jumped on the Jeep while we turned around as they commanded us to do. They put a big log across the road and with guns drawn asked us to get out of the Jeep and to show them our passports. We realized that we were in a forbidden zone in Kashmir that was in dispute between India and Pakistan. We apologized to them in Hindi the best we could. While we were detained, LeRoy fell and broke his arm. When the guards saw our distress, they finally released us, and we went back down the mountain to find the hospital. It was a very frightening experience.

We went home through Manali, a place where many Tibetans had resettled. When we greeted them in Tibetan, asking them how they were, they stuck out their tongues at us (a sign of respect). They answered us in a long Tibetan dialog. We had to tell them in Hindi that we had spoken all the Tibetan that we knew.

When we got back to Mussoorie, two of our Tibetan Tutorial students, Gedun and Tsewang, asked us if we could help them sell handmade Tibetan carpets to our friends. Many missionaries came to Mussoorie for their vacations to get out of the intense heat of the plains.

This was the time of the annual Woodstock School sale, when various missions sold wares made in their different areas. The school was transformed into a big bazaar for several days. We told Gedun and Tsewang that if they could get the carpets to us, we would help sell them. The sale was a big success, and many people bought homemade Tibetan carpets. Gedun and Tsewang told us later that this sale really saved the Tibetan carpet industry.

I frequently took missionary friends to visit the Tarings and to show them around the Tibetan school and homes. Although Mr. Taring was still involved in the Tibetan school, the Indian government was in charge. The Tarings were then part of the Tibetan Homes Foundation. Several years before, in August 1962, the Dalai Lama had told Mrs. Taring that he was concerned for the children living in the transit camps on India's hot plains. Many died because of appalling conditions. He wanted the orphans and those whose parents were working on the roads to be cared for in a loving way. The Dalai Lama had talked with the Indian government, and they had agreed to the establishment of the Tibetan Homes Foundation if Tibetans themselves would run the homes. He asked Mrs. Taring to establish a few pilot homes at that time. Each home had Tibetan houseparents who were responsible for twenty-five children. They were to be like real parents, responsible for everything related to the wellbeing of the children in their care. This included cooking, washing clothes, cleanliness, and discipline. Of course, the children helped a great deal. Mrs. Taring approached many relief organizations, and people around the world helped financially in this venture.

Before we went on our second furlough, the Tibetan Home Foundation in Happy Valley, Mussoorie, had established three homes as a pilot program to see how it would work. We were with the Tarings when the first seventy-five children arrived. Many of them had eye infections, skin diseases, and were severely undernourished, with bloated tummies.

By the summer of 1965, three years later, the Tibetan Homes Foundation had twenty-five homes in Happy Valley, Mussoorie. From the hot plains of India, five hundred healthy, happy children were in homes in Mussoorie. Relief organizations around the world had helped them purchase and remodel abandoned bungalows or helped them build new homes. There was the Swiss Aid to Tibetans home, the Save the Children home, the Dutch Aid to Tibetans home, etc. Five hundred more children lived in the dormitories of the Tibetan refugee school. By 1965, over one thousand children were in the school we had worked in a few years earlier. Many of Elcho's first students, including Anand Dawa, who used to live with us, were now married and served as houseparents in the homes.

Tibetan homes were also established in Switzerland, Germany, and England. Swiss families adopted other children. Through the efforts of Mr. Aeschiman, about two hundred Swiss families adopted Tibetan children. The plan was originally for only orphans to go abroad, but it didn't turn out that way. One day when I was with Mrs. Taring, a faithful Tibetan tailor came to her, very upset, and asked why his little girl couldn't go abroad too. She shouldn't be deprived of this opportunity just because he hadn't died in the trek out of Tibet like his wife had. Other parents came to her expressing their thoughts that it wasn't fair that, because they hadn't died, their children couldn't go abroad. They were willing to give up their children for adoption to be raised in another country by foreigners so they would have better opportunities in life.

When we were in Zurich with the Aeschiman family, we saw the tailor's daughter, and we were glad to see that she had adjusted well to her new life. Naturally, there were many pros and cons about this type of adoption, but at the time, it seemed to be a good idea.

30

Darjeeling, Nepal, and Aunt Mary's Visit

In 1966, our family went to Kalimpong and Darjeeling. Elcho and I had been there for a conference of people working with Tibetans several years earlier, but this time we took Mary Ellen, Miriam, and LeRoy for a two-week family vacation. We enjoyed the small-gauge train trip up the mountain to Darjeeling. Our Tibetan hosts arranged a place for us to stay. We went to bed early, since they planned to pick us up before dawn the next morning so we could see the sun come up over Mt. Everest.

Early the next morning, we went by Jeep to a place about fifteen miles up from Darjeeling. As the sun came up, we stood on a high lookout where we had a spectacular view of the towering Himalayan Mountains and four countries. To the east we saw Bhutan, to the west we saw Sikkim and Nepal, and we were in India.

The next day, we went to Kalimpong to stay in Ahawa, a lovely missionary guesthouse with a charming Norwegian hostess. Elcho's student, Wangden, and his friend were also vacationing in Kalimpong, so they introduced us to their Tibetan friends. They showed us around and helped us purchase two Tibetan hand-carved tables.

We decided that, since we were so close, we would drive home by way of Kathmandu, Nepal. The very narrow, bumpy road into Nepal was built on the side of a mountain. It had a high hill on one side and a deep cliff on the other. When a vehicle came from the opposite direction, we got as close to the side of the mountain as we possibly could. It was scary, but we finally made it to Kathmandu and had two days with our friends, Dr. Carl and Betty Friedericks, working with the United Mission to Nepal. Fortunately, the road back home was a different route through Raxul. We were thankful to get back to Mussoorie.

After the holiday, Tibetan Tutorial classes began again. A few young men didn't return to Mussoorie, and a few new ones enrolled. About thirty-five young men lived together in The Firs and studied in the classes at one time.

We invited Aunt Mary Marshburn to visit us, so she wrote early in 1967 that she would like to spend six weeks with us. Since those of us working with Tibetans were going to Kathmandu, Nepal, for a conference, we suggested that she meet us there. Elcho, LeRoy, and I flew to meet her on the specified date. Having been born in 1900, she was sixty-seven years old at the time. We stayed in a missionary guesthouse in Nepal, and our missionary friend, Dr. Jonathan Lindell, working in Nepal, showed us around. (His daughter, Nonie, was a good friend of our girls and often came home for the weekends with them.) After several days, we took Aunt Mary by plane, train, taxi, and rickshaw to our home in Mussoorie.

The Tibetan young people loved her. She was such a good sport and a big help in teaching the young men. The teenagers from the Christian schools often came to our home on the weekends. We had meals outside in our front yard, where we had a spectacular view of the snow-covered mountains. Inside, we sang while Aunt Mary played the piano, Elcho and Mary Ellen played the accordion, Miriam played the violin, and LeRoy the trumpet. We played ping-pong, volleyball, carrom, or chess. Aunt Mary enjoyed it all.

Aunt Mary spent hours talking with the Tibetan young people, and they enjoyed hearing her stories. She lovingly told them of her Savior, and it made lasting impressions on them. Many Tibetans and missionaries invited her to dinner, and the Tibetan school put on a special program for her.

Since our Jeep was giving us a lot of trouble, Aunt Mary helped us get a bigger, newer means of transportation. Elcho went to New Delhi and purchased an Indian-made vehicle. Our new "Jeep" was a pretty green color and looked something like a big pickup truck. The cab comfortably held three people, and the back had benches on the sides, where eight or ten people could sit. A canvas covering could be put on for long journeys or rain. We often crowded fifteen young people in the back for a ride.

Some days Aunt Mary and I went to each one of Elcho's classes, and some days she sat in our front yard, enjoying our fresh air and nice scenery, while making audio tapes for her children in California.

One day Aunt Mary received a phone call from California. Doug Marshburn, her sixteen-year-old grandson, had been badly injured in a car accident. His friend had been killed, and Doug was in a serious condition. So Aunt Mary decided to return home to be with her family. Although Doug lived through those terrible weeks, he recovered as a paraplegic. It's been a hard life for him, but Doug loves the Lord and has gone to Thailand to teach English several times.

Our family drove Aunt Mary in our new vehicle to see the Taj Mahal before her flight home. As we were running a little late, Elcho dropped us off at the New Delhi airport then went to park the Jeep. We waited and waited, and finally Aunt Mary had to board her plane without saying good-bye to Elcho.

31

Our Last Vacation in India: Kashmir Again

Mary Ellen wanted to return to Kashmir before she graduated from Woodstock and left India for the States. We decided to drive our new Jeep-truck to Palgoam, Kashmir. Each of the children took a friend. Mary Ellen took Nonie Lindell, whose father had so graciously showed Aunt Mary and us around Nepal. Miriam took her friend Karen Bowdish, and LeRoy took Geleg, who was living with us at the time. Elcho and I invited our good friends Canon Samuel Burgoyne and his wife Mary.

One afternoon, the ten of us piled into our Jeep with the tarp fastened overhead to drive to Kashmir. We all took turns riding up front with Elcho, who did all the driving, and sitting or lying in the back under the tent-like covering. We drove through the night, arriving at our destination of Palgoum, Kashmir, very tired at dusk the next evening. All along the journey, Mary Burgoyne gave us treats to enjoy. She had been saving goodies from her packages from home for just such an occasion. The scenery was breathtaking, but the narrow road was treacherous, with high mountains on one side and deep valleys and cliffs on the other. We had reserved two cabins, but the Burgoynes, veteran hikers that they were, opted to sleep in the little tent that they had brought along. We were quickly settled, and after a light meal that we cooked on a kerosene stove, we went to bed.

The next morning we woke up early, feeling refreshed. The air was clear, the sky was blue, and the scenery was beautiful. The next week, we went hiking and horseback riding. We played games and read books. One

LeRoy, Millie, Mary Ellen, Geleg Kyarsip, Nonie Lindell, Karen Bowdish, and Miriam.

day, when we went horseback riding along a narrow path, with mountains on one side and a deep cliff on the other, Elcho's horse became startled and threw him off. He narrowly missed falling hundreds of feet below. He landed on his camera that was strapped to his shoulder. While he was in pain for several days, we were thankful he had missed a tragic fall that would undoubtedly have taken his life.

It was a nice break from our routine lives in Mussoorie. On our return home, the next big step was Mary Ellen's graduation from Woodstock and sending her to California.

In August 1967, we wrote this in our letter home:

> Have you wondered what it is like to be a missionary child? Here in Northern India, high-school graduation means more than just receiving a diploma. It means farewells to childhood places and friends of many different nationalities. It means leaving parents and family and going alone ten thousand miles to your own country, where you have spent only two or three years of your life. Even though the farewells are difficult, you look forward to the new life that is ahead for you. So it is for our Mary Ellen and her classmates as they leave school here in the Himalayas for all parts of the world.

The full moon made the snow-covered mountains from Mary Ellen's bedroom window so picturesque. I went into her bedroom about two o'clock in the morning. She was standing at the window crying.

"What's the matter, honey?" I asked.

"I'm just reliving the many happy memories I've had here. It is just so hard to say good-bye," she said. "I wonder what is ahead for me." Although she didn't know what was ahead for her, she trusted the Lord to go before her as she went to California without us.

The graduation ceremonies and reception went well. Mary Ellen sang a solo, accompanied by her dad on the accordion. Many Tibetans, including the Tarings and Tessla Dorji, came to Mary Ellen's graduation. A few days later, she left India with the Charles Warren family and flew to Orange, California, to live with Aunt Mary until Biola classes began.

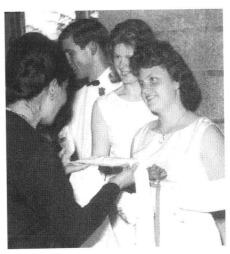

Tessla Dorji presented Mary Ellen with a Tibetan scarf at her Woodstock high-school graduation in June 1967.

32

Good-bye to India

The Tibetan young men in the tutorial classes and the teenage Tibetan students in the Wynberg-Allen School were all doing well in their studies. Along with their academic studies, all the students were required to take Bible classes, memorize Bible verses, and go to Union Church on Sundays.

In the fall of 1967, when it was time to renew our visas, we sensed resentment from the Indian police. We had never had any problems before. As we thought and prayed about the situation, we realized how it looked to the Indian authorities—we were foreigners working with other foreigners in India. We obviously had a good relationship with the Tibetans, and the Indians probably didn't understand this. We were well aware that we were not only Americans working closely with Tibetans under the authority of Indians, but we were also Christians working with Buddhists in a Hindu country.

One day our friend, Sonam, the Dalai Lama's personal interpreter, was in Mussoorie. As we talked with him, Elcho told him our situation. "Tell me frankly," Elcho said, "what do you suggest we do?"

"I'd go back to America before I was asked to go," he replied.

While his honest reply shocked us, we had been thinking the same thing.

"What do you think about us bringing several of the smartest young men from the tutorial classes to America for college?" Elcho asked.

"Let me talk to His Holiness, the Dalai Lama, about it," Sonam answered. "If you're serious, I'll talk to him and get back to you."

Some of the students at Elcho's Tibetan Tutorial classes present Mary Ellen with a Tibetan rug.

Miriam lacked only one English-class credit to graduate from Woodstock High School in December. Mrs. Burgoyne, her English teacher, agreed to give Miriam the credit if she did two book reports and sent them back to her at Woodstock.

Reluctantly, we made plans to return to the States, but again we both had peace about our decision.

Tibetan and missionary friends gave us fond farewells. It was hard to say good-bye to our many friends throughout India, yet, we realized that this was the best thing to do. As a ship was leaving Bombay a few days before Christmas for Trieste, Italy, we booked passages on it.

Many of the Tibetan Tutorial students took jobs in various Tibetan offices and camps in India. We turned over all our equipment and supplies to Mr. Gurgen, a Tibetan Christian who lived in a small town down the hill five miles from Dehra Dun called Rajpur. He knew English well and agreed to carry on classes with about fifteen young men from our school. Mr. Gurgen's sister, Mrs. Phunsok, was our friend and a charming Christian Tibetan lady. Their family was from Moravia, and their father

166 • Wherever He Leads

was the first to translate the Bible into Tibetan. We felt good about the Moravian mission carrying on our work in a limited way.

Missionary friends drove us to Dehra Dun, where we took the train to New Delhi. A number of Tibetans came to New Delhi to see us. Before we left Mussoorie, we got a telegram from Sonam, the Dalai Lama's interpreter, saying that the Dalai Lama would be in New Delhi, and he would be glad to have an audience with us. We telegraphed him that we would be delighted and arranged to see him there.

When we arrived in New Delhi for our interview with him, we were surprised to see many hippie-type American Buddhists trying to see him. Sonam told us that the Dalai Lama was so busy that he had accepted only two audiences: one with Indian Prime Minister Indira Ghandi, and the other with us.

During our time with the Dalai Lama, he was very gracious. His English had improved remarkably. We presented him with white silk scarves, and he presented scarves to us. He thanked us for our years of helping his people, and we assured him that the pleasure was ours. The Dalai Lama asked us what our future plans were. Elcho said he would like to bring several young men from the Tibetan Tutorial School to America for further studies. He liked the idea and gave us his approval.

Through the years, we've been asked many times how we, as Christian missionaries, had this close relationship with the Dalai Lama, his family, and other Tibetan leaders. It was easy to love the Tibetans and to help them in their time of need. We were in the right place at the right time. We were told that the Dalai Lama had told students in Christian environments to be like ducks in a pond, that is, to let the "water" of Christianity not affect them too much. We believe that the Dalai Lama, as well as the students, respected us for being firm in our own Christian beliefs. At the same time, we honored him as their leader. No doubt, he is a sincere, personable man, and he cares deeply about his people. As it happens, his birthday is the same day as mine, July 6 (he's ten years younger). Tibetans always celebrate our birthdays! We hope and pray that they saw that we love Jesus and serve a risen Lord.

We had walked through doors that had opened for us to help and be witnesses to the Tibetan people. My life verse, John 15:16, talks about fruit. We had many opportunities during nearly nine years living in

Mussoorie, but we had not seen much fruit in the way of conversions. However, we leave results up to the Lord.

Our Brahmin Hindu friend, Babu Kelkar, met the train when we arrived in Bombay. We checked into our favorite little hotel near the Victoria train station, and then he drove us to his home where his wife, Shaila, had prepared a delicious Indian feast for us—a real farewell to India. Our hotel was near stores where we did last-minute shopping.

As we went for a final day of shopping, Elcho reminded us that our things for the hold had already been checked aboard the vessel. Anything we bought had to be put into our suitcases and carried aboard the ship to our cabin. Also, we needed the funds we had to get us all the way to California. Even though I heard him say that, I fell in love with an ivory-inlaid, hand-carved rosewood table. The legs were hand-carved elephants. It was quite heavy, but the legs came out of the ivory-inlaid tabletop. The top fit into my suitcase, but none of us could get the legs into our suitcases. So, we each carried a leg onto the ship. When Babu came to the ship to bid us farewell, he laughed at us carrying wooden elephant legs to our cabin.

We embarked on the luxury liner, *Atlanta*. It was the sister ship of the *Victoria*, the ship that we had arrived on twelve years before. We had sold our vehicle to Mrs. Taring for the Tibetan Homes Foundation and, with the funds, ordered a Volkswagen hatchback to be picked up from a special mission agency in Hamburg, Germany.

The restful sea voyage was just what we needed. We had mixed emotions about leaving India, for it had been our home for eighteen years. Miriam finished her English term paper and book reports to send back to Mrs. Burgoyne so she could graduate with her Woodstock class of 1968. Mary Ellen was happy at Biola College, and Miriam wanted to go there too.

We didn't know what we would do after we got back to the States, but we knew that the Lord had led us this far. We were confident that He would continue to lead us. We reminded each other of one of our favorite verses, "I will instruct you and teach you in the way you should go; I will guide you with My eye" (Psalm 32:8). We looked up other promises in the Bible where God said He would guide His children. We also spent time as a family praying about what we should do next. We wanted to serve the Lord, but we didn't know where that would be. For now, it was time for us to enjoy our trip back to our own country.

Since the Suez Canal was closed, our ship had to go around the Cape of Good Hope. Our first stop was Mombassa, Kenya. We had about six hours ashore. We did a little sightseeing and then saw that an Indian movie starring Dev Anand was playing, so we went to see it. The theater was so filled with Indians that we wondered if we were really in Africa. Our next stop was Cape Town, South Africa. We spent the day with an Anglo-Indian family whose artistically talented sisters were among our friends in Mussoorie.

Our friends took us in their car around the beautiful, modern city of Cape Town. We went by the hospital where Dr. Christiaan Barnard had performed the first human-heart transplant the day before. We also saw the problems of South Africa in a new way—train stations for whites and blacks, separate trains for blacks, and segregated drinking fountains and restrooms. The Gordon family took us to their neat and comfortable home for afternoon tea and then back to our ship.

Elcho decided to get off the ship at the island of Cyprus. This is the third largest island in the Mediterranean Sea, located west of Syria and south of Turkey. Then he flew to Hamburg, Germany, to pick up our Volkswagen and would drive to meet us when the ship docked in Trieste, Italy. It was a good idea, but we made alternate plans, just in case he wasn't there to meet us.

When our ship slowly came into the port of Trieste, Miriam, LeRoy, and I were delighted to see Elcho standing on the dock waving at us! It was exciting to see our new cream-colored hatchback Volkswagen. We drove to the bed-and-breakfast pension, where we had made reservations.

The next day, we drove across the Italian border into Yugoslavia. We stopped to walk around awhile and to do a little shopping. When we got to the car, Elcho realized he had left the keys inside! What to do? There was no AAA to call. Finally, a nice stranger helped him find a wire coat hanger, and through the window that was left open a crack, he and Elcho got the door open. We happily went back to our pension in Italy.

One of the small purchases we made in Yugoslavia was a jar of delicious-looking berry jam. When we got back to our pension, Miriam was carrying it in a paper sack. Somehow the bottom of the sack broke, and the jar tumbled down a flight of fifty wooden steps where it crashed on the bottom. What a mess!

We knew this would probably be our last opportunity to be in Europe, so the next day we drove to Venice and then to Florence. We had seen a circus advertised, so after settling into our pension, we decided to go to it. It was a great evening with LeRoy and Miriam. In the plaza in front of the Florentine town hall, we saw the gigantic, 14.24-foot tall marble statue of Michelangelo's *David*.

The next day we drove south to Rome, arriving in the late afternoon. As our hotel was on a one-way street, Elcho let Miriam, LeRoy, and me out with our overnight luggage, telling us that he'd drive around the block. I had made the hotel arrangements, and I took the "important papers" briefcase with our traveler's checks, passports, and hotel reservations with me. We settled into the hotel and waited for Elcho. One hour passed. We went downstairs and stood in front of the hotel parking lot to watch for him. Another hour came and went with still no sign of him. We were getting concerned. By now, it was dark, and the streetlights were on. Finally, he drove up, and he was as elated to see us as we were to see him. There were many one-way streets, and they didn't run horizontally. Thinking he would recognize the street, he couldn't remember the name of our small hotel. He had gotten completely lost in a strange city with all the streets looking similar.

We went on to Germany where we visited several of our former students, including Dawa and Dickie, living in a Tibetan youth hostel. They were happy to see us and didn't want us to leave them. Although they were nicely settled, they missed Mussoorie. About fifteen Tibetan teenagers lived there with a Tibetan family. We enjoyed a delicious Tibetan dinner with them. They told us of another group of Tibetans in another city, so they made reservations for us to stop there the next day. This group of Tibetans also welcomed us and insisted that we share a meal.

We loaded a newly purchased steamer trunk, packed with the elephant tabletop, its three legs, and some clothes, in our new Volkswagen and put it on a ship bound for New York. Then we flew to London, England.

London was rainy and cold, but we enjoyed our time in that bustling metropolis. Genden Choden, a nineteen-year-old Tibetan girl who used to be in the Tibetan school and who came to our home in Mussoorie many times, was studying in London. When we called her, she was excited and wanted to meet us right away. We arranged to meet her at a designated tea shop. She cried when she saw us because she had been lonely and homesick. She said it was difficult to make English friends. Our hearts ached for her, and we wished that we could do more for her. Without hesitation, she accepted our invitation to go to dinner and to spend the night in the guesthouse with us. She and Miriam shared a room, and I think they talked most of the night.

Thubten Tenzin, who used to live with us when he was being trained to be an assistant to the Dalai Lama's cook, met us in London. In Mussoorie Elcho had helped him with private English lessons, and I taught him to make chocolate cake and Western dishes. He was now working in the Tibetan Pestalozzi Children's Village in England. He had many stories to tell us about his experiences in England. He said he was amazed that white people in London went to the beaches in the summer trying to get brown. In India, people with brown skin put on creams and powders, trying to be white. He took us to visit the Tibetan children in his care there. One of those children, Phuntsok Tashi, went back to India to help his people and became the director of the Vocational Training Center for Tibetan young people in the Indian state of Uttar Pradesh.

Part 4
Orange County

33

Following a New Path

In January 1968, our ship landed in New York City. A friend living there met us at the dock, and we piled her station wagon high with our hand luggage and rode to her home.

The next day, we put Miriam on a plane to join Mary Ellen at Biola. When we were alone in the guest room, I asked Elcho, "What are we going to do? We're not going back to India, so we have to make some decisions."

Elcho smiled. "First, we wait for our car and the things coming on the ship that arrives in a couple of days. We don't have to decide the future now."

I frowned. "But what can we do in the States?"

"We'll talk it over with our mission leaders when we get to TEAM headquarters," he said. "But now, let's pray." We knelt and committed the future to God.

Elcho, thirteen-year-old LeRoy, and I began driving across country in our Volkswagen. Along the way, we saw Niagara Falls and the home of Abraham Lincoln in Springfield, Missouri. We visited family and friends and spoke in several churches, arriving in Wheaton, Illinois, in time for our annual TEAM conference.

When we talked with mission authorities, they asked, "What are your plans for the future? Are you ready to be assigned to another field?"

We looked at each other. "Another field?" Elcho asked. "No, we don't believe our work with Tibetans is finished just because we returned to the States. We don't have any idea what we'll do now, but we hope to help some Tibetan students come here for schooling. We also would like to stay in the States with our three children for a while."

"But TEAM doesn't have any work in the United States," one mission leader said. "Why don't you take a few months of furlough, visit your family and friends, and get back to us later? We know God will guide you."

Since Aunt Mary Marshburn had invited us to stay with her in Orange, California, we continued our drive across country and arrived on her sixty-eighth birthday. She had a beautiful home with a large, covered patio. Apricot, kumquat, and orange trees grew in her big backyard. We were thankful to have such a lovely place of refuge.

Mary Ellen and Miriam lived in a Biola dormitory but often joined us on weekends. At first, LeRoy found it difficult to be uprooted from the only life he'd known and to adjust to life in America. All his friends were at Woodstock School in northern India. His junior-high peers were not friendly, and he didn't think like they did. He had seen very little television and knew nothing about the music they listened to or the movie stars they talked about. They, in turn, knew nothing about India, the Dalai Lama, or the Tibetan situation that had been part of LeRoy's entire young life.

I'm not sure if it was our love for the Tibetan people, a strong faith in the Lord Jesus, or that we were naive when we thought about bringing Tibetans to America. We knew we couldn't do it alone. We had no home, three teen-age children with two in college, and an insecure future.

Our stipend from India wouldn't go very far in Orange, California. We were grateful to Aunt Mary for opening her home to us until we knew what we were going to do. We didn't even know if we would be staying with TEAM.

Why weren't we anxious about what we were going to do? We knew the Lord would lead us and supply our every need if we trusted Him. He had done just that many times before, and we didn't doubt that He would do it for us again. On his accordion, Elcho often played one of my favorite songs, "His Eye Is on the Sparrow." We knew the Lord cared about our family and would open up another door of service for us to walk through. Two verses were special to us at this time: "Call to Me, and I will answer you, and show you great and mighty things, which you do not know" (Jeremiah 33:3), and "I will instruct you and teach you in the way which you should go; I will guide you with My eye" (Psalm 32:8). He did open up a new door of service for us, and He did "exceedingly abundantly above" anything that we could have asked for or thought (see Ephesians 3:20).

One day during our first week in Orange, we stopped at a gas station to fill our Volkswagen. We chatted with the good-looking attendant and discovered his name was John Komanapali from South India. He was a Christian student at Chapman College in Orange.

"Why don't you join us for dinner tonight?" I asked.

John smiled. "I don't get off work until six, but I'd love to come."

We had a great evening. He enjoyed talking about India and told us he missed his wife and two little sons who were still there. We were surprised that we knew his uncle, an evangelist in South India.

Elcho was delighted. "Before we left India," he said, "we met your uncle and found that he played the accordion. He wanted one for his evangelistic meetings and didn't have much money, so I traded my accordion for two lace tablecloths."

"Amazing!" John said. "We're having an international student potluck at my college next week. Why don't you join us?"

The following week, we attended the dinner and were surprised to see over one hundred international students from thirty different countries studying at the college—just two miles from our new home. Many were dressed in their national costumes. We enjoyed food and entertainment from around the world.

Meanwhile, Mary Ellen and Miriam told us about the international students studying at Biola College. Our girls, along with a number of other missionary kids, were part of the active international student club. Elcho enrolled in two classes at Orange Coast College and was surprised to meet many foreign students there as well.

During the summer of 1968, Miriam and Mary Ellen lived together in Glendale and worked long hours in a Christian nursing home to earn money to return to Biola College. At the end of the summer, Miriam decided she definitely did not want to go into nursing, and Mary Ellen never doubted that she wanted to be a nurse.

We soon learned California had more international students than any comparable area in America because of such attractions as Disneyland and Knott's Berry Farm, and we lived just five minutes from Disneyland.

We became convinced that a field "white unto harvest" surrounded us. We wanted to minister to international students, but how could this become a reality? When we contacted our mission for permission, they said again that they worked only overseas and not in the States. To do the work we felt called to, it looked as if we would have to resign from TEAM and start our own mission. We had a number of good friends who were willing to be on a board and support us in this change. We even talked with a lawyer about the details.

An elderly gentleman, Mr. Lewis "Dad" Gall, provided an example of what hospitality to international students could mean. He and his wife had befriended young Asian students and foreign military officers who were studying or taking advanced training in America. Some of those young people became like the Galls' own family. During World War II, many Chinese military officers trained in California. Mrs. Gall had been a missionary in China and knew the language well, so they invited officers to their home and later kept in touch with them.

In the 1950s, Akiko, a lovely Japanese girl, lived with the Galls while she attended Santa Ana College. She became a Christian, and the Galls provided a scholarship for her to study at Wheaton College in Wheaton, Illinois. At a summer retreat, she met Hiroshi Minato, a Christian Japanese scientist. They were married in the Wheaton Chapel after her graduation, and the Galls were a part of that special wedding. They said good-bye with mixed emotions when the young couple returned to Japan.

Twenty-five years later, the Minatos invited Dad Gall, now a widower, to Japan for a double celebration—the Minato's silver wedding anniversary and his ninetieth birthday. Dad Gall loved to show us pictures of that memorable visit with the Minato family, as well as many other internationals they had befriended in Japan.

"Hiroshi is coming for a conference and will stay with me," Dad Gall said one day. "Would you like to have him talk to international students?"

"That would be great!" we both replied at the same time.

We invited American friends and international students to our home one evening. Mary Ellen and Miriam invited students in the international club at Biola. About fifty came. After the introductions and singing, Hiroshi told how he became a Christian while studying in Chicago, how his wife found Christ while living with the Galls, and about his work

We enjoyed many happy times of singing around the piano.

as a Christian scientist in Japan. Hiroshi was known, not only as an outstanding scientist but also as a Christian. I had the pleasure of getting to know Akiko years later when we were working in Japan. She taught in TEAM's Tokyo Bible College and wrote a popular book about the influence of Christian women in Japan.

34

Changing Direction

Foreigners working with Tibetans in India were now almost nonexistent, and policies indicated that none would be allowed within a few months. We believed that God's plan for us in the first phase of working with Tibetans had been realized. We felt the second phase was still to materialize.

Elcho could not forget his promise to the Dalai Lama to bring Tibetan young men to America for further studies. This was more Elcho's idea than mine, but because it was important to him, I tried to get the proper visas for young men from his tutorial class in India to study in a local college. We didn't even know what an I-20 form was, but we found out about the regulations. We visited a number of colleges in the area to get the young men enrolled so they could obtain the coveted I-20 documentation.

"What formal education have these Tibetan young men had?" college authorities asked us.

"They've studied in our Tibetan tutorial classes," we responded. That wasn't enough, and they turned us away.

"If we can't get visas for these boys," I told Elcho, "we'll have to forget about helping them get here."

"Let's not give up so easily," he said.

We made one last attempt to get the I-20 forms at Southern California College in Costa Mesa, a small Assembly of God college. We told the foreign-student advisor about our situation. She also was about to turn us away when she suggested we talk with Dr. Causton, the dean of students.

He was a kind, elderly gentleman who had been a missionary in India and had spent several summer vacations at Childers Lodge in Landour, Mussoorie. Childers is a big bungalow on the same winding, narrow road around the bend from Seaforth Lodge, where we had lived. In fact, we passed it every day going to The Firs, where Elcho had his Tibetan Tutorial School. Dr. Causton had met Tibetans while on vacation in Mussoorie and was interested in our project. He gave us eight signed I-20 forms and said the college would be happy to have the Tibetans as students.

Now, where was the money to come from? Bob Bowman of the Far East Broadcasting Company was interested in our project. He took us to lunch and introduced us to a poultry farmer, who gave us a check for three thousand dollars to pay for the Tibetans' transportation. Other friends said they would help in any way they could, and Aunt Mary let us use her old family home for the students to live in for one year.

Elcho carefully, prayerfully, and wisely chose eight Tibetan young men. We invited Gedun, Wangden, Donyu, Tsewang, Tenzin, Lobsang, Sonam, and Renchin to come as soon as possible, hopefully in time for the fall semester. They got clearance from the Dalai Lama's office and the Indian authorities. The United States government offices in New Delhi gave them student visas. We were amazed at how quickly the paperwork was done. We arranged for their tickets, and before we knew it, we had a phone call that they were arriving in plenty of time for the September registration.

One day in early September 1968, just six months since we ourselves had arrived from India, Aunt Mary, Dad Gall, and our family went to the Los Angeles airport to welcome seven of our former Tibetan students to Southern California. Knowing something about red tape, especially in India, we could not believe how quickly everything happened, and that was before such things as fax and e-mail. Geleg, his mother Lhadun, and his uncle Lobsang Tenzin, would arrive in a couple of days. The Indian government had allowed the young men to each bring only eight dollars out of India. Not much with which to start college life!

The newspapers reported, "Tibet Comes to California." Yet, the young Tibetans were in a precarious position financially, and so were we. They had traveled twelve thousand miles from the Himalayas to Southern California on prepaid air tickets and arrived with the price of a couple of meals in their pockets. Complicating the situation was the fact that

Elcho worked to bring some of the best students in his Tibetan Tutorial classes to the U.S. for further studies. He is shown here with two of them, Gedun and Donyu.

their student visas did not permit them to hold regular jobs, and we had no promised income, living back in our homeland for the first time with three teenagers!

Since we had spent many years in a foreign land, we sympathized with the feelings of loneliness and frustration of the international students studying in our local colleges. They had to learn to turn on water faucets, find numbers in phone books, dial telephones, handle banking procedures, shop in supermarkets, and drive on the "wrong" side of the road. Actually, we ourselves also had made many of these same adjustments, since we'd been out of our own country for almost two decades.

When Elcho heard about a Christian stewardship conference at Disneyland Hotel, he decided to attend. The first day of the conference, he met Hal Guffey, the newly elected president of International Students, Inc. (ISI).

Excited, Elcho called me. "I've met a man here that has a mission doing just what we want to do," he said. "May I invite him for dinner to talk with both of us?"

"Yes, of course," I replied. "I'd love to meet him."

We liked Hal and agreed with everything he told us about ISI. We learned that the mission was only fifteen years old and had about twenty

Elcho's folks loved being with us and enjoyed getting to be a part of the lives of the Tibetan students with us in Orange.

full-time staff members. The headquarters was in Washington, D.C., just a block or so from Capitol Hill.

"Elcho," Hal said, "why don't you come to our annual conference in June? You could meet the board and other staff members. In fact, I'd like you to seriously consider joining our staff."

So Elcho flew to the ISI headquarters in Washington, D.C. for their conference. He was impressed with the friendliness, integrity, and dedication of the board members and staff.

We officially became ISI staff members and began work in Orange County, California. TEAM gave us their blessing, and most of our faithful supporters stood behind us as we changed the direction of our ministry. One night in the fall of 1968 in Orange, California, we went to bed as TEAM missionaries and woke up as ISI missionaries. We continued to do what we had been doing since we arrived in Orange a few months earlier.

Elcho and I were very happy in our home and ministry in America. Elcho was always a big help in the kitchen.

Aunt Mary decided to move to Escondido, California, to be near her children and grandchildren. She wanted us to buy her home at a reduced rate, but we had no funds. Instead, ISI bought her beautiful, spacious home, and our housing allowance made the payments. The house had a huge living room, an attached den, and a large, glassed-in lanai. It was an ideal home for entertaining large crowds of international students. Showing hospitality had always been our family's lifestyle.

The more we got involved in our outreach to foreign students, the more convinced we were that the Lord had prepared us for this ministry. With the permission of the ISI board, Elcho continued classes at UCLA to finish his master's degree in teaching English as a Second Language (ESL). I spent full time in hospitality and meeting students on campuses. Elcho and I had always been a team, and I was considered just as much an ISI staff member as he was. More than one staff person has told us, "When Elcho joined International Students, we got an entire family for the price of one staff member."

The Tibetan young men adjusted well. They lived in Aunt Mary's old family home, did their own cooking and housekeeping, and studied hard. They usually had Sunday dinner with us and were at our home much of the time. None of them knew how to drive, so until they learned, we picked them up in our van and took them to the college and then picked them up every evening.

The Tibetan students gave Tibetan-catered meals in homes, churches, and clubs to raise funds for their college expenses.

The young men were good cooks, and we took orders to serve Tibetan meals in various homes and many churches. All the profits went toward their expenses. Some of them had brought Tibetan carpets, and their families sent them carpets after they arrived. We sold them to our friends to give the Tibetan students their own pocket money.

35

An Open Home in California

We began having international student meetings, which we called "rallies," in our home on the last Friday of every month, with eventually about a hundred attending. We made fliers and invited internationals from six colleges in Orange County. The invitations told about the program and a Christian movie or special program that would be shown.

LeRoy helped get the house ready and ran the movie projector to show films. Mary Ellen and Miriam were active in the international club at Biola and invited internationals and missionary kids to come. It was a family ministry, and our three teenagers were a big part of it.

We had dinner between six thirty and seven thirty in the evening, followed by introductions and singing. Various international Christians led the meetings and gave inspiring testimonies. We showed Moody Science films and other Christian films. One movie put out by Gospel Films, *Something to Die For*, was a favorite of ours because it had a powerful message and was in an Asian setting.

While I did much of the cooking for these events, our friends in various churches helped us as "culinary missionaries." Students often brought snacks or food from their homelands. After the meetings, we chatted and became better acquainted over dessert, coffee, tea, or punch.

Since students came to our gatherings from different countries and colleges, they enjoyed getting to know young people from other lands, as well as from their own countries. More than one student would meet

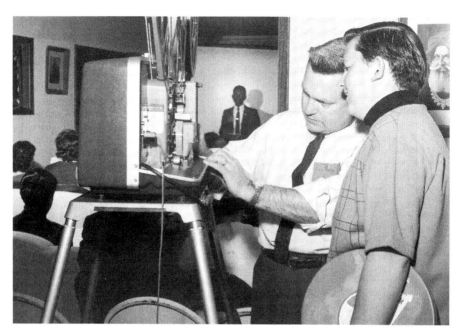

LeRoy helped his dad to set up the projector to show Christian films at our monthly international student rallies in our home.

someone, not only from the same country but also from the same town. One night, two students realized they lived on the same street in the same town thousands of miles from Orange, and they met in our living room!

In the winter of 1968, Joan Fitzroy, my widowed Anglo-Sinhalese friend in India, wrote us about her oldest daughter Kathy. She had graduated from high school in Mussoorie and wanted to study in America. I'd always liked Joan and her girls, and I wanted to help. Through various contacts, we got her a scholarship at Biola College. Almost immediately, she obtained a visa. Soon we welcomed her to our home, then helped her get settled in a Biola dorm with Mary Ellen and Miriam in time for the new semester.

Every day seemed full of opportunities. We thanked the Lord for the challenging work among international students. Our student gatherings continued to be well attended. Everyone enjoyed the Christian films and fellowship. Even more thrilling for us were the students who came by ones and twos during the week.

In the spring of 1969, we had a Pakistani family named Rahman stay with us. Dr. Rahman had received his Ph.D. in America and would soon return to his homeland to be a professor at the University of Dhaka. Had we been in Pakistan, we would never have met him or his family, but here in California, they were our guests, and we became close friends.

We took the Rahman family and Dad Gall to visit Universal Studios. As Dad Gall purchased the tickets, he whispered to me, "I know lots of people wouldn't think of this as missionary work, but I do."

Soon after the Rahmans left, a Korean doctor, his wife, and four children came to our home. This lovely family told us they had known real Christian love when they stayed with the Galls as students in Orange County, and because of that love, they had given their lives to the Lord for His service. From all over the world, we heard of students now in the Lord's work, who, ten or twenty years before, had known the hospitality of the Gall home—further illustrating the importance of extending Christian hospitality to international students studying in America. Dad Gall may have paid the bills by working as the manager of a supermarket, but he and his wife were missionaries to the world from their home in Santa Ana, California.

For a while, we had twelve young Tibetan men living and studying in Orange. Two had come from other parts of the States to stay with our students. The Tibetan students finished their first year of college and did very well. Although they were happy at Southern California College, they decided to separate and go to different colleges. Through various contacts, we were able to get them scholarships at junior colleges with lower tuitions.

After a year with us, Geleg went to live with his mother who was teaching at the University of Minnesota. His father had been left in Tibet guarding the Potala Palace in Lhasa and was presumed dead. Geleg and his mother had been separated much of his short lifetime, so they needed to be together.

Since she was interested in linguistics, Miriam studied at the Summer Institute of Linguistics (SIL) at the University of Washington during the summer of 1969. There she met Hiroko Oguri, the first Japanese candidate to join Wycliffe Bible Translators. Miriam asked me if Hiroko could stay with us for six weeks while she prepared for Wycliffe's jungle-training camp in southern Mexico.

We had a busy home with many international students coming and going all the time. This is our family with some of the Tibetan students and the three Fitzroy sisters who lived with us for awhile in Orange County.

At that time, Wycliffe Bible Translators and the SIL headquarters were near us in Santa Ana. Four of my Yakima Victory Club friends, who had gone to Biola with me, were full-time Wycliffe missionaries along with their spouses, so we knew the mission well. Dad Gall was glad that Miriam was interested in SIL and was excited about Hiroko coming to live with us. Since he was a good friend of Wycliffe's founder, Cameron Townsend, Dad Gall called one evening to see if he could bring "Uncle Cam" to our home. Over tea and cookies, we talked about missions. The Lord has used Wycliffe translators and support personnel to get the Word of God translated in many countries and to enable people to read it in their own languages. We ended our time with prayer, especially for Miriam and Hiroko, as they were both considering careers as Bible translators.

It was a joy to have Hiroko in our home and to help her prepare for jungle camp. One day she told us why she wanted to be a missionary translator. When she was a teenager in Japan, someone gave her a Bible. As she read, she knew that this was different from anything she had ever read before. Someone explained it to her, and she gave her heart to Christ. The Word of God had made such a change in her that she wanted to help others to have the Bible in their own languages.

I took Hiroko to Wycliffe's headquarters where she took classes and received a list of things to buy for jungle camp. We went shopping to buy the supplies she needed. She asked me to help her buy a small "millol." I couldn't figure out what she wanted and finally discovered it was a mirror. We also bought her a pair of walking boots, and she walked about four miles home in them. What a sight she was! This dainty little Japanese girl in a pretty, pink dress walked the streets in high-top walking boots that almost reached the hem of her skirt. She soon went to jungle camp and passed with flying colors.

Hiroko became a part of a linguistic team that translated the New Testament into an Indonesian tribal language. When we later worked in Japan, she visited us on her furlough. Over dinner, she told us about her life as a linguist and that she was supported entirely by Japanese churches. In June 2006, after thirty-five years in Indonesia, she retired to her homeland of Japan.

Hiroko Oguri (at left) was the first Japanese to work in Wycliffe. She spent time with us while preparing to go to the field. Army nurse Mary Ellen came home before she was stationed at Tripler Hospital in Honolulu, Hawaii. At the far right is Peter Cheng.

We attended the ISI staff conference in June 1969. Besides meeting other staff and board members, we enjoyed seeing the sights of Washington, D.C. As we walked out the door of the ISI headquarters, we faced the United States State Department. ISI President Hal Guffey took us there for lunch one day. We felt privileged to be affiliated with ISI and its outreach to international students.

We had heard the story of Prem Pradan when we were in India. In the 1950s, he became a Christian while studying in the United States. When he returned home to Nepal, he was immediately jailed for his faith. Later, he was released and returned to his home in Kathmandu. When Prem Pradan visited Orange County in 1969, he spoke in our home to about eighty people and told of the situation in Nepal at that time.

36

Meeting Wichit

As I was preparing Thanksgiving dinner in 1969, the phone rang, and Elcho answered.

"We have an emergency," ISI staff worker Max Kershaw said. "Six internationals were on their way to San Francisco when their van broke down. They're stranded near Bakersfield. They're going for a conference and sightseeing as guests of church families."

"How can we help?" Elcho asked.

"I know this is asking a lot on Thanksgiving Day, but could you folks pick them up in your van and spend the holiday there with them?"

"Give us the necessary information, and we'll see if we can work something out," Elcho assured Max.

Since we had a house full of company, I couldn't go. Elcho had other commitments, and Mary Ellen had a big nursing examination coming up.

"Kathy and I can go!" Miriam volunteered. "I got my driver's license this week, and I've driven on the freeway to Los Angeles."

Elcho frowned. "Miriam, you've only driven the freeway once. How can you drive our new fifteen-passenger van that thousand-mile trip?"

"I'm sure I can! And we're the only ones who can go."

Elcho and I weren't so confident.

Just as Miriam and Kathy were going out the door, Mary Ellen spoke up. "Wait a minute!" She turned to us and said, "If I take my nursing books along, I can help with the driving. I won't do any sightseeing or go to meetings, but I'll stay in our room and study for my exams." It sounded like a good idea to everyone.

The three girls drove off in our new van to rescue the stranded international students waiting by a freeway. After the girls found them, they continued on to San Francisco. They arrived too late for the opening session of the conference, but they found their host families and had a good night's sleep. The next morning, they joined the group for the morning session of the conference.

In the afternoon, they went sightseeing in our van. Miriam was nervous about driving in downtown San Francisco, so Mary Ellen decided she'd better help. She took along her big nursing book in case she had a chance to study.

One rescued young man was a Northridge University of California graduate student named Lee. He noticed that Mary Ellen was tired, so he offered to help drive.

"Do you have a valid California driver's license?" she asked. "And can you drive a big van?"

"Yes to both questions. My father owns a bus company in Chiang Mai, Thailand, and I used to drive one of his buses." Lee drove the van for the day's sightseeing and much of the way home.

When the girls arrived back in Orange, they told us about this "cute little fellow" from Thailand who had carried Mary Ellen's heavy nursing book when they rode a streetcar and helped with the driving.

We were planning a winter retreat at Big Bear, a tourist area in the San Bernardino Mountains where our friends had a large lodge. We asked the girls to invite Lee to go along. They said they had already invited him to come the next weekend for the international student rally in our home. They would invite him to the retreat then. We later found that Lee's real name was Wichit Maneevone (pronounced Mun-EE-wun). He worked part-time for a man who couldn't remember his name. "Wichit is too difficult. I'm just going to call you Lee," his boss told him.

Wichit started coming to the student rallies and was helpful with our yard work. He joined us for the winter retreat and was interested in the singing and the Bible message, but as he talked, we realized he had not yet accepted the Lord as his own Savior. Not only did he seem interested in talking about the Lord but also in talking to our younger daughter, Miriam.

"Why do you think Wichit is coming around so much?" I asked Max. "Is he interested in the Lord or in our daughter?"

He smiled. "I think he is probably interested in both!"

Max proved to be right. Wichit continued to come to our home almost every weekend. He asked questions and enjoyed being at our home. He was especially interested in our international student rallies the last Friday of every month. As he continued to learn more about the Lord and was around Christians, the more he wanted to find a purpose in life.

Mary Ellen telephoned me from her Biola dorm. "Mom, may I join the Army Nursing Corps? I talked with the recruiting officer on campus, and he wants to talk with you and Dad tomorrow. I can come home then, too. Is that okay?"

The next day, the recruiting officer and Mary Ellen came to see us. It was what she wanted to do, so we agreed with her wishes. She enlisted in the United States Army as a private.

"The World at Our Doorstep" was the theme of our ISI banquet at Knott's Berry Farm in April 1970. Early in the year, we sent invitations to friends and churches in Orange County. Many churches put the announcement in their bulletins. After a couple of weeks, we called those we had invited to ask if they knew how many were coming. Each church had a coordinator who took reservations and promoted the banquet.

Our inner circle of friends was made up of the "youngest" older people in their seventies, eighties, and nineties that we had ever met. They prayed for us, supported us, and encouraged us. They loved us and our international family, and we all loved them. Aunt Mary Marshburn came from Escondido. Dexter and Lenore Lutz, veteran missionaries to Korea and India and the parents of our friend and missionary to Nepal, Betty Friedericks, came from Westminster Gardens. Agnes "Grandma" Dunn, former missionary to India and a retired school nurse, came with friends from Calvary Church of Placentia, and Dad Gall came with his friends.

At the famous Mrs. Knott's Chicken Dinner Restaurant at Knott's Berry Farm, we made reservations for three hundred people. The dinner was free to our guests. We wanted to tell more people about how we in ISI were reaching the "world" that had come to study in Southern California. We needed more volunteers to get involved and to collaborate with us.

Our friend and ISI board member Bob Welch was the master of ceremonies. Hal Guffey came from Washington, D.C. and brought a challenging message of people in the Bible who had become Christians away from home. Then he told stories of world leaders who had been discriminated against in the West, such as Mahatma Gandhi. He compared them with students like Bakht Singh, who had been exposed to Christian hospitality in America then returned home and made a difference for Christ.

Mary Ellen and Miriam sang duets. Cornelius and Lydia Ritau, a young couple dressed in their Indonesian attire, also brought special music. Emmanuel Ephraim from Ghana and Liberia gave an inspirational testimony. We invited our Tibetan young men, Wichit from Thailand, and students from our international rallies, so each table had a few international students seated among the American guests.

This banquet was a "friend-raiser," not really a fund-raiser. However, envelopes for a freewill offering were on each table. We provided ISI literature and cards to fill out for those interested in getting involved in this foreign mission field in Southern California. By the end of this wonderful evening, we not only had enough money in the offering to pay for all our expenses, but there was some left over for other needs.

Through the outreach of these banquets, we met fine Christians from churches in Orange County. Many became friendship partners and are still involved in an outreach to internationals today. We continued to have these banquets every year throughout the 1970s. They proved to be an important part in promoting the message of "Reaching the World at Our Doorstep."

On June 14, 1970, Wichit Maneevone accepted the Lord as his personal Savior. What a change! Later, Wichit gave his testimony at an ISI conference at Star Ranch in Colorado Springs, Colorado. The mission asked him to put his testimony in writing, and this is what he wrote:

> Alone under a tree on the campus of the University of Pittsburgh, I pondered my plight. I had problems. It was hard to understand the language and customs of the people around me. When I tried to speak, no one took time to listen to my stumbling speech. I missed my family and friends. I did not enjoy eating American strange, bland food. Why was I here?

In Thailand, I had done well in high school and at the university. It is the custom in Thailand for a young man to become a monk and to study in a monastery for one year before he goes to graduate school. I persuaded my father to let me do graduate studies in the United States before fulfilling my year in the monastery. This would give me more social prestige and a better job. Had I made a mistake?

I had sold a piece of land my father had given me and bought a ticket to Pittsburgh, where I had a Thai friend. On arriving, I found little of the glamour and fun portrayed in Hollywood movies. Instead, I found America to be a lonely place. I had taken an intensive English course for four months, but I could not find anyone who would stop long enough to let me practice. So I longed to return to Thailand. I felt that nothing—not even saving face for myself and my family—could be worth the sadness and emptiness I was experiencing.

Then a total American stranger came and sat down beside me. He talked with me and invited me to his home. Such a thing had never happened to me before. I was delighted to see the inside of an American home. Fred Wolfe and his wife asked about my family and me and explained about American customs. Someone cared.

Later, I found they were on the staff of ISI. Although I did not care about their religion, I went to church with them because I wanted to practice my English, and the people at church were friendly and happy. I wondered why they were different. Why did they seem to genuinely care about me? I had nothing to give them. Yet, I could call them anytime I needed help. One day Fred told me that Jesus Christ had made him a different person than he used to be. I had much to ponder.

Pittsburgh was too cold, so I moved to Los Angeles. I met more of the ISI staff and Christian families through them. They were good to me, and I could see by their lives that I lacked something. One ISI couple, Elcho and Millie Redding, took me on special retreats, and I felt welcome to stay in their home any time I wanted. They told me more about the Lord Jesus. Rather than pressure me to make a decision, they let me have time to think things over for myself.

After reading John 3:16 and John 14:6 over and over again, I decided to accept Jesus Christ as my Savior. I immediately wrote to my father and told him of my decision to believe in Jesus and to become a Christian. He did not reply for several months. When I finally received his reply, he expressed bitter disappointment in me and said I was no longer his son. Sadness would have overwhelmed me had it not been for the entire Redding family, who helped me and showed great love and concern. They assured me that I now had a heavenly Father who loved me and wanted the best for me.

Since I was the only son in the family, the duty fell on me to spend time in the Buddhist monastery to gain enough merit for my parents' salvation. Now my father feared there was no hope of gaining sufficient merit to ensure his salvation. In anger, he cut off all my financial resources. I was left with no income to pay for my rent, food, and school expenses. But God supplied my every need.

37

Retreats, Rallies, and the Ritchies

One day the counselor at Orange High School was on the phone. "We have a student named Peter Chang who will have to return to Hong Kong unless you can help us," the counselor said. "May I bring him to your home so you can give us some advice?"

Peter came from a wealthy family in Hong Kong. He was living alone in an apartment in Orange. However, this was against school policy. All students needed to live with adults who were responsible for them. His mother hoped to join him in a year or so. In the meantime, LeRoy agreed to let Peter share his room in our home. In the spring of 1970, Peter joined our extended family and went to high school with LeRoy.

Elcho was active in the Teaching English to Speakers of Other Languages (TESOL) program and attended all the California and national conferences. He saw teaching English as a way to enter closed countries. Without formal training, he had taught English to Tibetans for many years, so he was glad to learn that he'd been doing many things right. He received his master's degree at the University of California at Los Angeles (UCLA) in June of 1970. He made international friends in his classes, and many came to our home for our monthly international student rallies and attended other ISI events.

One student he brought home was Fauma, a tall young man from Burundi. His girlfriend, Karitas, came as well. They were married after their graduation from UCLA that summer, and we were special guests

at their wedding. They asked if they could come to our home for their honeymoon. We agreed and took them to Disneyland as a wedding present. It was great fun, and we had another opportunity to tell them about our Lord.

The Burundi government had sent Fauma to America for his education, and he was destined to rise high in the politics of his country. He told us he wanted to be Burundi's ambassador to the United States and would see us again someday in that capacity.

At the end of the summer, Fauma and Karitas returned home. We heard from them only once. Soon after, we read in the newspapers of a political coup in their land. We continued to write, but sad to say, our letters remained unanswered.

One day Aunt Mary called me. "I'd like to go to Joanna Ritchie's wedding in Garden Farms near Santa Margarita," she said. "Would you please drive me?" Joanna had helped in the monthly international dinner rallies in our home, so I was happy to go.

The lovely wedding took place in a rural church in a wooded mountain area of northern California. The pastor, Dwight Ritchie, the father of the bride, performed the ceremony. At the reception, he and his wife, Winnie, told me that they had just been accepted by ISI and would be moving to Los Angeles to work with the Kershaws. Dwight was an engineer and a seminary graduate. The Ritchies had been in Kabul, Afghanistan, for four years with USAID and two years with Village Missions before joining ISI. The wedding was the beginning of a long friendship for the Elcho Redding and Dwight Ritchie families.

Throughout the school year, we continued to have international student rallies in our home the last Friday of each month. Our lovely, spacious home was well suited for this, but as the group averaged about one hundred each time, we knocked out a wall to enlarge our living room.

We represented ISI at many missionary conferences throughout Orange County. As a result, many people became partners in our outreach to internationals. Friends in a number of churches in Orange County hosted students for weekends and helped provide food for our rallies.

During the 1971 spring break, we took fifty international students on a camping trip to Yosemite National Park. It was a beautiful day, and the scenery was spectacular. After checking in, we ate in a cafeteria before finding our campsite. We had made reservations months in advance, so we had a nice spot near a stream on one side and modern bathroom facilities on the other. We put up two good-sized tents in which to change clothes.

To prepare meals, we put up two folding tables and two propane stoves. Winnie and I had made supper the night before we came, so preparations for the first meal would be easy. As soon as we were settled, people scattered to roam the park until suppertime. Winnie and I relaxed nearby to watch our belongings and get supper ready. After eating, we tied our leftover food in hammocks we made by tying ropes to trees. Park authorities told us that all food had to be either left in a locked car or strung high, away from the black grizzly bears that sometimes roamed the park at night.

With Elcho playing the accordion, we sang around the campfire. Several people shared testimonies, and then Elcho gave a short devotional. We roasted marshmallows and talked around the campfire for a long time. Winnie and I kept pans, lids, and heavy spoons nearby to make loud noises if bears came around. Under the starlit sky, we unrolled our sleeping bags beneath magnificent tall trees and fell asleep.

At about three o'clock in the morning, I woke up with a start and saw a huge black bear sniffing Mary Ellen's head next to me. I was petrified! I prayed and tried to find the noisemakers, but they were all near Winnie's head, and I was sleeping at her feet. I tried to call her, but I had no voice, so I closed my eyes and sent up a quick prayer. Then I sensed motion and slowly opened my eyes. The bear was moving away. Simultaneously, I heard a male voice shout, "I'm coming in!" as a man ran into the ladies' bathroom, seeking shelter from the bear.

One of the most outstanding students to become a part of our international family during the seventies was Ahn Soo Lim. As a young boy in Korea, Ahn Soo went to the beach one day. He saw a shiny object in the sand and picked it up to see what it was. As he was playing with it in his hand, it exploded in his face, and he lost his eyesight. The Dexter Lutzes were veteran missionaries in Korea, and "Mother" Lenore Lutz had met Ahn Soo and his family before the accident. As the director of the Seoul School for the Blind, she noticed that Ahn Soo did extremely well academically.

"Mother" Lenore told us that Ahn Soo was teaching in Seoul but wanted to come to Southern California for graduate studies. We arranged for him to come to summer school at Chapman College in Orange, and he lived with us. Since Miriam had just graduated from UCI, we asked her if she would go with him to his classes and help him not only in the adjustments but also in the transportation. She was delighted and enrolled as a graduate student herself. He taped the lectures and then put them into braille. In the evenings, he and Miriam studied together and both did well.

I learned much by having Ahn Soo in our home. More than once, I came into a dark living room, turned on the lights, and asked him what he was doing in the dark. He'd say, "Mom, you forget that it doesn't make any difference to me." Once I asked him if he'd like a glass of buttermilk. When he said that he would, I gave him a tall, cold glass of it. He took a gulp, made a face, went to the sink, and spit it out. "That is terrible!" he said. "It's spoiled milk!" Another time, he ran his fingers across our glass windows and said, "These are dirty. Let me wash them." I gave him the supplies, and he did just that. They had never been so clean before and were never that clean again. I will never forget taking him to Disneyland. I talked so fast as I described the Haunted House and the Pirates of the Caribbean that we both laughed and laughed.

Aunt Mary liked Ahn Soo and invited him to her home, so I drove him to Escondido to spend a few days with her. Chiawat Roongrooshi, a Thai student from Chiang Mai, Thailand, who had been living with her, had just returned to his homeland. She excitedly told us of experiences that she had enjoyed with him in her home that year.

The next year, Ahn Soo's sister got married, and we were invited to the wedding in Seoul, South Korea. At the same time, Chiawat wanted Aunt Mary to visit him in Chiang Mai, Thailand. She also wanted to meet Prasan, a fine Christian Thai young man she had sponsored in Singapore Bible College. She asked if I would be her companion and go with her.

Our first stop was Tokyo to see students who had been in our activities. We went

Aunt Mary Marshburn, Ahn Soo Lim, Millie, and Ahn Soo's niece in Seoul, South Korea

on to Bangkok to meet Prasan and then to Chiang Mai to be with the Maneevone family, Chiawat, Dr. Jiron, Wichit's good friend, and other students who had been in our home. We stayed for five days in a quaint hotel that seemed like something out of a storybook. I still remember the wonderful haircut and massage that I got for three dollars.

In Seoul, South Korea, we stayed with longtime Presbyterian missionaries, Dr. Dick and Carol Underwood. Dick was principal of the International School in Seoul at the time. Carol is the daughter of Dexter and Lenore Lutz and sister to our good friend from Nepal, Betty Friedericks. We had a wonderful week with them as well as with Ahn Soo and his family. His sister had a lovely Christian Korean wedding.

38

Special Events

Miriam and Elcho both enrolled in the Ph.D. program at Claremont Graduate School and began classes in September 1971. She was the youngest in the class, and he was the oldest. Many graduate students were from foreign colleges. Naturally, Miriam and Elcho invited their classmates to come to our home and to ISI activities, and they made lasting friendships. And so did we.

Sutin and Wanpen, a charming couple from influential families in Bangkok, Thailand, were among the graduate students who became our good friends when they came to our home. Several years later, when Aunt Mary and I went to Thailand, they were gracious hosts.

An influx of Iranian students was at Orange Coast College and Chapman College the fall of 1971, and many came to our activities. On Thanksgiving weekend, ISI was holding a conference in San Francisco, so we hired two Greyhound buses as transportation. We left Los Angeles together at about ten o'clock on Wednesday night and planned to arrive at Walnut Creek Presbyterian Church in time for breakfast and to meet the American host families. The bus I was responsible for was more than half-filled with loud-talking Iranian students. The others came from other countries. Many students on our bus talked all night, keeping the rest of us awake, so we were exhausted in the morning. The other busload slept.

When we arrived at the church, we were ushered into a large gym where we met international students from various parts of California.

About one hundred and fifty students were in one part of the gym, and American host families were in the other. The students went home with their host families to enjoy a typical American Thanksgiving. The next morning, we all met at the church for the conference. The ISI staff did a good job of arranging for host families and planning sightseeing, sing times, fine speakers, and discussion groups. After the conference, our Iranian students were so tired that they slept all the way home.

Miriam and Wichit Maneevone were married on December 18, 1971, in Calvary Church of Placentia. It was a beautiful wedding, and the church looked lovely with Christmas decorations. President Hal Guffey of ISI and Elcho performed the ceremony. International students, our family, and friends filled the sanctuary.

Wichit's family was opposed to his marrying an American Christian girl. "There are a lot of pretty Thai girls," his parents wrote. "Why do you want to marry an American?" His family never accepted the fact that he had become a Christian, and for him to marry an American Christian was hard for them. No one came from Thailand for the wedding, but Wichit had a new family in the many believers who loved him.

Our international student rallies on the last Friday of every month continued to be well attended, and our church friends as friendship partners helped with the food. One day, a lady in Santa Ana Calvary Church visited us and said she wanted to wash dishes and clean up the kitchen, if I would let her. Would I let her? She had to be kidding! She did this during every rally until she moved away three years later and was as committed to it as if she had been leading the meeting. Her service freed me to visit with students after the

Mary Ellen went back to India in 1971 while she was studying at Biola. Here she is with the Dalai Lama at that time.

meeting. LeRoy ran the movie projector and helped put the furniture back in place afterwards. With so many helpers, we found it easy to have about a hundred people in our home one day each month.

Mary Ellen graduated from the Biola nursing program in June 1972. She had worked hard to earn her R.N. as well as her bachelor of science degree. She also was commissioned as a first lieutenant in the United States Army. She went to San Antonio, Texas, for basic training and was stationed at the Beaumont Army Hospital in El Paso, Texas.

ISI bought Star Ranch in Colorado Springs, Colorado, from Young Life in 1972, and the headquarters moved there from Washington, D.C. The founder of Young Life, Jim Rayburn, used to come to the Firs Bible Conference Center in Bellingham, Washington, when I went there as a teenager. The Rayburn family home was remodeled and made the ISI headquarters building. Over the next few years, our family went to Star Ranch several times a year.

After ISI moved its headquarters, Dwight and Winnie Ritchie were transferred to work at Star Ranch. ISI needed Dwight's expertise as an engineer, and Winnie became the conference hostess. We missed working with them in the Los Angeles area, as we were a good team.

Elcho went to India in the summer of 1972 to visit his former students and the Tarings. He had his fifth audience with the Dalai Lama and told him about the Tibetan young men we had brought to America and about our family. When Elcho was in Mussoorie, he attended a big celebration for the Dalai Lama's thirty-seventh birthday on July 6. Elcho sat on the platform as a special guest and was honored as an American who had done much for the Tibetan people.

While in India, Elcho visited young people who were studying or had studied in Christian schools. Many of them had spent time in our home, and he wanted to know how they were doing and to encourage them to find God's plan for their lives.

On August 22, 1972, family and friends helped us celebrate our twenty-fifth wedding anniversary. Hal and Betsy Guffey from ISI headquarters came for the occasion, as well as many American and international friends. I was glad I could still wear my wedding dress. We were thankful for our years together and especially that our three children were not only walking with the Lord but also wanted to serve Him.

At Christmas 1972, Elcho wrote a letter to our friends:

> Hundreds of international students were contacted in our home and on the campuses in Southern California. There are many students that we would like to tell you about, such as Hiroko, now back in Japan preparing to go to Indonesia with Wycliffe Bible Translators; Peter from Hong Kong, studying at Biola College; the sixteen Tibetans here in Southern California; Chaiwat, Pongso, Vichai—all graduate students from Thailand; and many others, but we will tell you briefly of one in particular: Ahn Soo Lim of Korea.
>
> Ahn Soo lost his eyesight during the Korean War. As a boy, he attended a school for the blind in Korea, supervised by our dear friend, Mrs. Dexter Lutz. Now, twenty years later, Ahn Soo has earned his master's degree at Chapman College in Orange, and more recently graduated from the International Guiding Eye School in Los Angeles. He acquired Zara, a beautiful black seeing-eye dog, the first to ever go to Korea. Now he has just returned to his homeland. Besides his advanced degree, his seeing-eye dog, and his two-hundred volumes of braille books, Ahn Soo also took a renewed faith in Christ as his Lord and a new dedication to serve Him among his own people.
>
> I visited our Tibetan young people in India this summer and sought to encourage them about God's plan for their lives. In every Tibetan office that I entered anywhere in India, I saw my former students. My hosts in northern India were the Tarings. Mr. Jigme Taring, with his lovely wife, is director of the Tibetan Homes Foundation. I also had another long conversation with the Dalai Lama of Tibet (this was my fifth audience with him). Besides our Tibetan friends, I called on Indian families whose sons and daughters are studying in Southern California. Such a welcome I had never experienced during the more than eighteen years we were there as missionaries.

Our family is doing well. In August, Millie and I celebrated our twenty-fifth wedding anniversary. Lt. Mary Ellen works in the emergency room in an El Paso, Texas, hospital. Miriam has completed her Ph.D. qualifying examinations. She and Wichit are expecting their first baby soon, and that, no doubt, will change all of our lives. LeRoy is a senior in high school and plans to major in psychology.

I continue to contact foreign students and their families through the evening classes that I teach (English as a Second Language). The classes have added considerably to our opportunities of extending friendship and giving a positive witness for Christ to our international guests.

Please mark your calendar and save February 23 for our next ISI banquet at Knott's Berry Farm. Hal Guffey, president of ISI, Mark Hanna, and several internationals will share in testimonies and music.

Now that the holiday season is just around the corner, we are reminded that our international friends who are far from home may feel especially lonely at this time. Use this opportunity to extend friendship and hospitality, and pray with us that they will come to know that Jesus came to bring them salvation.

Miriam and Elcho completed their Ph.D. qualifying exams and were working on their dissertations. Then we learned we were going to be grandparents, and Leonie Frances Maneevone was born on January 26, 1973. Our lives would never be the same again.

LeRoy graduated with honors from Orange High School in June 1973, and went with us to Star Ranch in Colorado Springs for our ISI annual conference. Wichit, Miriam, Leonie, and Watcharee, Wichit's sister visiting from Thailand, also came. Wichit and Miriam had been working with ISI as volunteers while in Claremont. Mary Ellen was able to join us from El Paso, Texas.

Later that summer, I took Aunt Mary and Lenore and Dexter Lutz to the Friends of ISI conference at Star Ranch for a wonderful time of

Christian fellowship. Mary Ellen was again able to join us from El Paso for a few days.

Wichit had a desire to study God's Word in a deeper way. Dad Gall provided the tuition for him to attend Dallas Theological Seminary for a year. The seminary had a special program for those who had graduate degrees and wanted an accelerated Bible study. Since Miriam had completed her basic studies, their family decided to move to Dallas, Texas. Wichit's sister, Watcharee, lived with them and did the cooking and cared for baby Leonie so Miriam could write her dissertation. They had very little money, and Wichit raved about Watcharee's cooking, which he liked better than Miriam's bland American cuisine. This was difficult for a young mother who was under a great deal of pressure. In addition, studying Christian theology was difficult for a young man who had recently been converted from Buddhism. Nevertheless, they grew in the Lord and in their relationship as a family—and Miriam learned to prepare delicious Thai food!

When LeRoy enrolled in California State University in Fullerton in the fall of 1973, I became acquainted with the foreign-student advisor there. She invited me to help in her office as a volunteer. I met many internationals, and she said I could invite them to our home and our activities. I started going to the National Association of Foreign Student Advisors (NAFSA) conferences with Elcho at the regional and national levels. I continued to be involved for several years, and he preferred attending the Teaching English to Speakers of Other Languages (TESOL) conferences.

In the fall of 1973, Mary Ellen, now a captain in the U.S. Army, was transferred to an Army hospital in a little town named Bad Kreuznach near Frankfurt, Germany. She decided not to live in the officers' quarters but in a small apartment in the home of a German family. The family next door was good to her, and they became friends. She often played their piano and sang for them, and they took her on vacations around Germany and Austria. Since they knew very little English, she had to communicate in simple English and German.

One rainy day, Mary Ellen was driving from the Army hospital to her apartment when she saw a tall gentleman and two little boys walking briskly in the rain. She stopped the car and offered them a ride. They hurriedly jumped into the backseat, and she started a conversation. The man saw her Bible on the seat and exclaimed, "You must be a Christian! So are we. Praise the Lord!" They were missionaries to Yemen with the Red Sea Mission. After that, Mary Ellen spent a great deal of time with that family, whose name was Stumf.

Wichit and Miriam applied to ISI as staff members in early 1974. That spring Miriam and Leonie joined us in Orange. Wichit was finishing his course at Dallas Theological Seminary, and his sister did his cooking and housekeeping. Miriam had finished writing her dissertation and needed her dad to help her type it. This was in the days before the word processor, and the dissertation could not have any typing mistakes. Therefore, Elcho typed her entire manuscript, and she received her Ph.D. in June 1974. We had a reception for her in a nice restaurant in Claremont. Our special senior group was there—Dad Gall, Lenore and Dexter Lutz, Aunt Mary, and Grandma and Grandpa Redding. Another dear family friend, Dr. Leonie Soubirou, founder of Biola's nursing program, was also there.

Even though Aunt Mary Marshburn had moved to a lovely home on a hilltop in Escondido, I remained close to her. I often visited her and took her to visit her brother in Three Rivers, California. One day soon after Miriam's graduation, I was driving Aunt Mary to visit her brother.

Dad Gall, Miriam (holding Leonie), Millie, Wichit, and Dexter and Lenore Lutz celebrate Miriam's graduation from Claremont Graduate School.

She said she was going to sell her lovely home in Escondido and move into a retirement home or a mobile home nearer to me in Orange. I was surprised, as she had told me so many times how ideal the home on the hill in Escondido was for international student work. When I told her I coveted that home for a student ministry, she replied that ISI didn't have any staff to put there, and she couldn't wait for them to find someone. When we stopped for gas, I went to a phone booth and made a quick call to Hal Guffey at ISI headquarters. "If Aunt Mary gives her home to ISI," I asked, "could Wichit and Miriam move there right away?" He replied that it would be possible, so it was arranged. Aunt Mary gave ISI the 1.8 acres of property situated on the top of a hill with a lovely home surrounded by one hundred orange trees.

In May 1974, we heard that Biola was launching a new semester-long program in Germany for sophomore students. This appealed to LeRoy, so he applied to Biola's German program. He was accepted and left in midsummer to spend time in Germany with Mary Ellen before classes began. When the time came, he joined the Biola student group, which was comprised of seventeen girls and three boys. The Biola Abroad program in Germany was possible through the cooperation of the Greater European Mission. The students lived and had most classes in a youth hostel in nearby Zwingenberg. They studied the German language and culture, English literature, and European history, and went to the mission for Bible classes. The excellent program lasted for four months and included trips around Germany. LeRoy wrote in a letter to us, "I think I've met the girl I'm going to marry. We haven't had a date yet, but we've seen lots of castles and other historical sights with the group of twenty. Her name is Carol Roth, and she's from Albany, Oregon." Before the students left Germany, they took a trip to Austria where *The Sound of Music* was filmed. The beauty and serenity of the area left a lasting impression on the young people.

LeRoy arrived back home in Orange in time to go with us to our winter retreat at Big Bear and to Miriam and Wichit's Christmas party in their home. There we met three Vietnamese Navy men. One of them, Hung Viet Nguyen, endeared himself to our family. We gave him a cordial invitation to come with his friends to our home anytime.

LeRoy moved into the Biola men's dormitory in January 1975. Now it was his turn to become part of the international club. He informed the students of our activities and brought many home in our fifteen-passenger van. He and Carol began dating, and she often came with him for the international student rallies.

We had a spring retreat for the internationals at Forest Home, a Christian conference center in the San Bernardino Mountains. Wichit and our friend and fellow ISI worker Sam Ooman joined in this venture.

We also had another Friends of ISI banquet at Knott's Berry Farm. That year we first met Ridge Ryan, pastor of Saddleback Bible Church in Mission Viejo, California, and his wife, Margo. Ridge had met the Galls when he was an army officer during World War II. Their church became involved in our outreach to internationals, and the Ryans have encouraged us through the years. They are now retired after working many years with J. Vernon Magee's *Through the Bible* radio program.

On April 30, 1975, Hung Viet Nguyen was among a group of Vietnamese Navy officers in our living room as we watched the fall of Saigon on television. They all had family in Vietnam. Some had wives and children, as well as parents, brothers, and sisters. We wept with these young men in their time of sorrow and uncertainty. Some had become Christians while they were with us. We tried to assure them the Lord would uphold them, and He did. As American rescue planes flew into the El Toro United States Marine base in Orange County, we met many flights and helped several refugee families relocate. Hung remains particularly special to me. Through the years, he has given his love, encouragement, and support to us, and he still thinks of us as his American family.

In June 1975, Elcho received his Ph.D. from Claremont Graduate School. It was quite an accomplishment for a busy fifty-one-year-old man. He was sure his degree would open doors for us someday, and it did.

Right after Elcho's graduation, we had a Biola alumni gathering in our home, and our friend, Biola president Dr. Richard Chase, came. We had known his in-laws, Dr. and Mrs. Sam Sutherland, and had attended Biola with his wife. As we visited with Dr. Chase, he invited Elcho to teach at Biola. Elcho discussed it with the ISI leaders, and they agreed to let him teach the English as a Second Language classes for the internationals and a class in the history and development of the English language.

That summer of 1975, we spent a great deal of time at Star Ranch. We had our annual conference there in June. In July, I took Aunt Mary and the Lutzes by plane to the Friends of ISI conference. In August, LeRoy and Elcho drove a van of internationals to the international student conference at Star Ranch. They brought back a report of good times of Bible study, worship, and fellowship.

Malina Esther Maneevone was born on November 15, 1975. Now we had two darling granddaughters to adore.

Mary Ellen got out of the Army and applied to Johns Hopkins University for her master of public health (MPH) degree and a midwifery certificate. The school told her she needed experience in public health nursing before she would be accepted into the program, so she moved back home and got the required job as a visiting home-care nurse for Orange County.

39

More Special Events

During the 1975 Thanksgiving weekend, LeRoy and Carol drove our van with students from Orange County, and Sam Ooman drove the Hollywood First Presbyterian church bus with students from Los Angeles to the annual ISI conference at San Francisco. We had a sense of pride seeing LeRoy take leadership with the students, and Carol related well to them.

Hung and some of his former Vietnamese Navy officer friends were with us for Christmas. LeRoy told us that he and a former officer named Tai were driving one day when Tai said he didn't know the Lord but would like to. LeRoy pulled over to the side of the road, and Tai accepted the Lord. They both came home so happy. We have lost track of Tai but trust he is continuing in his Christian walk.

LeRoy and Carol Roth were married on June 25, 1976, at the Lebanon Mennonite Church in Oregon. It was a beautiful wedding with her sister Helen as the maid of honor, Mary Ellen the bridesmaid, Leonie the flower girl, and Gedun and Wangden as attendants. ISI president Hal Guffey and Elcho performed the

ceremony. Elcho actually tied the knot, as he had for Wichit and Miriam several years before.

After a short honeymoon in Victoria, British Columbia, Canada, LeRoy applied to ISI for a part-time staff position, and he and Carol went to Star Ranch for training and were accepted. LeRoy spent time with his Tibetan friends, who were working for an insurance company at the time.

During the 1970s, Melodyland Christian Center near Disneyland, had good Christian musicals. The building was originally a circular theater with a stage in the middle. *He Is Risen* and *A Savior Is Born* were two musical performances that blessed us so much that we took students several nights in a row.

We also enjoyed hearing Corrie ten Boom at Melodyland. Her book, *The Hiding Place*, had been released in 1971, and the film of the same name had just been released in 1975, so Corrie was in the area a great deal during that time. I took others with me to hear her whenever I could. Her actions and accent not only reminded me of my Dutch grandma but of our day together at India's National Celebration in 1961. Also, she always had something worthwhile to say that blessed me.

One evening at Melodyland, Corrie told a story about forgiveness: In 1947, she spoke in a church in Germany. Afterwards, an overweight, bald man approached her. She recognized him as one of the cruelest former Ravensbrück prison-camp guards. He told her that he was now a Christian and Jesus had forgiven him. But he asked for her forgiveness. She was reluctant to forgive him but silently prayed that she would be able to do so. Only when she remembered how her Lord had forgiven her was she able to forgive him. They grasped hands for a long time—the former guard and the former prisoner. Corrie added that when other victims of Nazi brutality had forgiven, they could rebuild their lives.

Corrie held up the backside of a tapestry with its tangled threads. Then she showed us the right side with its beautiful pattern. Finally, this dear Dutch lady, now in her eighties, in front of three thousand people, quoted this poem:

The Weaver

My life is but a weaving
Between my Lord and me.
I cannot choose the colors
He worketh steadily.

Oftimes He weaveth sorrow,
And I in foolish pride
Forget He sees the upper
And I, the underside.

Not 'til the loom is silent
And the shuttles cease to fly
Shall God unroll the canvas
And explain the reason why.

The dark threads are as needful
In the Weaver's skillful hand
As the threads of gold and silver
In the pattern He has planned.

—Author Unknown

Corrie moved to Orange near us in 1977, when she was eighty-five-years old. Soon afterwards, she had a series of strokes that left her unable to speak. Our Missionary Aviation friends, Grady and Maureen Parrot, who were close to her, took us to visit her. She died on her ninety-first birthday.

During the Labor Day weekend of 1976, the phone rang late one night at LeRoy and Carol's apartment, and he heard a frantic woman's voice. She was at the Los Angeles International Airport and had just arrived from Nairobi, Kenya. Lucy Wainaina was a new student at Biola, but no one was at the airport to meet her. She had tried to call the school but received no answer. Could someone pick her up? LeRoy and Carol jumped in their car, found Lucy, and brought her to us. That was the beginning of a special relationship for our family.

During her four years at Biola, Lucy came to our home often. She spent most weekends and holidays with us and brought other African girls. She was an outstanding Christian and a smart girl, but she had boyfriend problems. I told her how important marriage was. The young man she liked didn't match her level of intelligence and Christian maturity. Fortunately, she didn't continue the relationship, and the Lord had someone better for her. She now has a fine Christian husband, Maina, and three clever children.

During the Thanksgiving weekend of 1976, Lucy and ten other Biola internationals joined LeRoy and Carol when they took a group from Orange County to San Francisco for the ISI conference. Wichit brought students from San Diego, and Sam Ooman brought students from the Los Angeles area.

The monthly international student rallies continued to be well attended. We involved the Christian international students and missionary young people as much as possible. At the February rally, thirteen international doctors and students from twenty-seven different countries were there. Nearby Chapman College had a greater percentage of international students than any college in America at that time.

In March, three ISI banquets were held in Southern California. Sam Ooman had one at the First Presbyterian Church of Hollywood, Wichit had one in Vista Community Church, and we had one again at Knott's Berry Farm.

LeRoy and Carol graduated from Biola in June 1977. They both did well in their studies, and we were proud of them. Carol's parents, Glen and Naomi Roth, came from Oregon for the ceremony. We were pleased to sit in the same section as Roy Rogers and Dale Evans, whose granddaughter was graduating as well.

Evangelist Luis Palau brought a dynamic message at the graduation ceremony. He told about the Biola graduate who had been a missionary in Argentina, where he told Luis about the Lord when he was a boy. That young missionary was Keith Bensen, one of Elcho's roommates at Biola. I had spent two summers with Keith in a children's outreach on Manhattan Beach with Dr. and Mrs. Hooker from Biola.

Soon after graduation, LeRoy and Carol moved to Dallas, Texas, so he could attend Dallas Theological Seminary. They were still on a part-time status with ISI and made an effort to get people involved in the ISI ministry at their new church, Scofield Memorial. They also became good friends with a number of internationals studying at the seminary, including Ramesh Richards.

That summer, Mary Ellen was accepted at Johns Hopkins University. She found a small apartment in the home of a surgeon, a friend of ISI. She studied hard but was glad to spend an occasional evening with friends and international students. Her hard work did not curb her desire to witness to her international classmates from forty-five countries. Many of them later became health leaders in their homelands.

In the fall of 1977, a number of older students from Saudi Arabia were studying at Chapman College. We especially liked one married couple, Aziz and Fatia, who came to our home often for dinner, and they had us in their home as well. One evening, we were having refreshments and talking in our covered patio with its hanging ferns. "We could never have so many plants in our country," Aziz said. "We don't have enough water. We dig for water, and all we get is oil."

Fatia was bored with nothing to do at home while her husband was in classes, so she attended beauty school. She wanted to be qualified as a beautician in her country. "The ladies have to wear veils when they go out," she said, "but they would feel better if their hair looked nice."

Fatia was a petite, attractive girl who dressed stylishly. "Will you be able to dress like this in your homeland?" I asked one day.

"No," she said, "never in public. My father would rather see me come back home in a coffin than in a dress like this."

Wanida Ellen Maneevone was born on January 31, 1978. She was an active little bundle of joy from the beginning. Miriam had her hands full with three little girls, all less than five years of age. Besides that, she had about eighty international students in the International Christian Fellowship (ICF) in their home every Friday night.

We loved being grandparents. It was such a joy when Miriam and Wichit brought the girls to stay with us for a few days. For the most part, they played well together, and I was never happier than when we had a picnic by the fishpond on our patio. Leonie learned to read very early and almost always had a book with her. It wasn't long before the girls played school, with Leonie as teacher to her younger sisters. When Miriam took her to enroll in kindergarten, the teacher asked Leonie to read and do simple math. The school put her into first grade instead of kindergarten. Today Leonie is a high-school teacher in San Diego.

Malina loved the outdoors. She often came into the house with a ladybug cradled in her hand. She liked to watch the birds and pick flowers. When she was about four years old, we bought her a little nurse set. She loved to put on the little white hat and the stethoscope around her neck, and then play that she was a nurse. As an adult, she not only became a nurse but also a nurse anesthetist.

In June 1978, we helped our dear friends Dexter and Lenore Lutz celebrate their sixtieth wedding anniversary where they lived in Westminster Gardens, a Presbyterian retirement home in Southern California. It was the beautiful celebration of a shared life that radiated sweetness. They were a testimony to all who loved them—family, friends, and international students.

We were shocked to hear that our dear friend Dwight Ritchie was tragically killed in an auto accident in Afghanistan. His wife, Winnie, was also in the accident and was near death for days. Her loving children flew to be with her and make funeral arrangements to bury their father in Kabul. Thankfully, Winnie recovered and has been going "full speed ahead" ever since.

Our ISI staff convened at Colorado Springs to celebrate the organization's first twenty-five years. We rejoiced in God's blessings and dedicated ourselves anew to serve Him more fervently. Special emphasis was given to reaching the Muslim world. We heard several speakers who worked with Muslims say that it took at least one hundred different positive contacts over several years before a Muslim was ready to accept the Lord.

In August, Wichit, Sam, and Elcho took three vanloads of internationals to join others from around the country for an International Leadership Conference for mature Christians at ISI's Star Ranch. Seventy key internationals gathered for a week of intensive Bible training and prayer times for the Christian witness in their countries and their willingness to be used in any way the Lord chose. Many did go back and make a difference in their homelands.

One day, the pastor of a large church called us. "A Japanese movie star is coming to Orange County, and we wonder if you can let him stay with you and teach him some English," he said. "A contact in Tokyo gave us your names." It turned out that Ken Joseph, a former Biola student who had come to our rallies, was now a businessman in Tokyo and had met this movie star. He had called the pastor of his former church and had given him our names.

We couldn't imagine what a Japanese movie star would be like, and we didn't have room to let him stay with us at the time. However, to have him come to our home to learn English was a different story. Therefore, Tomokaza Miura stayed with the music pastor of the church and came to our home every day for two weeks. He was a friendly, charming, and good-looking young man.

Every weekday morning, Tomo drove his big, black rented car into our driveway, studied English for several hours, and learned about the American way of life. He said he was engaged to a famous Japanese singer and was going to have a Christian wedding in a large Tokyo church.

"Are you a Christian?" Elcho asked.

"I've been to church a few times, but I don't really know what a real Christian is. I'd like to know," he said.

After Elcho explained the way of salvation, Tomo accepted Jesus as his Savior and Lord. For the next six days, Elcho gave him Bible verses to assure him of salvation.

The first weekend, Elcho gave Tomo some homework: "What are the advantages and disadvantages of being a famous movie star in Japan?" On Monday morning, Tomo could think of only one advantage—having lots of money and being able to buy anything he wanted. The disadvantages were many. He couldn't go to a store and buy toothpaste. He couldn't walk in a park or a shopping mall without causing a near riot. He literally had lost his freedom to be himself. In America, no one knew him, and he gradually relaxed. Tomo asked if he could go shopping with me. I proudly took him to the grocery store, to the hardware store, and anywhere he wanted to go. Befriending an international student had never been so much fun.

Tomo's reputation followed him when he went with me to Biola. One day, I had to set up an ISI booth for the school's annual missionary conference. As we entered the gym, he was fascinated with all the various booths. Then several Japanese girls saw him and got excited. They put their hands to their mouths, giggled, and started screaming.

A year later, I was in Hong Kong and saw magazines with Tomo's wedding picture on the covers. The first movie we took our Chinese students to see in Chongqing, China, was in Japanese, and Tomo was the leading star. I talked to him on the phone several times in Tokyo.

Kong Mian Jen, an attractive young Chinese lady from Shanghai, came to visit us one day in the late spring of 1979. She was one of the very first young people to come to the United States from the Peoples Republic of China in the crack in the new open-door policy. She asked if she could live with us and if we would help her learn English and teach her about life in America. I'm not sure how she heard about us, but I believe the Lord sent her to us. We both taught her English, with Elcho giving her formal lessons, and I giving her practical lessons. She liked to go with me wherever I went. She was a good cook and often made Chinese dishes for our supper. She and I liked driving to Escondido to see Miriam, Wichit, and the girls, as well as Aunt Mary, who now had moved into a mobile home in Escondido nearer her family. We enjoyed having Kong Mian living with us.

Since we were seventy miles apart, I found it difficult to help Miriam as much as I would have liked. We always enjoyed having the girls come to visit us, but I didn't take the girls often enough. I was busy and didn't realize until later how very busy Miriam was with her young family and helping Wichit in the ISI ministry. They had an open home with international students there almost continually. Their ICF was growing, and Wichit spent most days on different college campuses visiting students, so Miriam always had too many irons in the fire. ISI work is not merely an eight-to-five job, especially if it is a home-centered ministry.

In May, we took the train to Dallas, Texas, to visit LeRoy and Carol at Dallas Theological Seminary. Although it was hot in their student apartment, we enjoyed meeting their friends and seeing the campus. We were thankful that our only son had this opportunity to attend an excellent seminary. We became acquainted with one of their friends, Ramesh Richards, a student from India. Today Ramesh is an outstanding international Christian conference speaker and a professor at Dallas

Theological Seminary. His sister married the son of our former coworkers in India and in ISI, Sam and Ruth (Stam) Thiagarajian.

In June 1979, we flew to Baltimore, Maryland, for Mary Ellen's graduation from Johns Hopkins University. She had worked hard and had done well, and we were proud of her. She flew to Orange to begin a three-month internship in midwifery at the Los Angeles County Hospital.

Elizabeth Ann Redding was born to LeRoy and Carol on August 1, 1979, in Dallas, Texas. Now we had four granddaughters. We could hardly wait to see her.

In September, the international student rallies began again. We both were involved in the follow-up with students and in hospitality. Mary Ellen and Kong Mian were living at home with us. They got along well and did many things together. Kong Mian was a good student, a charming young lady, and was interested in learning everything.

Both husband and wife had to be qualified to be on staff of ISI in those days, and both of us had to be actively involved in the ministry. However, with the board's approval, we could also be involved with educational institutions. Elcho continued to teach six hours a week at Biola College and four hours a week at the William Carey University in Pasadena at the World Missions Center. Since all the students planned to be overseas missionaries, Elcho encouraged them to come to our rallies and get to know international students. When several came and helped me, I wondered if Elcho had given it as an assignment.

Stuart Hamblen and his lovely wife, Susie, invited us to bring thirty or forty internationals to their home in Hollywood one Friday night. Stuart Hamblen was a cowboy singer who had become a Christian at a Los Angeles Billy Graham crusade. After his conversion, he wrote a number of Christian songs. "Until Then" and "It Is No Secret What God Can Do" are the best known.

The Dalai Lama of Tibet came to Los Angeles in November. Our Tibetan young men helped with the arrangements and security. Gedun arranged for us to have a private audience with the Dalai Lama. Our family had a nice visit with him in a private room in his hotel. He seemed happy to have a picture taken with Leonie, Malina, and Wanida.

Christmas in 1979 was a happy time with our immediate family. LeRoy, Carol, and baby Elizabeth came from Dallas; Wichit, Miriam,

Leonie, Malina, and Wanida came from Escondido; Elcho's folks came from Oregon. My dad joined us, and Mary Ellen was living with us. I remember the genuine happiness I felt to be in our lovely Orange County home, surrounded by loved ones. Many international friends had sent gifts and cards, and Kong Mian gave us a beautiful thirty-two by fifty-inch needlepoint picture of the Great Wall of China. This has hung above the fireplace in Wichit and Miriam's home in Escondido since 1980. Peter and the Tibetan young men came for visits during the Christmas season.

In the joy of that season, it didn't enter my head that we would never be all together again in Orange, California.

One Sunday morning in early February 1980, Pastor Mike Fisher made an announcement in our church service: "Someone in our congregation was riding the bus this week and sat next to a man from mainland China," he said. "His name is Yi Ling. He's in our congregation today and desperately needs a place to stay for a while. If anyone has any idea of a room for him, please talk to him after the service." We invited Yi Ling to stay with us, and he moved in the next morning.

Yi Ling had been in the States for only a few days and was here on a work visa. He was the father of three teenage sons and a grade-school daughter. His wife, Jane Wang, and their children were still in Shanghai. He had a job with a company in Irvine. He stayed with us for three months until he had saved enough money to find a place of his own.

Elcho was taking a Chinese language course at Orange Coast College. One day, he looked at me and said, "I'd like to live overseas again, preferably in China."

I was shocked. "Well, I enjoy living in California in a nice home with hot running water, hot showers, flush toilets, a furnace to keep us warm in chilly weather, and some of our children and grandchildren nearby. After all," I explained, "we're fifty-five years old. If we're ever to live overseas again, it will have to be soon." I was accustomed to the luxuries that America afforded. In fact, I took them for granted. I certainly was not anxious to give them all up and move to Asia again.

40

A New Door Opens to China

In early March 1980, Elcho attended a Teaching English to Speakers of Other Languages (TESOL) conference in San Francisco. On the second day, he called. "Three men are here from the People's Republic of China's National Education Department," he said. "They have come to select twelve teachers to teach English at several prestigious universities in China. May I apply and be interviewed by them?"

"But you don't even have an updated resume, do you?" I asked.

"I sent one of mine to Peter Cheng a couple of weeks ago. He had to write his resume, and he didn't know what one was, so I sent him mine as an example. He's coming tomorrow to have lunch with me, and he'll bring my resume then."

"How many people are at the conference?" I asked.

"About five thousand."

"Well, do what you want, I guess." I was so sure that our friendship with the Dalai Lama, which certainly was no secret, along with our advancing years, didn't give Elcho much chance of the Chinese choosing him.

When he came home, he was walking on air. He just knew the Chinese officials liked him and planned to select him. Every time the phone rang, he wondered if it was the Chinese embassy. The officials at the conference implied that the chosen ones would know within a couple of weeks, as the selected teachers had to be in China when the August classes began. So we waited.

Working with ISI in Orange had been rewarding. The six guest books, which had been filled during our twelve years there, reminded us of the privilege of showing hospitality to people from around the world. But we realized that the ISI ministry in Orange County would continue without us. Herb and Gloria Baker had been accepted by ISI and were raising their support to go into the ministry full-time. They had a home in Placentia, California, and had been working with Vivian Max in the international outreach of the Fullerton Evangelical Free Church.

At the end of April and six weeks after Elcho had applied, Kong Mian's father phoned us from Shanghai. "Dr. Redding was chosen to teach at Chongqing University," he said. "The Ministry of Education is making the announcement today."

"Chongqing! Where is that?" I asked. We got out our encyclopedia and saw that it was at the head of the Yangtze River. Although Elcho's appointment had been announced in China, we were told we would have to wait until we received official papers before we made final plans.

We called ISI headquarters and talked with Hal Guffey. We and the mission had to make big decisions right away. He was encouraging and felt that the Bakers could take over the work. Hal told us that ISI did not want to continue owning property. The home in Orange that Aunt Mary had sold to ISI at a reasonable price, where we had been living and paying rent to the mission for twelve years, would be sold for four times the buying price and the money added to ISI's general fund. Arrangements were also made for Elcho, Wichit, Miriam, and me to buy the house in Escondido that Aunt Mary had given to ISI. Hal was concerned that we all would have security in our retirement years since ISI had no retirement plan for its workers at that time.

Even though the Chinese government would give Elcho a salary, we wanted to stay associated with ISI. Our monthly stipend would remain if our friends and churches kept sending funds to ISI for us. We would use those funds for ministry outings, extra travel expenses, and supplies for our work with the students at Chongqing University. Every obstacle had been removed. China was a wide-open door.

Without a doubt, God had been preparing us to go there. Elcho had his master's degree in TESOL from the University of California at Los Angeles (UCLA) and a Ph.D. in education from Claremont Graduate

School. We had wanted to go to China (or Tibet) for many years, but with the government changes in 1949, that had been impossible. Now the Chinese government had invited us as honored guest teachers and was even paying us to go! Elcho was excited about the opportunity but sad about leaving our children and grandchildren. Another grandchild was to be born soon.

We had had the joy of showing hospitality to several young adults who had been among the first young people to arrive from China in 1979. Kong Mian, her friend, Yau Mao, and the young businessman, Yi Ling, were all from Shanghai. They had all lived but a stone's throw from each other, yet met for the first time in our living room in Orange, California. They were formerly the elite of Chinese society. We believed that these God-appointed visitors had come to us in His perfect timing.

While I had a sense of excitement about being among the first English teachers to go to China, I had mixed emotions. The work with international students had been going well. We had been happy for over twelve years in the ISI Orange County ministry, but as I prayed and read the Scriptures, I had peace about this decision. If the door really was opening for us to go to China, I was willing to go, even if a bit reluctantly.

While we waited for official word, we divided our personal belongings five ways. The most important things would go to our three children. We would give another pile to international students or anyone else, and the fifth would go to the dump.

We went to Escondido so Elcho could spend a little time with Wichit, Miriam, and our little granddaughters, Leonie, Malina, and Wanida, before he left for China. He also wanted to say good-bye to Aunt Mary Marshburn.

Mary Ellen had rejoined the Army Nurse Corps and was assigned to Tripler Army Medical Center in Honolulu, Hawaii. The Army would pick up her things to move her there in a few days. As they would pay the moving expenses, we decided to send our grand piano, dining-room set, and some of our things from India with her.

The very day they came to pick up her things, we got an official letter from China: "Acting on the recommendation of the Foreign Experts Bureau of the State Council of the People's Republic of China, Chongqing University has invited Dr. Elcho Redding to teach graduate students and teachers in colleges in Sichuan the methods of Teaching English as a Second Language. Contract to begin August 1, 1980."

ISI staff members in Hawaii invited Mary Ellen to stay with them until she had rented a condominium in downtown Honolulu. They also got her involved in the international student ministry on the University of Hawaii campus.

On June 15, 1980, Elcho left for China with only two suitcases. He was anxious to get going, and I planned to join him in a month or so. Wichit, Miriam, Leonie, Malina, and Wanida came to say good-bye. We had Elcho's farewell luncheon at the lovely Lawrence Welk Resort in Escondido. Elcho then left California and flew to Washington State, where he visited LeRoy, Carol, baby Liz, my mother, and his folks. LeRoy was on an internship

Aunt Mary, Gedun, Miriam, Leonie, Malina, and Patty Marshburn gave us a farewell send-off at the Lawrence Welk Resort.

with Dallas Theological Seminary, working as a youth pastor in Yakima. Elcho stopped in Honolulu for the weekend to visit Mary Ellen in her lovely condominium with its spectacular view. His next stop was Hong Kong, then Chongqing, Sichuan, China.

Part 5
China

41

Elcho in China

On June 22, 1980, Elcho wrote me:

> I arrived last night at 9:09—right on time. Hong Kong was as beautiful as ever. Met Opal Anderson, a good woman. You will love her. She has been in China and Hong Kong many years. She is a retired Evangelical Free missionary and lives in the YMCA. Trip up by train was very nice all the way. Did not have to touch the luggage anywhere, except in Hawaii. Chinese trains are very nice. The food was superb.
>
> Four men met me at the Guangzhou (Canton) train station. One was the government representative of education in Canton; another was from China International Travel. An interpreter, Mr. Lao Tung, came from Chongqing (two days and two nights), representing Chongqing University. The Canton Educational representative took us to a restaurant in the middle of a lake. I have seen pictures of it in travel books. It was a beautiful setting. We had nineteen courses with a variety within some of the courses. Lao Tung took care of all my expenses, travel, and food on the train coming to Chongqing. I spent Chinese yuan today for the first time to get tea, a bath towel, washcloth, cards, stamps, this stationary, cookies (for guests), an umbrella, etc. I have an interpreter, and he is with me whenever I need him.

You will love China. The country coming up was gorgeous. Everything is so green. Fields are neat as a pin. The whole country is like one big park—lots of rivers, irrigated fields, mountains, and terraced paddies.

It's hard to describe Chongqing—strange, but I have seen few bicycles. I think that the city is too hilly. I rode around the city quite a bit. People travel mostly by large buses. Very few cars, and drivers honk when they start up, go around corners, and when they stop. Progress is very evident. Lots of building going on. I have a chauffeur, a good driver. He works for the university and drives me around in one of the university's six cars.

I will meet the head of the foreign language department tomorrow. I am sure that you will be asked to teach some classes. The students are in need of English conversation. My students are teachers of Russian and now will be teaching English. I have met several students going to or coming from the dining room. I am glad that I came early. I am in a room next door to where we will be living. We will have two rooms on three

Elcho was hired by the Ministry of Education to teach this class of teachers from colleges all around Sichuan Province.

sides with lots of windows in a brand-new building. No one has lived in it yet. Lao Tung said that it was "air-conditioned," but he was not kidding. He thinks many windows and air circulation is air-conditioning. The bed is solid comfort with no mattress. I will try to find out where I can get one. My interpreter does not know the word in English and was surprised to see the Chinese word. Guess no one uses a mattress.

Han Chi-Shun is head of the foreign language department here. I had a long talk with him this morning. He came to my room, and I must say he is very kind. He reminds me of the Dalai Lama's first interpreter. From what I learned, I will have twenty students who have already passed a score of 450 on a TOEFL test. Their English then is quite good. They are language teachers in many different colleges in Sichuan.

For hot water, I use three large thermoses. They are filled at night, and twenty-four hours later, the water is still boiling hot. Someone downstairs did up some of my shirts and underwear.

I have only to wish, and it is done, it seems. Someone is looking into getting a mattress. I mentioned church, and the interpreter will take me tomorrow. On Monday, I will see the library and the texts already in use. Students need help in conversation skills.

Mr. Han visited Shanghai and met someone there who had met you at a conference in Monterey, California. He said that the man gave a glowing report of you and the conference.

On July 7, 1980, Elcho wrote:

What did you do for your birthday? Hope that it was a nice fifty-fifth. Did you get my telegram wishing you a happy birthday? I have not been able to get any air forms here. No post office in a town of six million people has any air forms. Hard to describe how everyone is so kind.

A major problem is the language. Han Shi-Shua, the head of the foreign language department, said he would try to get a teacher for me for two hours a day. The problem is to find someone who has the time and knows both Mandarin and English.

I am comfortably situated in a room with two sitting chairs with a table between, an *almirah* [a cupboard, cabinet, or chest of drawers], and a long hard bed with a mosquito net. I didn't sleep the first night here because of the mosquitoes, in spite of the fact that Lin set off two anti-mosquito incense joss spirals that burned until morning. Also, I have a washstand with an enamel basin and a towel rack, a small desk, a chair for it, and four teacups with lids. It is hot here, but the fan is adequate.

The people are good to me—yet I am very lonesome for you and wish so much that you were here now. I miss Leonie, Malina, Wanida, and Liz. I have written to them all. Wonder if Miriam has had her baby yet? I have my family pictures out and look at them all the time. I show them to everyone who visits me.

I was taken to church today and met the pastor who knows English, Pastor Tsai. I am sure I was quite conspicuous. We arrived at eight thirty in the morning, and the place was almost full. I asked a man there to save me a seat and then went across the street to a barber—then back to church. Glad that I asked to have a seat saved, because there was no room. Unfortunately, the saved seat was right down in the front of the church. I felt all right during the prayer and opening remarks. Then we stood, and I felt like Paul Bunyan or Gulliver—or like an elephant.

The first song undid me completely. I knew the words of all the verses in English and thought them through as they sang in Chinese. "He leadeth me: O blessed thought! O words with heavenly comfort fraught. Whate're I do, where're I be, Still 'tis God's hand that leadeth me." Could not keep the tears back—flowed like the Jordan River. However, I don't think anybody saw because I didn't make a motion to wipe my face—just let the tears flow. I did not understand the sermon. However, I was much warmed and blessed by being with others who know the Lord. I am the first foreigner to be in the church since it opened in December, six months ago.

The shower is so very cold, but I did not say anything. Lin told me that he was requesting the university to put in a heater for a warm shower for us. Therefore, by the time you get here, you can have a warm shower.

Now Han is coming by for me at six fifteen in the evening. The president, two vice presidents, and the department heads have invited me to dinner. I don't handle these "banquets in-honor" very well. Sorry you're not here to help me through it. One of the teachers said it is usually quite a party. I am reminded of the feast in Dharamsala that the Tibetan educational department gave us before we left India.

I will save some space to tell you about tonight's dinner. I have been doing a lot of reading on TESL programs. Somehow, I think that twenty weeks is too short a time to learn all that I think these students should have. From what I gather, the emphasis in these programs has been only on learning English grammar and some oral (far too little) and vocabulary building. However, I think they need to learn the principles of teaching it. Han Chi-Shun is taking me to the library tomorrow.

Ten thirty at night: Well, what a feast! Vice President Jin, Vice President Dun, Vice President Chan, Dean of the Foreign Language Department Hun, and Lao Tung, who are slated to become big administrators, were all on hand at the banquet. Three of them came to fetch me at 5:45. We talked a long while and then walked to the university dining hall. Formal greetings and cold water were offered in Vice President's Jin's office.

Then we went into the dining room. The table was beautifully set with seven different kinds of appetizers. Then the dinner: roasted fish (yummy), sliced beef, peanuts with eggs, cucumber with bean oil, gizzards in salted water, rabbit, and Sichuan-style sausage. A shredded something was in the center. I sat between Vice President Jin and Vice President Dun.

The dinner began with a formal welcome in English by Vice President Jin (graduated from Purdue University in 1930), which was also translated into Chinese for Vice

President Chan and Vice President Dun. They were well-chosen words and a cordial, warmhearted welcome. Then Jin and Dun loaded my bowl with delicacies.

It was time for another toast, and then they served flavored duck; peacock in its pride (This was a masterpiece. Only someone who knows Chinese dishes could possibly explain it, but it was very beautiful and tasty); sea cucumber; sizzling rice of three flavors (scrumptious); first-rank bean curd. Then more toasts and sliced pork with mustard; sliced bamboo shoots with cream (actually beaten egg whites); chicken with eggs; and gourd with shrimps. Then more toasts and more toasts and a special soup; silver-ears mushrooms (which I understand are extremely costly); fried dumplings; cake of egg with milk; peach preserves; and Chinese apple pie. How's that for a welcome feast?

Vice President Dun offered a toast to you. Quite a few toasts. I'm afraid it's a custom I'll have to live without. My drinking glasses were as full when we ended as they were when we began. However, I did toast and touch glasses with the others. No one seemed offended that I didn't drink. I like Han Chi very much, and Vice President Jin is most gracious. Others were very nice. Jin, Han, and Dun escorted me home, and we talked for about forty-five minutes. Jin is anxious for us to see Chengdu, which is further up the Yangtze with spectacular gorges. He told me that Chengdu has forty thousand Tibetans (or was it four thousand?).

The campus is on one thousand acres, but not all the acreage is right here. Students need English conversation and seem eager to practice with me. I'm sure you will be very happy here. While I think of it, please bring two bottles of white liquid eraser stuff—you know what I mean—and three bottles of thinner. We really must have the copier, so please give it the priority of things you bring. Having seen the vice president's office today, I know it will be appreciated more than can be said. Tung is showing me the campus tomorrow. Han is showing me his office and library. Jin has ordered a citywide tour this week sometime.

On July 9, 1980, Elcho wrote:

> I just had a talk with Han (head of the foreign language department), who has talked with Vice President Jin. I will teach linguistics and methodology to three different classes four hours each week for the first twelve weeks, plus lectures to the university teaching staff itself. I will also help with your classes and do some teaching there too.
>
> Han said they would like for you to be a faculty member and teach twelve hours a week. There is not enough time for teachers and students to talk together, and it's the oral practice they need so much. I had three nice young men, ages seventeen, twenty-four, and twenty-five, here last night from seven thirty to nine o'clock. Two had been here before. One had been given the name Stephen by a teacher. I told him about Stephen and showed him his name in the book of Acts. Then he asked me, "Do you think I'll ever be worthy of the name?" He's a very insightful young man. "Yes," I said, "perhaps one day you will." Then Robert wanted to know if his name was in there and felt let down when he found out it wasn't.
>
> A television is here but is in a common room downstairs— quite unhandy. Han is giving us this room as a study. So actually we have half of the whole second floor. I'm going to get measurements of windows in the end rooms. You will want panels. The way the rooms are arranged, we can be inspected on two sides by four sets of neighbors (four stories) on both sides, eight different households. I just know that you will be very happy here. Can hardly wait for you to get here.

Elcho wrote this letter to our dear friend, Dexter Lutz, on July 9, 1980:

> I thought of you so many times as I came up country from Guangzhou (Canton) by train. The trip was two days and two nights of traveling through extremely beautiful country. Everywhere I looked, there was sheer beauty—rice fields, brooks, rivers, mountains, and terraced countryside. The vegetation was lush and, if under cultivation, was kept like a garden. The

country seems to be one giant park. I saw rice in all stages of growth from newly planted shoots to ready-to-harvest. There also was taro, tapioca, cane, water chestnuts, peanuts, and soybeans. I saw bamboo, eucalyptus, pine, and banana trees. My strongest impression has been the beauty of the country, which is only surpassed by the friendliness of the people.

Millie has been appointed as a staff member to teach twelve hours a week to younger English major students. Couldn't find a better teacher, could they?

Our quarters here are ample, a four-room suite, which takes up half the second floor of the building. I have been to church three times but find it difficult because of the language. I know all of the hymns but can't read the Chinese script fast enough, so I have the script romanized. I don't know if I'll ever master the Chinese characters. The church was full—about three hundred people—all over fifty years old.

I have been here four weeks and count sixty-six names in my guest book, so you see how friendly everyone is. I am so happy, and I know that Millie will be too!

42

Joining Elcho in China

Meanwhile in California, the house needed a lot of work to get it ready for the market. My seventy-seven-year-old dad painted the house inside and out and got the yard in tip-top shape. Each time I opened a closet, I had more decisions to make. I had to get rid of thirty-three years of belongings of a family of five. Miriam and Wichit took whatever they wanted. He was more interested in the staghorn ferns than in the sofas and chairs. That was a good decision, for the sofas and chairs are long gone, but the staghorn ferns have multiplied many times and look as nice on their deck as they did on our patio years ago.

We separated things for LeRoy and Carol and packed them into our big van. A friend then drove it to Yakima, where LeRoy was working as a youth pastor. Elcho asked me to send our three sets of encyclopedias, *National Geographic* magazines, English books, and Bible-study books to him. Friends also donated books, and my cousin Gordy and I packed nearly fifty boxes of books for Chongqing University.

I will never forget the farewell luncheon that the ladies of Emmanuel Faith Community Church gave me. Miriam had just given birth to her fourth daughter, Anjuli Miriam Maneevone, on July 14, 1980, and was overwhelmed at the thought of saying good-bye. She had her hands full with three little girls and a newborn. With tears in her eyes, Miriam spoke of when missionaries go to the field, their parents send them, but she was in a reverse role. She had to send her parents, and it was difficult for her.

We had said many good-byes in our missionary career, but this was by far the hardest time for me. Yet, the Lord gave me peace. After the good-byes at the San Diego airport, I flew to Yakima, Washington, to say good-bye to my mother, as well as LeRoy, Carol, and baby Elizabeth. Then I flew to Honolulu for a couple of days with Mary Ellen and on to Shanghai. When I arrived in China with my earthly belongings in two suitcases, I knew that was where I should be and was doing what I should be doing.

Until 1976, Americans had been forbidden to visit or trade with China. The story behind this momentous thaw is worth retelling. I am reminded of how far we have come since Richard Nixon, then the newly elected United States' president, set out to change the world in defiance of the foreign policy of our government. China was still convulsed by mass upheaval in the Cultural Revolution that had begun in 1966. The Soviets had invaded Czechoslovakia, the Vietnam War was raging, and Hanoi's Soviet allies were not helpful in ending the war.

The United States had boycotted China since the Communists had seized power in 1949, and Nixon resolved to end this. The first major public sign of change came in April 1970, when Chairman Mao invited the United States table-tennis team to China, and the phrase "ping-pong diplomacy" was coined. The breakthrough came in July 1971, when, with the help of Pakistani mediation, Secretary of State Henry Kissinger secretly led the first official delegation into China in twenty-two years. Coincidently, that summer we were invited to the headquarters of Wycliffe Bible Translators, where we personally met President Nixon when he dedicated an airplane donated to the organization.

In February 1972, President Nixon visited China for a week, and this led to China's momentous shift toward capitalism. Soon the Watergate scandal would engulf Nixon, but he is credited for the diplomatic breakthrough into China. The Cultural Revolution ended in 1976 with the death of Mao Zedong. The process of economic reform began in earnest in 1979 when Chinese leaders concluded that the Soviet system, which had been in place since 1950, was making little progress in improving the Chinese standard of living. It was failing to close the economic gap between China and the industrialized nations. This was the situation in China when we went there in 1980.

I had a royal welcome in Shanghai. Besides Elcho, the families of Kong Mian Jen, Yi Ling Wang, and Yau Mao were all there to greet me. Elcho looked good and was very glad to see me.

As we drove through the streets of Shanghai that beautiful day in 1980, the Jen family told how the Red Guards had been especially cruel. In 1967, the Jens buried their treasures in their backyard. Soon after, the Red Guards smashed the precious artifacts that remained in the home. Mr. Jen's family had owned the Swan cotton factory in Shanghai for many years. The factory manufactured many kinds of cotton goods, which the average Chinese family used. Underwear and towels from their factory were sent to many parts of the country. When Communists overwhelmed the country in 1941, they took over the factory and put Mr. Jen's father in charge. Later, Mr. Jen himself was in charge. In the late 1960s, the Red Guards took over the factory and the Jen's lovely home in Shanghai.

Soon the taxi arrived at the Peace Hotel where Elcho had checked in the night before. We were guests there many times in the next few years. The Peace Hotel symbolized the most luxurious "number one in the Far East." It was first called the Cathay Hotel when it opened in 1929. Through the years, it has been well known for its luxury and magnificence.

The Jen and Wang families were a big help to us in China. Kong Mian Jen and Yi Ling Wang had lived with us for several months in Orange, California.

Shawn Chen's parents often welcomed us into their home for tea or a meal. We especially enjoyed those times with them.

Distinguished guests from all over the world have stayed there. It was the scene of Generalissimo and Madame Chiang Kai-shek's engagement party. It was filled with Italian marble floors and hand-blown stained glass. However, when we stayed there on that hot summer day in 1980, the ravages of the Cultural Revolution were still evident. Because the Red Guards hated everything that the hotel stood for, they had destroyed much of its splendor. Our room looked as if we'd stepped back into history. Maintenance had been neglected, but it still had an air of past splendor.

The next day was Sunday. We made plans to spend the day with Jane Wang, whose husband, Yi Ling, had lived with us in Orange, California. She had written a note for us to give to the taxi driver so we wouldn't get lost. We were glad to see Jane waiting for us outside of the church when our taxi pulled up early Sunday morning.

It was a thrill to be in a crowded church in China. The familiar hymns, sung in Mandarin, were "music to our ears." The congregation was made up mostly of older people, many of whom had been educated in mission schools. But young people were there too and were hearing these hymns for the first time. The church was full for two services. Afterwards, Jane introduced us to the pastor, and we had a nice visit with him in his office.

After the early church service, we went with Jane to the small apartment that she shared with her children and her in-laws. We had a nice lunch and a good visit with the family. We later learned they had used valuable food coupons for our meal.

Jane's father-in-law, Dr. Wang, had graduated from the University of Pennsylvania. His father was the former secretary of the treasury for the People's Republic of China. Dr. Wang talked about the brutality of the Cultural Revolution. He told us that if he had seen us on the streets of Shanghai a few years earlier, he would have ignored

Chongqing is one of the largest cities in the world. It was a very old and polluted city in 1980—very different from today. We knew we were very privileged to be among the first "foreign experts" welcomed there.

us, even though he would have been delighted to befriend us. We asked him what would have happened if he had talked to us. "Probably I'd go to prison," was his reply.

The family told us how they had been forced to hide in the small attic of their own apartment. Dr. Wang asked us to look out the window to a high-rise building and sadly said, "My younger brother jumped from its roof during those terrible times."

Jane's nine-year-old daughter, Dorothy, played the piano beautifully for us. She is now an international lawyer.

The next day, we went by train with the Jens to Hangzhou, which is famous for its West Lake. An old Chinese saying declares, "There is heaven above and Hangzhou below." Centuries ago, Marco Polo called Hangzhou the most enchanting city in the world. The hills of the city embrace West Lake on three borders. This lake has inspired painters for centuries. We enjoyed walking around the lake with Kong Mian's parents. As there were many places to stop and rest, we enjoyed wonton soup, tea, and cookies. The next day, we went with Mr. and Mrs. Jen and a friend, who was an official, to see more of the city and to have an authentic Chinese dinner in his home.

Since Jane had some free time from the university where she was teaching, she came to Chongqing with us. I knew she could help me buy things that would make our living easier. On trains in China, there are no "classes" (i.e., first, second, and third class, as we had in India) but rather "soft seats" and "hard seats." The soft-seat tickets are reserved for government officials, high cadres, and foreign experts like Elcho and me. Jane, Elcho, and I had a comfortable sleeper cabin with access to our own special dining car. It was a pleasant two-day train ride from Shanghai to our new home in Chongqing.

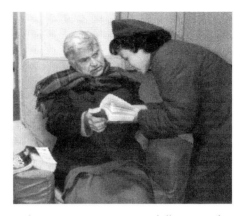

Wherever we went, even on chilly train rides, young people wanted help with their English.

Chongqing is a hilly city with government apartments built on the steep hillsides. At last, we moved into our comfortable, new apartment on the of Chongqing University campus. We felt the university was trying hard to make us feel welcome. It was a strange situation, for as far as we could tell, no foreigners had lived in Chongqing for thirty years. Then the policy changed in Beijing, and the university authorities were now responsible for us.

Our second-story apartment had whitewashed walls and bare cement floors. Although we hunted through the stores, we could not find a rug or carpet to cover the bare floors. The weather was either very hot or very cold. We wore layers of clothes to keep warm in winter, since we had no central heating. We were fortunate to have the use of a university car and driver, but the university took the expenses for the car out of our salary stipend.

Being among the first foreigners to teach had special challenges. Elcho had told the university authorities that since I would be teaching, I would need help at home. He knew we would want to eat in our own apartment rather than the university's central dining room. The school found a retired cook who could help us as needed if we paid his salary. We were thankful for our cook. He could make tasty dishes with limited supplies (mostly cabbage, potatoes, and onions), so he prepared one meal a day for us during the week.

The kitchen had a small wooden table, a washbasin, a small hole in the cement floor for water to drain, and a larger hole with a chute to go down the two floors as a waste disposal. If I had not lived in India for nearly twenty years, those first few days living in China would have been more difficult for me. As it was hot in Chongqing, the one thing I really wanted was a small refrigerator. Jane and I went to town to buy one. In a city of over six million people, it seemed we could not find a single refrigerator! Finally, we found a small one for sale, and I was so thankful. I found out that the average family had a small icebox and bought ice from the market—a reminder of my childhood.

Our quarters were adequate. We had three rooms that were all separate and led onto a small cement balcony. The kitchen and bathroom were separate off the balcony. We even had the luxury of a Western-style toilet. We had been told that it had been ordered just for us.

Each room had an automatic lock, so if the door closed accidentally, we were in big trouble. During my second week of teaching, I got a frantic note that Elcho needed my keys. He had gone into the bathroom in his shorts and robe, and the bedroom door had locked behind him. But he needed to get back into the bedroom so he could dress for class. He had managed to flag down someone from the second-story balcony to communicate his situation. After that experience, we were both careful not to let doors close behind us without keys.

Chinese older people took care of the babies and toddlers so mothers could work. Most babies seemed well cared for and well dressed. When we walked to our classes or in town, we would see older adults caring for the children. The little parks were filled with children and grandparents. We admired the cute, chubby children, and everyone stared at us.

When we were in the university car with the driver, the people were curious and crowded around us. Some held up their babies so they could get a better look at us. Young people wanted to practice their English with us, and others just wanted to look. We smiled and tried to communicate in our limited way. Elcho knew much more Chinese than I did, but I tried.

The veteran teachers in Elcho's classes used to teach Russian, but now they were assigned to teach English in colleges scattered throughout Sichuan Province. They did well in written English, but their speaking skills were limited. However, they were serious students and learned a great deal about teaching English as a second language.

The babies were all chubby and cute. With China's one child per family policy, the children are extremely doted upon by parents and grandparents. People crowded around us wherever we went.

The students loved our library of knowledge of the world. They did well in English and wanted to learn.

We were both assigned to teach classes of thirty-five students in the teacher-training classes. These young students stole our hearts. They were sixteen-to-twenty years of age in their third year of college. We enjoyed the classroom teaching, but we came to know each other in our apartment and on outings. That's when lasting friendships were made.

During the Cultural Revolution, most English literature had been destroyed. We had many English books, including three sets of encyclopedias and lots of *National Geographic* magazines. The latest editions of the encyclopedias were a big hit. The students could take many books home, but we kept the encyclopedias for them to look at in our apartment. We set up a nice library in one of our rooms, and students spent a lot of time looking at the books. We had our private devotional and Bible-study books in a small part of the library marked "personal books." No doubt, they looked at those too.

Six girls and twenty-nine boys were in this special teachers-training class. They had all been given English names, which made it easier for us, but we wanted to learn their real names.

Usually eight or ten students came to our apartment on afternoons and evenings. We never did find out how they decided who was going to

Left to right, Ben (with camera), Elcho and Chen "Craig" crossing the Yangtze River with some students on an outing.

come. They seemed interested in us and enjoyed seeing pictures of our family. They came to study, do puzzles, visit our library, play games, or to sing and play music. They liked to hear Elcho play the accordion, and a couple of them played it too. We had bought a little electric organ, and many enjoyed playing it. One played the violin and another the harmonica. Our apartment was a happy place where students relaxed. If we were just too tired or had too much to prepare for our classes, we put a sign on the door telling them so. The next day, they would ask us what the matter was. The students had to sign in with the guard at the building's entrance and tell their purposes before they entered.

The young people asked us questions about many things. We tried to answer them as best we could. The Lord gave us wisdom as we daily asked Him to do so. If they were hungry, they could make themselves meals in our little kitchen, as long as they cleaned up.

Professor Han, the head of the English department, came often to check on how we were doing with our classes. The university president and vice

The university let us rent one of their trucks and drivers to take the students on all-day field trips. It was a lot of fun.

president showed us pictures of their children, and we showed them pictures of our five granddaughters and other family members. The men seemed genuinely interested.

On several Saturdays and holidays, we hired a school truck for the day to visit various places around the Chongqing area. We rode on the back of the open truck with twenty-five or so students who chose to spend time with us. As we had no idea where to go, we let the students decide and make arrangements. These were great times for us, not only to see historic and scenic spots but also to be with young people away from the university. We would have lunch in a park somewhere. Sometimes we took a boat across the river to another town.

We often had parties in the classroom. Favorite games were Musical Chairs, Simon Says, Shoe Scramble, Black Magic, and other such games. The students often asked us to sing Indian songs in Marathi and Hindi. We usually brought oranges, peanuts, and crackers for refreshments.

On Sundays, Shawn or Gary, our student interpreters, made reservations for the university car and driver to take us to church. We were honored to be the first foreigners in the church. All the people, except

On Sundays, Shawn hired the university car and would act as our interpreter when we went into the city for church and shopping. We often went to his home afterwards. This photo was taken outside his parents' home.

our two students, were over fifty. Even though we couldn't communicate much, the people were friendly.

One day we saw several big packages in the church. They were Bibles for church members only, and they had to sign for them. We surmised that the purpose was to discover who considered themselves Christians.

After church, the boys usually took us out for lunch (we paid). Sichuan food is spicy, but we liked it. Freshly made steamed buns were delicious. However, restaurants were greatly lacking in cleanliness. People threw bones on the floor as they ate. Often chickens were in the dining area, eating scraps that had been tossed.

Life for the average citizens in Chongqing was meager and hard. Families lived in small, crowded government housing with few modern conveniences. People outside the city worked hard under difficult circumstances.

We were not tourists but rather teachers living with the people. It had been thirty years since foreigners had lived in this city of six or seven million people. Even older ones dimly remembered foreigners. Naturally, everyone was curious. We knew that living there was a privilege.

One morning I woke up with a high fever and felt very weak and sick. The university doctor checked me then decided that I should go to the hospital. What an experience that was! Two or three students stayed with me day and night to translate and to make sure I was well taken care of. The head dietician had gone to a mission school as a girl and, although she had not spoken English for three decades, she often came to my room to speak English and to make sure I had the food I wanted. Always three doctors and at least two nurses discussed my condition at any one time.

One day, the nurse brought me a basin of warm water to wash as usual. I used my new washcloth, but afterwards, I couldn't find it. When one of the boys came, he asked the nurse, and she said she must have thrown it out the window with the water. Someone three floors down got a new washcloth!

I don't know what medications they gave me or what ailment I had, but I gradually got better. After ten days, I was glad to go home and happy to be alive.

43

Christmas 1980

Christmas came to Chongqing for the first time in thirty years. In early December, students asked us the meaning of Christmas. They had heard about it on the British Broadcasting Company programs. They asked if they could have a party and sing Christmas songs.

When we were in the States, former missionaries had told us that in the 1940s, they had a large ministry among college students in Chongqing. Many of our university administrators had studied in America and had

Christmas came again to Chongqing after three decades of Communist rule. Shawn is decorating our Christmas tree with lights and chocolate candy kisses wrapped in silver, green, and red foil.

celebrated Christmas there. They also had suffered greatly and had been "reeducated" during the Cultural Revolution. However, they granted us permission to have a Christmas party and, as part of our English class, to teach the students Christmas songs. We began by stringing colored lights on our balcony. Since I was going to Hong Kong to get the copy machine fixed, I promised to try to buy Christmas carol books.

I asked Pastor Tsai at the church what I could bring him back from Hong Kong. I thought he'd suggest warm jackets for his family and was surprised when he said, "Please bring Bible-study books in Chinese. All our Bible commentaries and Bible dictionaries were destroyed during the Cultural Revolution. We desperately need them."

On Christmas 1980, we were far from our families but glad to be in China.

I stayed at the YMCA in Hong Kong and again had great fellowship with Opie Anderson. We went to many Christian bookstores. I bought Bible commentaries and Bible dictionaries for the pastors, but I couldn't find Christmas songbooks.

One evening, I went to the Evangelical Free Church monthly missionary supper and prayer meeting. They asked me questions and promised to pray for us. One missionary invited me to the Bible school where she taught and asked me to speak at their chapel service, which I did.

Later, I purchased an oven that sat on the fire, like we'd had in India, so I could make treats for the students. I bought cake mixes that could also be used to make cookies, but I still couldn't find Christmas music and carol books for the students.

On Sunday I went to church with Opie, and after the service, a young couple asked me if I were Elcho Redding's wife. When I told them I was, they hugged me and said that he had been their professor at the William Carey Missionary Training School in California. Now they were missionaries in Hong Kong and hoped to go to China soon because of Elcho's challenge to them. I was glad to see some fruit from our work in California.

Since I'd been in Hong Kong almost a week, I had to get back to Chongqing, even though the copy machine wasn't ready. I decided to go home without it or the Christmas songbooks. That afternoon, I was sitting on the roof of the YMCA having tea and my quiet time. I was like Elijah sitting under a juniper tree, feeling sorry for myself (1 Kings 19:4). I wished I were back in the States with my family for Christmas, and I was discouraged that I couldn't find songbooks.

Before long, Opie came up on the roof. "Would you like to go out to an early supper with me?" she asked. When I said yes, she added, "Afterwards, we can go to a hotel where they're having a meeting of Christian leaders. They're praying for China and talking about different ways to get there."

At the meeting that evening, some speakers were Chinese nationals living overseas. Various circumstances prevented their return home. Other speakers had yet to visit China and desired to take advantage of the current government's willingness to allow foreigners in. Most expressed what they hoped for the future.

Finally, I told them that I was in China as a foreign expert, teaching English as a second language. It was sometimes lonely, difficult work, but my husband and I both felt that this was the way to go. Then I said that the church in China needed Bible commentaries and Bible dictionaries and how I had been searching for Christian music tapes and especially Christmas songbooks for the students.

The leader asked me where I was staying and how long I was going to be there. The next morning, I was surprised to receive two visitors. A Christian and Missionary Alliance leader gave me fifty beautiful Christmas songbooks in English and Chinese, and an Asian outreach leader brought Christmas tapes and Bible-study books. The Lord encouraged me through His people.

As I hugged Opie good-bye and boarded the plane, I was glad to be going back to Elcho and the students waiting for me in Chongqing. The plane ride was quite an ordeal. The seat belts would not fasten, and my plastic cup containing green tea leaked.

Upon my arrival, I had a warm welcome. It was a good thing Elcho and the students brought a truck to pick me up because I had so much baggage. And, with the little oven that went on the kerosene burner and the cake mixes, coffee, black tea, cocoa, and other treats, we had lots to eat when students came to our apartment. Ben, one special student, either liked to cook or liked to be with us, so he was a big help in fixing these treats.

By Christmas Sunday in 1980, the church had been open for a year! It was the first time we saw young people in church. The choir music was good, and the choir members looked nice in their white robes and red scarves. Someone had painted a Christmas scene on the front of the whitewashed wall, and we sang familiar carols. During a baptismal service, over one hundred people were sprinkled. Since the church was very cold, I couldn't blame them for not opting for total immersion. The Christmas painting stayed on the whitewashed walls until Easter, but we enjoyed the manger scene with the big camels during those months.

University President Jin heard about our singing Christmas carols. He wanted someone to film the students singing carols during our English class so this could be broadcast on closed-circuit TV to all classes in the university. We were happy to arrange it!

A couple of United States embassy representatives visited us after the first of the year. They were surprised at the freedom we had with the students. Then, later in the month, two men came from the ministry of education in Beijing. They also saw the freedom that the students had with us. After that, guards at the entrance to our apartment building were much stricter about letting students come to see us. We sensed that "party members" were closely watching us, but we didn't know who they were. Soon, the students didn't come as often as they had before. Something was different.

One day in January, a student in Elcho's English teachers' class, George, and his friend came to our home with a gift of a tea set. He said that it was in gratitude. Then he apologized for keeping a book he had borrowed from our personal library for so long. It was a *Daily Light*, with Scripture readings for morning and evening. He said that when he read it, he had such peace, and he wanted to keep that peace. His friend said the reason he took so long was that he'd hand copied the entire book.

"When did you have time to do that?" I asked.

"I copied it at night after lights-out, under the covers with a flashlight."

"How many notebooks did it take to copy it?" I inquired.

"Nine of those blue exam books," he said.

I went into the bedroom and got a couple of brown leather-covered *Daily Light* books that I'd just brought from Hong Kong. I gave one each to George and his friend.

While the students didn't come to our place as often, they still invited us to go places with them. We enjoyed being a part of our students' all-university sports days. Several students were good athletes, and the rest

Shawn and Ben joking with Elcho, trying to get the oranges from his hands

of us cheered them on. The People's Hall was a popular place for the students to take us. We sometimes had dinner there. One evening we saw the Shanghai opera in the big hall.

We had to go to the main telephone company downtown to make a telephone call to the States. It took several hours, and Shawn Chen usually went with us. Sometimes on Saturday or Sunday, he invited us to his home for dinner or a tea party. It was unusual for a student to invite his professor into his home, but we were comfortable with him and his family.

We liked visiting the students at their homes and in their dormitories. They all appeared to come from influential families and seemed glad to have their families meet us. Ben Leo was one of our favorite students. He often brought his friends to us and took us around town. Sometimes we went with the students to movies and programs at the outside theater where several thousand students gathered.

44

Happiness and Heartbreak

I met our granddaughter Leonie at the Hong Kong airport on her eighth birthday, January 26, 1981. She flew by herself from Los Angeles to Hong Kong. We celebrated by having high tea at the Peninsula Hotel with Opie. Then we flew to Chiang Mai, Thailand, to spend time with Leonie's relatives there. We saw some beautiful places and enjoyed a few days with Wichit's family. They showed us real hospitality.

From Chiang Mai, we flew to Kathmandu, Nepal, to be with long-time friends from our India days, Dr. Carl and Betty Friedericks. Betty was the daughter of our dear friends, Dr. Dexter and Lenore Lutz.

From Nepal, we flew to New Delhi, India, where our TEAM missionary friends, Charles and Anita Warren, hosted us. We visited a number of former Tibetan students, including Thubten Dawa, who was one of the young people who used to spend his holidays with us when we were in Mussoorie in the 1960s.

The Sunday-evening services of Delhi Bible Fellowship, where Charles Warren was the pastor, were exciting. Missionaries had seven or eight small groups of believers who met throughout the city. On the first Sunday of the month, they all met together in the ballroom of the largest hotel in downtown New Delhi. About five hundred people, many of them young people, met on the Sunday afternoon we were there. I met many old friends and former students that day. I was glad to see how the Lord's work was prospering under difficult circumstances.

Leonie and I stayed with our long-time friends Carl and Marie Flickner in Agra and saw the beautiful Taj Mahal. We took the train to Dehra Dun and then proceeded on to Rajpur to stay with Jigme and Mary Taring. They had been reunited with their three daughters, who had just been released from Tibet. When we worked with the Tarings in Mussoorie in the early

Mrs. Taring and Millie with Mrs. Taring's three daughters, Una, Peggy, and Betty

1960s, Mrs. Taring would often talk about her two daughters Una and Peggy who had been left in Tibet. Because they were from an aristocratic family, she knew they would be suffering under the Chinese occupying forces. Peggy's son Tenzin was a teenager and had just arrived in India when we visited them. Later, he came to the University of Washington and often visited our home in Bellevue. We took a day trip to Mussoorie to see our missionary friends and the Woodstock school again.

We took the train to New Delhi and then flew to Bombay to be with Babu and Shaila Kelkar. Babu's niece was getting married, so we had the joy of being a part of the wedding celebrations, eating delicious Indian food, and seeing our Indian friends again.

From Bombay, we flew to Hong Kong, the last leg of our adventure. The plan was for Leonie to go to Chongqing with me, but when we got to Hong Kong, she became sick. I took her to the mission hospital, and the American doctor made many tests, including giving her a spinal tap. He advised us not to take her into China, so Mary Ellen flew from Hawaii to take her back home. I flew back to Chongqing to return to Elcho and my Chinese students who were waiting for classes to begin.

While Leonie and I were traveling in India, the university had a two-week vacation over the Chinese New Year in February 1981. Elcho decided to stay in China to visit Kunming and Chengdu. He took Shawn Chen, a student in our teacher-training classes, as his interpreter. They traveled by train from Chongqing to Kunming in Yunnan Province to Chengdu and back home. Shawn's sister Shawna joined Elcho and Shawn in their sightseeing in Kunming. They visited some ethnic tribes, including Tibetans.

Shawn heard about a pastor who had just been released from prison. He asked Elcho if he'd like to meet him. Of course, he would. Pastor Win had been imprisoned for many years. Although he had suffered a great deal, he was rejoicing in the Lord. Elcho got there just in time to take communion with this

Elcho with Shawn and his sister, Shawna, in Kunming on winter break

pastor and forty of his flock. The barnyard fowl were the spectators. Elcho was so moved that he could not stop his tears. No church was officially open in Kunming at the time, but many came to know and love the Savior.

From Kunming in Yunnan Province, Elcho and Shawn went by train to Chengdu to meet some students and their families. On Sunday, they went to church. The pastor was an older man who had also been imprisoned for many years. As he was enthusiastically preaching, his false teeth flew out of his mouth and onto his Bible. He quickly put them back into his mouth and said, "When I preach about Jesus, I get so excited!"

One evening, while Elcho was eating fish in a local restaurant, a fish bone got caught in his throat. He could feel it there, but he couldn't get it out. So Shawn took him to the hospital where a doctor extracted the bone. Elcho knew he was fortunate to have been near medical help during his emergency.

Soon after Elcho got home, he came down with a high fever. Classes had not started, so only a few students were on campus. As Shawn lived in Chongqing, he went to see Elcho one day. Elcho didn't come to the door, but Shawn heard him groaning. Somehow, he got a key and went in. Elcho had not eaten for three days and was burning with fever. Shawn got the doctor, who gave Elcho medication. Shawn then stayed with Elcho and made sure he ate, drank fluids, and took his medication. That was the second time that God used Shawn to get emergency medical help that saved Elcho's life.

It was good to see Elcho and hear of his adventures, and I was sorry for not being with him during his illness. Now, however, he was well, and we were soon busy teaching classes again. We continued to be amazed to see the openness of our friends there. We were experiencing the reality of John 15:16, "You did not choose Me, but I chose you."

Yet, something seemed different. We didn't know what the remainder of 1981 held for us, but we planned to stay in China as long as the door was open.

With the help of Chongqing University authorities, we got visas for Aunt Mary Marshburn to come with her six college-age grandchildren. University President Dr. Jin contacted Beijing, and we got the proper papers—a miracle indeed. I met them in Hong Kong and took them to Beijing for a couple of days of sightseeing. They especially wanted to walk on the Great Wall of China. Wes, Aunt Mary's oldest grandson, carried her and her wheelchair up the steps so she too could walk on the wall.

We flew then to Chongqing. Talk about attracting a crowd! The six Marshburn teenagers were the first American young people in Chongqing for three decades. Our students liked talking with them. We had a party with the students, and Wes showed slides of his Palomar College campus. We hired a bus to sightsee with our American friends and any Chinese students who wanted to come along. Later, they played basketball together. We were glad to see barriers broken down and friendships made.

After four full and exciting days, Elcho took the young people to Guangzhou to visit a university there and then put them on a plane to Hong Kong for their flight back to California.

Aunt Mary stayed with us and helped individual students in English conversation. She had visited us on the Tibetan border when we were working with Tibetan young people. She was as good with our Chinese students as she had been with the Tibetans. She was interested in them, and they were interested in her. They often asked her questions like, "What have you learned from your long life?" and "Are you afraid to die?" They couldn't imagine an eighty-year-old lady traveling all the way from California to China.

Elcho kept asking the authorities about our contract for the next year. They acted like this was no problem and gave him hope for the next semester. But we were beginning to doubt if there would be a new contract.

Since our classes were over at the end of May, I made plans to take Aunt Mary back to California, visit our children and grandchildren, and then meet Elcho back in China if we were given another contract. Elcho wanted to stay in China and study more of the language. He had even arranged for a teacher in Beijing.

The university authorities gave us a huge banquet that even surpassed Elcho's welcome banquet. They flattered us in their toasts. Although the words were nice to hear, I felt they weren't telling the truth. Elcho still wanted to believe them, but deep down, he had his own doubts.

It was raining when the university car and driver took Professor Han, Elcho, Aunt Mary, and me to the Chongqing airport. A university truck drove a load of our students to the airport too. I had mixed emotions as I said good-bye to them and to Elcho.

Miriam, Wichit, and their four little girls met us at the San Diego airport. While it was wonderful to see them again, we were all concerned about Elcho. We didn't hear from him for nearly two weeks. Then he wrote that his contract with the university had not been renewed, and he had to leave China within two weeks.

"Which bonsai do you want?" Vice President Jin asked Elcho in Chongqing University's garden. Elcho was so disappointed that his teaching contract had not been renewed that the bonsai tree was a small consolation. University officials had lied to him and given him false hope until almost the end.

Jane Wang's youngest son, Kevin, had joined Elcho after Aunt Mary and I had left for the States. The university authorities made reservations on a ferry for Elcho and Kevin to go down the Yangtze River through three gorges—something Elcho had wanted to do. He enjoyed the trip, and it gave him time to digest what was happening in his life.

Leaving was sad, but we were thankful for a wonderful year with the students at Chongqing University in Sichuan, China. We wondered whom among them the Lord had chosen, and what they would do with the rest of their lives. We had walked through an open door to teach some special young people. We would never be the same, and neither would they.

What was next for us? We had no idea, but God did. "'For I know the thoughts that I think toward you,' says the Lord, 'thoughts of peace and not of evil, to give you a future and a hope'" (Jeremiah 29:11).

45

Led Down an Unexpected New Path

"What's this?" the immigration officer asked Elcho as he deplaned on United States soil in Hawaii.

"It's a bonsai plant—a gift from Chongqing University in China."

"You can't take any soil into Hawaii," the officer explained. "If you want the rocks and plants, we'll have to wash all the dirt off of them." And that's what they did.

Mary Ellen had graciously invited us to stay with her in her lovely condominium in Honolulu until we knew what we would be doing next. We had remained affiliated with ISI while teaching in China, and we wanted to continue with the mission.

Hal Guffey, the president of ISI, told us on the phone to take time to relax in Honolulu with Mary Ellen. That was not hard to do. She was an officer in active duty in the United States Army, working as a nurse in Tripler Hospital, so we had military privileges. We enjoyed the tourist attractions of that island paradise. It was nice being with her and meeting her friends, both in the military and in the church.

We prayed that our Lord would guide us in the next step. Although Elcho still believed we would go back to China, together we claimed the Lord's promise: "I will instruct you and teach you in the way you should go; I will guide you with My eye" (Psalm 32:8).

One day after church, a professor at the University of Hawaii told Elcho that he had all the qualifications for a position that had opened there, and he was on the search committee. "Elcho," he said, "are you interested in heading up the English as a Second Language (ESL) program and teaching linguistics at the University of Hawaii?"

"No, thank you," he replied. "I want to go back to China."

Levi Elcho Redding was born August 18, 1981, in Yakima, Washington, the town of my youth, where LeRoy was a youth pastor. LeRoy, Carol, and Liz were happy to welcome their new son and brother. We could hardly wait to see him—and all of the family.

The phone rang. It was Max Kershaw calling from Chicago. "Elcho, would you like to teach English in Japan?" he asked. "Hideo Ojiro is a pastor there whom we befriended when he was a student in Chicago. He has an English program in his church, and the teacher who was supposed help him is in the hospital. He desperately needs a foreign teacher. I think you'd be great for the job."

"Thanks, but no thanks. I want to go back to China," Elcho replied.

"Why did you say that?" I asked him.

"I don't want to go to Japan. I want to return to China!"

"Elcho, we can't go back to China without an invitation," I said. "And we can't continue living with Mary Ellen. We're fifty-six-years old and in good health, so I'm sure the Lord has something more for us to do."

Elcho quietly left and drove around the island for several hours. When he came back, he asked me to get Max on the phone again. I called the Kershaw home in Chicago. Max's wife Pat said that Max had just left for a conference, but she would try to contact him.

After several hours, Max called back and gave Elcho Pastor Hideo Ojiro's phone number and more information. The young student had accepted Christ, attended seminary, and was now an Evangelical Free Church pastor in Hamamatsu, Japan.

Elcho called Pastor Ojiro, and after a lengthy conversation, Elcho agreed to go to Japan to look the situation over. Taking only a small carry-on and dressed in casual Hawaiian clothes, Elcho left by plane the next morning for Tokyo. He planned to stay just the weekend and took only one change of clothes.

"Welcome to Japan," Pastor Ojiro said to Elcho as he greeted him at Narita Airport on that summer day in 1981. "I'll help you get your things from baggage."

"This is all I have," Elcho said.

Pastor Ojiro was shocked.

When they got on the bullet train for Hamamatsu, Elcho was surprised to see all the men dressed in white shirts, ties, and black suits.

That evening, over one hundred prospective students met at the church. Pastor Ojiro introduced Elcho as the new foreign English teacher.

Later, Elcho told the pastor, "I would like to stay and help out, but I don't have the right clothes. All the men I've seen here are so small, I doubt I'd ever find clothes to fit me." Then, as an afterthought, he said he would ask me to airmail a few clothes until I could join him in Japan.

"If you stay and help us, I'll have a new suit tailored for you," Pastor Ojiro said. "Or I could take you to a store that sells men's clothing in extra-large sizes."

That is how we agreed to go temporarily to Japan to help the Evangelical Free Church of Hamamatsu, Shizuoka Prefecture, in their English program outreach.

Pastor Ojiro and his wife, Kane, were dedicated Christians and hard workers. They were convinced that the English program was an excellent way to win the intellectuals of Japan to the Lord. So they, the students, and the people in the church welcomed Elcho warmly.

We had scheduled several meetings with family and friends on the American West Coast. It seemed best for me to attend those meetings and then join Elcho as soon as possible.

Part 6
Japan

46

Helping the Church in Hamamatsu, Japan

After a few days, Elcho wrote me from Hamamatsu, Japan.

> Yes, from Japan! How strange to be writing from here. I certainly would prefer that the above address were from any place in China, but it seems not to be God's preference. I confess that I am a blind follower. I don't mind in the least, since I know who I am following, and He gives great contentment. He does lead beside the cool waters and makes me lie down in green pastures. Nevertheless, like the cow, I suppose I'd rather be in the pasture across the fence. I constantly think about China and the students, young and old, that we know there and the families like the Wongs and Jens. I confess that I really do miss China more than I thought I would.
>
> Japan is easy to adjust to physically. It is much like the United States except that everything is miniature and compact—the roads, houses, and chairs. Food is no problem. The supermarket across the street from the church has almost everything that is offered in the States plus a great deal more—various Japanese foods that I'm anxious to taste. Some American goods are very expensive, such as beef, walnuts, coffee, and raisins. The Japanese either don't like them, or they are not produced here.
>
> We will definitely need a car because the assignments are in various parts of Hamamatsu. Some classes are held in homes,

and I like this idea, because the influence of the gospel is spread over a greater area. Classes are in both Christian and non-Christian homes. I think that you will drive more than I as the homes are far from the bus lines. I don't know of a single family that doesn't have a car, and most of them have two. Pastor Ojiro and I will go to Tokyo early next week to find a good secondhand car. I think he is anxious not to have to drive me to the classes. Now that I have met the students and the hostesses, I believe that I can find the classes on my own.

Hamamatsu itself is a nice city with a mild climate. Tea grows here. I go through fields of tea to some of my classes. I think that those classes will be yours because they are children's classes, and I don't have the patience with youngsters that you do.

The city is known for its musical instruments, including the Yamaha piano. A couple of major-brand motorcycles and Seiko watches are also made here.

The abnormality on my face has been removed, and the biopsy report was good—no malignancy. The doctor who first examined me is chairing the International Dermatological Convention to be held in Tokyo in 1982. He's in London now to work on the arrangements. Two dermatologists are my students! So, you see I am in good hands. Another student is a noted pediatrician and chairs a pediatrics conference the end of this week. His wife, a writer of several books, is also my student. She will be your student when you come. I've never really counted the students, but I have twenty-five classes and over one hundred fifty students. Some classes are large, and others have only one or two students.

The Ojiros handle all of the arrangements, including funds and arrangements for my (our) classes. I know the doctors and lawyers all pay a lot for each lesson. The church gives us a place to live and a small stipend for utilities and hospitality.

The students are from varied backgrounds. They range in age from five to eighty! We are evidently in a high-middle-class community, judging from the homes that I teach in and the occupations of the families. Besides the lawyers and doctors, my students are nurses, students, teachers, managers of personnel in hotels and factories, journalists, and designers of musical and other instruments.

A few are Christians, but most aren't, and that is why we are here. I find there is great hunger for the Lord, but they don't seem to know it. They seem receptive to the gospel message but don't take it to heart. Most believe the gospel story, but like the Tibetans and some of the Chinese we worked with—pride stands in the way. I asked one of our Tibetan students why he didn't embrace the Lord since he believed that the story was true, and his answer was, "I guess it's just pride."

Every mother of children in the children's class is required to attend at least one hour of Christian instruction each month. The ladies' class has a short Bible lesson every day as part of the English class. I know of no working mothers. All are homemakers.

Yesterday, Sunday, we had a youth "singspiration" in the afternoon. There were about twenty there—all in their late teens or twenties. They love to sing and quickly catch on to the new tunes. I need the accordion, so please bring it. Also, please bring about thirty chorus books for times like this.

I believe you'll enjoy it here. Japan is a beautiful country. The most popular tourist attractions are all within several hours from here. I have been studying the Psalms lately. I also have been studying Japanese. The language has a few words similar to Chinese. But the languages are similar only in a few words. The syntax is quite different. The Japanese language has three different—widely different—scripts. I've managed to learn the Hiragana script and will now tackle the next to the easiest, the Katakana. If we stay here long enough, I'll begin to learn Kanji.

The Japanese prefer green tea to black. I'm getting used to green tea, which reminds me of a bland soup. Black tea is available here but is very expensive. I'm not sure about squid, octopus, and eel, but it seems to be prepared in such a way that the fishy taste is quite delicate. The people are very generous. I have received many gifts, everything from dolls, pictures, food, socks, and a sweater, to soap and toilet paper. I had dinner in the Christian home of one of my students. He is a lawyer in our church. Sho and Shigeko have a loving Christian family. He played a Christian Western music tape. I think they will be our friends while we are here. Come soon.

I was glad to finally be reunited with Elcho in Japan. The people in the church gave me a warm welcome, and soon I began teaching a class of high-school students at the church. Young adults came from six different high schools and seemed eager to study English with me.

Elcho and I taught five children's classes together. We usually had a mother as a hostess/interpreter to help. I was glad that I'd brought flannelgraph materials, easy English as a Second Language (ESL) materials, and Sunday-school supplies. We put simple Bible quotations on used Christmas cards and gave them to the children.

Soon Elcho and I had thirty weekly classes. Some we individually taught, and some we team-taught. While the children's classes were the most difficult to teach, this was a great outreach for the church. We both enjoyed private classes with doctors, lawyers, and university students. Dr. Furuya, a leading neurosurgeon in Japan, was preparing to go to England to study pediatric microsurgery. She and I had many enjoyable discussions about life and eternity.

Elcho preached one Sunday a month, with Pastor Ojiro translating. One couple in the church befriended us and helped us adjust to life in Japan. Sho Ishizuka, a young lawyer, and his wife invited us to their home many times. Since they had three youngsters, we had a children's class in their home. She also was in my English class and my women's Bible study, and Sho was in Elcho's men's night class.

We taught a women's English class at the Hamamatsu Evangelical Free Church. About fifty women came every Thursday morning for a short devotional and singing, followed by an English lesson. Elcho taught the advanced class, and I taught the lower level.

Elcho played his accordion for our retreats, and people always enjoyed it when he accompanied our singing.

Before long, several ladies in my English class asked if I would teach a Bible study. In the regular classes, I had taught them simple Christian choruses and mentioned the Lord, but a few ladies wanted a real English Bible study, using their bilingual Bibles. I was delighted.

We decided to start with a coffee-and-snack time in our home at ten every Friday morning. I wanted the ladies to feel free to ask questions and to speak simple English. Since we had pictures of our family on the walls, I told them about our children and grandchildren. I encouraged them to bring pictures of their families and talk about them too. Then we sang choruses and hymns. The women especially enjoyed having Elcho accompany us on his accordion. We closed with a simple English Bible lesson. Once a month, we had lunch together, and I encouraged them to bring their friends.

Elcho usually did the laundry in our little washing machine on the verandah. My Japanese friends were surprised that he helped with the cooking and washing. This is something that their husbands and fathers would never do.

In December, we had several small Christmas parties and a big one for all the English students. Elcho gave a Christmas message, which Pastor Ojiro translated. This closed the English classes for the year.

Elcho was glad to sing *The Messiah* with several hundred Japanese singers in Hamamatsu. He had sung this in Biola's choir as a student, and it always thrilled him.

Fumie was a pretty lady and a new Christian in the ladies' English Bible class. Her husband Masahiro was a Toyota engineer. Many Sundays after church, we had lunch with Masahiro, Fumie, and their young son. We taught them the meaning of "Dutch Treat," and they took us to many interesting restaurants.

Japan has many sushi and noodle shops, fast-food places, family-style restaurants, and elegant, expensive restaurants. Elcho was glad to discover McDonald's and Kentucky Fried Chicken. Plastic replicas of the food offered hung outside the entrances of most restaurants. This was a big help to us, especially when we ate alone. The first time we ordered ice cream cones, we got cold corn soup!

The students in our English classes did well, and we were glad to be part of their lives. We knew we were where the Lord wanted us to be. Gradually, Elcho stopped talking about China.

47

JSJ Japan and Eiwa School

We had been teaching at the church for six months. The school year ended, and new classes would begin after a short break.

One day we received an unexpected phone call. "Our mutual friends told us about you," a voice said, "and we wonder if you and your husband would like to teach at a Japanese Christian girls' high school in Kofu?"

"Thanks, but no thanks," I replied. "Your offer sounds good, but we are committed to the work here."

Later that day, Pastor Ojiro called and asked us to meet him for lunch. He seemed troubled, and we knew something was wrong. As we ate our meal, he sadly told us that the church had not voted for him to stay on as their pastor. The board felt he was spending too much time with the English-program outreach and not enough time shepherding the flock of believers. He wanted to start a new church with the same English program. While it was a good idea and he eventually did that, we did not want to be a part of a church split. We told him not to worry about us.

I phoned the earlier caller. "We weren't interested in your offer this morning," I said, "but we are this afternoon." We liked the idea of teaching English in a Japanese girls' junior and senior high school. So the next day, we visited the school and had an interview with the principal. When he invited us to teach English and have chapel services, we happily accepted the invitation.

Although Yamanashi Eiwa was affiliated with the United Church of Canada, a local Japanese board ran it. Three Eiwa schools are in Japan: Yamanashi Eiwa in Kofu, Shizuoka Eiwa in Shizuoka, and Toya Eiwa in Tokyo. It was a privilege to be involved with these schools for twelve years.

We went back to Hamamatsu, filled our station wagon with our earthly belongings, and drove the one hundred eighty miles to Kofu. The city is in a valley surrounded by mountains on the opposite side of Mt. Fuji from Hamamatsu. Kofu is surrounded by the Japanese Southern Alps and the Northern Alps.

The school provided us with an apartment on the fifth floor of a new building in the center of town. We were really on the fourth floor, but as the number four means "death," there is no fourth floor in Japan. I used to wonder why all tea sets came with five cups.

Our home was small but comfortable. The bathroom was comprised of two small rooms. A small washing machine stood in the same room as the washbasin and an *ofuro*, a Japanese style bathtub and shower. The toilet was in a separate little room. We had a double bed and a chest of drawers in the bedroom, but the room was so small that both of us couldn't be there unless we were on the bed!

Okajima, the largest department store in town, was almost next door to us. We had fun shopping for furniture for our new home. Fortunately, the dollar exchange rate was good at that time.

Elcho and I each taught English conversation twenty-two hours a week to girls in junior and senior high, with forty students to a class. Elcho took half the students, and I took the other half.

One day soon after we started teaching, Madoka, a sophomore student, asked if I would teach her privately. I was happy to do so. Within days, she asked if I would also teach her mother Miko. Madoka had been born in the United States when her father was doing special research there. Miko's English was good, but she didn't have a chance to speak it in Japan. I liked her so much from the first time we met that she is still one of my special friends.

We taught the girls at Eiwa during the daytime. In the evenings, we taught classes at the YMCA, and English and Bible classes in our home. We often invited students in the adult classes to our home for potlucks and sing-alongs. They, in turn, took us on picnics and invited us to their

Elcho's class of junior high girls at Yamanashi Eiwa

homes. They were so eager to speak English. All Japanese adults have had many years of English grammar but no practice in speaking it. Japanese teachers usually teach English by speaking Japanese.

One day in the spring of 1982, my sister Polly called to say that my father was sick and not expected to live more than a few days. I quickly bought a ticket to fly home, but before I boarded the plane, Polly called again to say that he had already gone. Thankfully, he died peacefully in a Los Angeles hospital in the arms of Sam Ooman, a dear Christian Indian friend and an ISI coworker. Sam and my dad had become close while we were in China, and I will always be thankful for that friendship.

Before long, we flew to Hawaii for Mary Ellen's wedding. She and Bert Kubo were married in Kapahula Baptist Church in Honolulu, Hawaii, on July 24, 1982. It was a beautiful wedding, and everyone in our family was involved in this lovely event: Elcho performed the ceremony; Miriam, Mary Ellen, LeRoy, and Carol sang; and our beautiful little granddaughters, Leonie, Malina, Wanida, and Elizabeth were flower girls. After the happy couple left on their honeymoon, the rest of us explored parks and beaches, ate in interesting restaurants, and sang together.

During this time, Miko was also in Hawaii with friends, and we three "Mrs. Reddings"—Elcho's mother, Carol, and I—met her for breakfast.

While we ate, Miko suggested that when Elcho and I returned to Japan, she and her husband, Ken Horikawa, could meet us at the Narita Airport and drive us to Kofu in their car. We accepted her kind invitation.

The two-hour drive to our Japanese home was beautiful. By the time we reached Kofu, we felt as if we'd known Ken and Miko all our lives. Ken had obtained his engineering degree in Japan. Then he spent two years in the States as an intern in several American companies. He was then CEO of the Japanese-American manufacturing company TEL-GenRad that made electronic test equipment for computer circuit boards.

Another friend, Kuni Ogawa, who taught at Yamanashi University in Kofu, had earned his doctorate degree from the University of California at San Diego (UCSD). He was the director of the Japan Broadcasting Corporation (NHK) English-language television programs. One day, he asked Elcho if he would help with the contents of the TV programs. Elcho was happy to do so.

We wanted to introduce Ken and Miko to Kuni and his wife Yasuko so we invited both families to dinner at a traditional Japanese restaurant in Kofu. Although these couples didn't move in the same circles, they became friends and have remained so ever since.

After being a part of Mary Ellen and Bert's wedding in Hawaii, Miriam and Wichit Maneevone went on to Thailand to see his family. He had

Elcho worked with Dr. Kuni Ogawa on the NHK (Japanese National Television) English teaching programs for radio and television.

272 • Wherever He Leads

not been home for seven years, and three of their girls had never been to Thailand. Besides his family, Wichit also visited many students who had been influenced for Christ while studying in the States. He wanted to see how they had adjusted back in their homeland.

Wichit, Miriam, and their girls stopped to see us on their return to the States. We hardly saw him, as he visited students he and Miriam had entertained in their home in California. When he wasn't on the Shinkansen (the bullet train) to visit students, he was on the phone talking to them and arranging to see them. Of course, we were delighted to have Miriam and the girls with us and to show them around.

A special treat for us was a visit from Hiroko Oguri. She had studied linguistics at the Summer Institute of Linguistics (SIL) at the University of Washington with Miriam. She had stayed with us before going to Wycliffe Bible Translators' jungle camp in Mexico, and later as she prepared to go to Irian Jaya as a missionary with Wycliffe. We were glad to get an update on her translation work and to hear that Japanese Christians were supporting her.

As we all wouldn't fit in our little car, we rented a van during Miriam's family's visit. They came to our Eiwa classes, spent time in town, and visited our friends. Kofu is famous for delicious grapes, strawberries, and oranges. Grapes are grown differently in Japan than in the vineyards of California and Washington State. They grow very high, and each bunch of grapes is wrapped in paper until almost ripe. Ken and Miko invited us to their home, which also had a nearby vineyard.

Although they were young, our granddaughters were interested in Japanese people, food, and customs. However, they were happy to find an American-style "Makudonarusu" (better known as McDonald's).

We also took Miriam and the girls to Hakone, a resort town a two-hours' drive from Kofu, where we stayed in a Japanese-style hotel. The girls loved riding a "pirate" ship across the lake and driving little swan boats. When the Maneevone family returned to California, we got busy in our regular routine.

Kuni Ogawa told us soon after we met him that our best friends in Japan would not be those we worked with but those we met outside of the workplace. That proved true for us. Our best friends were those who had studied in the United States, as they were anxious to be our friends.

Yatsuko Hashimoto taught with us at the YMCA. She was a graduate of Stanford University. Her father had been a professor at Stanford, so she had grown up in California.

Etsuko Nonogaki was an English student of Yatsuko. Etsuko's husband Kengo was CEO of Okojima, the largest department store in Kofu. Both Kengo and Etsuko were interested in improving their English, especially since Kengo traveled a great deal outside of Japan. Although he was a busy man, he came often to our home so Elcho could teach him. He was especially interested in learning about our idioms.

We were glad to introduce Ken, Miko, Kuni, and Yasuko to Kengo and Etsuko Nonogaki and Kentaro and Yatsuko Hashimoto. They were all highly educated and had spent time in the United States. We enjoyed being guests in their homes through the years. Kentaro was a medical doctor who taught in the government medical college in Kofu. He was raised in the home of his uncle, who at that time was prime minister of Japan. We enjoyed hearing about their time in America. Fortunately, they had all had good experiences while studying abroad. That is not always the case.

On Christmas 1982, we had an ISI Japan Christmas party, and Mark Komaki organized the evening. Mark had attended an ISI conference at Star Ranch in Colorado, where the leader had challenged him to follow up with returnees and reach out to internationals studying in Japan. On returning to Japan, Mark became busy in his job at Mitsubishi. However, when Judge Pressler, the chairman of the ISI board, visited Japan, Mark showed him around and was again challenged about student work. Masaki Kagatani had been on ISI staff in Atlanta, Georgia. He and Mark established and registered ISI Japan in 1978.

Elcho played the accordion and gave a Christmas message, and Mark was emcee. That evening, we again saw the importance of International

Students, Inc. (ISI) around the world. Fifty returnees to Japan told about their experiences while studying in the States. Several were from Wichit and Miriam's group, and three had been in our home in Orange County, California. They were glad to talk about their experiences in America. It was a good evening, and Mark and Masaki asked us to join the planning committee. We decided to have an organized activity every three months.

48

Living in Japan and Visiting China

During our two-week winter break in December 1982, we returned to China to visit our former students. We flew to Shanghai, where Jane Wang met us. We stayed a night at the Peace Hotel, and Jane helped us get "soft-seat" train tickets to Chengdu.

When we arrived, we saw a big banner reading, "Welcome to Chengdu, Dr. and Mrs. Redding!" Shawn Chen and his friends met us at the train station at two o'clock in the morning and took us to our hotel. The next day was busy as former students came to visit us. The following day, Shawn went with us to Chongqing, where we settled into our room in the People's Hotel. We had eaten with students there many times.

We had a constant flow of visitors, most of whom were former students. We spent much of our time in Chengdu and Chongqing, but we also visited students in Xian and Guangzhou. They all seemed glad to see us, and we were happy to see them.

Madoka Horikawa graduated from Eiwa high school the spring of 1983, along with over three hundred other girls. We were surprised that Ken was the only father at the graduation ceremonies. Many Eiwa girls told us that they hardly knew their fathers. Most of them left for work before the girls went to school, and they came home late. Many men worked in cities hundreds of miles away from their homes. They often gave their paychecks to their wives, and the wives gave their husbands allowances.

When the graduates received their certificates and were leaving the auditorium, they sang, "God Be with You 'Til We Meet Again" over and over. As they sang, all the girls cried, no doubt because they hated to part from their friends. Perhaps in one way they were glad to leave the school since Eiwa had strict rules about dress, hairstyles, academics, and dating. Beauty parlors were booked months in advance the day after graduation so girls could get perms or their hair colored, as these were prohibited for high-school girls, not only in Eiwa but in most high schools in Japan.

On Valentine's Day, Elcho was showered with flowers, candy, and gifts. I got nothing! Only men receive gifts for Valentine's Day in Japan. However, Japan has "White Day" in March, when men give women and girls small gifts, like handkerchiefs or lingerie.

Micah Zaire Susumu Kubo was born August 8, 1983. Mary Ellen's lifelong dream of motherhood came true when our second grandson was born in Hawaii.

Christmas is not a national holiday in Japan. However, it is widely celebrated as a commercial holiday, especially in large department stores. Japan is a big gift-giving society, and the commercial world capitalizes on that. Since schools have an end-of-the-year vacation, January 1 is a big day. People go to their hometowns—that is, the places where they were born and raised. They get their accounts in order, clean their homes, and prepare special food. Hence, we often went to the States to visit our family for a few days between Christmas and the first of the year.

On December 1, students in Japan put on their winter uniforms. No matter how hot the weather gets, they cannot wear their summer uniforms until the end of May.

In 1983, after Eiwa exams, Christmas programs, YMCA, and ISI Christmas parties, we went to Colorado Springs, Colorado, where LeRoy was a pastor. All our family came together for a great Christmas. LeRoy and Carol were living in a home next to the church. They were gracious hosts, and with their home and the church basement, we had plenty of room for all the family to sleep and eat, even when it was cold outside. The children loved making snowmen and having snowball fights. Even though it was the Christmas season, we gave the ISI leaders a report of our work. Soon it was time to say good-bye again and return to Japan.

Eiwa girls wearing their winter uniforms

Since most Japanese study English for at least six years, they know English grammar very well. In fact, they probably know it better than the average Americans. They don't like to make mistakes and want to be perfect in their English speaking. We tried to tell them that English conversation is about communicating, and they didn't have to use perfect grammar. Conversation is not just answering questions. It is not like a bowling game but more like a volleyball game, using both questions and answers. In our classes, we insisted that the students spoke English. Since the material was appropriate for their level of English, they seemed glad about that requirement.

Bert, Mary Ellen, and Micah came to visit us in March 1984. Eiwa had a spring break at this time, so after a few days of visiting with our friends, we drove to Hiroshima. Both sets of Bert's grandparents had come from that area of Japan, so he wanted to visit there. We were anxious to see it too.

As we were near Hakone, one of our favorite places, we spent our first night there. We drove around snow-covered Mt. Fuji and reached the Tomei Express the next morning. We drove through Nagoya and Osaka and stopped for the night at the historic town of Kyoto. We checked into our reserved hotel and went sightseeing.

We got on the road again early the next morning. Beside the expressway, there were often "P" stops where we could buy cold drinks, snacks, gifts, and noodles. Free green tea and hot water were always available. We arrived in Hiroshima about noon and toured the war memorial before we boarded a ferry that took us to the island of Miya Jima, where we stayed in a Japanese inn. We slept on *futons* on the floor and had interesting food served in our room in the evenings.

After taking Mary Ellen, Bert, and Micah to the Narita Airport, we returned to Kofu.

Spring is a lovely time of year in Japan. When the cherry blossoms bloom, everyone seems to be in a good mood. People picnic in temple gardens in the shade of cherry trees. Since most Japanese do not have large yards, they enjoy going to parks with their abundance of lovely flowers.

In May 1984, we went on an ISI retreat in Nikko. The highlight was seeing Yashiko Kinji again. We had first met her in 1978 when we were part of the ISI staff in Orange, California. Every Thanksgiving from 1969 to 1979, we and other staff members took busloads of internationals from San Diego and Los Angeles to San Francisco for an American Thanksgiving homestay, sightseeing, and a Christian conference. That was the first time that Yashiko had heard about Jesus. The following Christmas, she went with Wichit to the winter retreat at ISI headquarters at Star Ranch in Colorado Springs. There she accepted Christ as her Savior. In the summer of 1979, she returned to Star Ranch for another conference where she dedicated her life to Christ and was baptized.

Another couple I was glad to see again was Akio and Mary Oka. They had met as students in San Diego State University where Wichit and Miriam had an ISI outreach. Wichit invited them to their home for their International Christian Fellowship meeting. They came and had a good time. Mary was a dedicated Christian and had told Akio about the Lord. He accepted Christ, and they courted at the Maneevone home and in their ISI activities.

July 6, 1984, was my fifty-ninth birthday. One of the YMCA classes surprised me with a birthday cake. Our Japanese friends told us that only children celebrated birthdays, and they were surprised that we adults did. Nevertheless, they liked the idea. As we all liked a party, we were glad for any excuse to eat delicious Japanese cake.

Ken and Miko showed us much of Japan. For my birthday present, they took us for a vacation trip to Hakubo, Matsumoto, where we stayed in a nice pension. The food was advertised as "the best food in the world," and we all agreed. We drove high in the Northern Alps of Japan and saw many historic places. Akio and Mary Oka joined us one day. Since it was hot in Kofu, it was pleasant to stay in the cool mountains.

Keiko Arai, a sweet, happy girl in Elcho's class, tried hard to communicate in English. She was a favorite of his. One morning we were saddened to hear that, as she was riding her bicycle to school, a car hit and killed her. Her Eiwa book bag was still on her crushed bicycle under the car that had hit her. The Kofu police came to the school and told the principal before notifying her parents. The entire school was in shock after hearing the tragic news. We were invited to the funeral, and her parents were glad that we came to show our grief.

49

Welcoming Visitors

I was surprised when Elcho's eighty-five-year-old parents said they wanted to spend six weeks with us in Japan. On his mother's birthday, February 20, 1985, we met them at Narita Airport and drove them home to Kofu. Since the Japanese respect older people, our friends were all good to them. Elcho's parents enjoyed eating all kinds of food and became skilled with chopsticks. Raw horsemeat is a delicacy, which I had never tried to eat, but Elcho's dad did. Madoka and Miko took the folks around Kofu and entertained them while we were teaching our classes.

Eiwa School had a two-week semester break in March. As Elcho's folks wanted to go to China, we took them to Hong Kong to get visas. Our good friend, Opie Anderson, arranged for us to stay at the YMCA, and we obtained our visas for China with no difficulty.

LeRoy and Carol were expecting their third child at any time. Since we couldn't make overseas calls from the YMCA, we went to the phone company six blocks away. We wanted news from Colorado Springs before we went to China. At midnight, we got through to Mary Ellen. She told us to wait by the phone, as LeRoy wanted to tell us himself. We still had no idea if the baby had been born and if "it" was a boy or a girl. Soon LeRoy called. "It's a girl!" he said.

Leah Joy Redding was born March 19, 1985. Our eighth grandchild had come safely into the world. Now we could take the train from Hong Kong into Guangzhou, China.

Our former student, Gene, met us at the train and took us to the hotel he had arranged for us. He showed us around the city and helped us get plane tickets to Shanghai. Jane Wang met the plane in Shanghai. It was good to see her and her extended family again.

Jeanie, our former student at the University of Chongqing, traveled by train two days and nights to see us. Again we stayed at the Peace Hotel, where we had often stayed during our time in China. We took Elcho's folks sightseeing and then boarded a ship to Hong Kong to return to Japan.

In June 1985, the Redding siblings gathered to take their children to Disneyland. Having fourteen people in the same house for a week worked out better than expected. In the evenings, they showed old 16-millimeter movies of us getting ready to go to India, traveling on the ship, and some of our time in India. LeRoy ran the projector while Bert and Wichit took videos. Mary Ellen, Miriam, and LeRoy commented on what they remembered when different scenes of their past were shown on the screen. The old projector has been disposed of, and the reels of movie tapes are stored in a trunk, but how glad we are to have those VHS video recordings now.

When we returned to Japan, Mary Ellen called one day. "Guess what?" she said. "Bert got a job at the U. S. Navy base in Yokosuka! We're to begin there by the middle of August. We're so excited!" They soon came, and after two weeks at the Yokosuka Naval Base, they settled into their two-story home in Kamakura.

Before long, Miriam called. "Leonie and Malina are not finding school a challenge anymore," she said. "They want to spend several months with you and learn about Japan and its culture. I talked with their teachers, and they say it is a great idea. How about it?"

Of course, we agreed to the plan, and soon we picked them up

at the Narita Airport. Now we were seven family members living in Japan. We had a great time with them, but I'll let them tell you about it. In the front of Leonie and Malina's book of memories, filled with many pictures, they wrote this:

> We have put this book together to help us remember and to share with our family and friends the fun-packed days we had in Japan. We left our home in Escondido, California, on September 1 and returned on November 30, 1985— three whole months of exotic experiences. We lived with Grandma and Grandpa Redding in Kofu and with Uncle Bert and Auntie Mary Ellen and Micah in Kamakura.
>
> We renewed old friendships with Ken, Miko, and Madoka Horikawa, as well as with Yatsuko Hashimoto, and Sachiko. We also made many new friends. We shared in outings with Japanese friends—fishing, barbecuing in the Japanese Alps, joyriding in a famous amusement park, viewing Mt. Fuji and the beautiful fall colors. As guests, we enjoyed the hospitality in several Japanese homes and went to various parties and an ISI retreat. We went many times to Eiwa School where Grandma and Grandpa teach, and even sang at a multi-million-yen wedding reception.
>
> All of these wonderful experiences taught us a lot about Japanese culture, but most of all, they deepened our love for the Japanese people. We hope to go back again some day.

On Christmas 1985, we were having dinner at Ken and Miko's with our special group of friends when Kuni asked Elcho if he was happy teaching young girls at Eiwa.

"I like Japan, and I like you friends here in Kofu," he said. "However, I'm tired of teaching giggling girls."

"How about teaching in a university?" Kuni asked. "I'm sure that something is available, even in a government university. But there's not much time before the spring semester, and your age may be a drawback. A private college usually doesn't have such strict age requirements. However, I don't know of anything here in Kofu, so you may have to move to another part of Japan."

Elcho was enthusiastic. "No problem with that. Sounds good to me!" He was ready for a change. He much preferred working with university-age adults than with young girls, and he certainly didn't need a Ph.D. to do what he was doing.

Things moved quickly after that. A week later, Kuni told us about an opening at a prestigious government university in Shizuoka. The main problem was that the deadline for applications was less than a week away. Elcho asked his University of California in Los Angeles (UCLA) teacher, Dr. John Oller, to send a reference to Dr. Suzaki, the head of the selection committee at the University of Shizuoka. Dr. Oller was now the head of the linguistic department at the University of Arizona. Since we knew him and his family well and he had helped us in the ISI ministry in California, we knew he would give Elcho a good recommendation.

Elcho worked on his resume and was going to drive the two hundred miles to Shizuoka and back when Ken said, "Why don't you send a facsimile?"

"What's that?"

"I have a machine at the factory, and you can send a copy of the resume by a machine that uses the telephone line, and then send the originals by mail," Ken informed him.

Kuni talked to Dr. Suzuki, and he agreed that would be fine. However, he also said that they had a number of other promising applications. We prayed and waited. Then Kuni said that Dr. Suzuki had called him, and Elcho was among the final three choices. The selection committee wanted him to come for an interview. He drove there immediately, had the interview, and was selected! We were moving to Shizuoka in time for spring classes.

In February, I was called to the Yamanashi Eiwa principal's office. The Shizuoka Eiwa principal, Mr. Sho, and the head of the English department, Mr. Ishikawa, were there also. They invited me to teach in their school. I accepted their offer without hesitation.

We resigned from Yamanashi Eiwa and finished our teaching there by the middle of March. Dorothy Martin, who had come from Vista, California, to teach English, took over my classes. Interestingly, her mother and I had been friends in high school. Our friend, Kengo Nonogaki arranged for movers to transport our things to Shizuoka.

As Shizuoka is on the Shinkansen (bullet train) line, we realized it would be easier to follow up with returnees and work with the ISI Japan team in quarterly get-togethers.

We were no strangers to change. Actually, we were happy about the move, especially as it would be a good change for Elcho. We were glad to find a Japanese TEAM church a block away from our new apartment. We had attended several churches in Kofu but had never felt at home in any of them.

On a beautiful March day in 1986, we drove around Mt. Fuji to our new home in Shizuoka, a lovely city on the Pacific Ocean. Our lives would not change much, as we both liked living in Japan and teaching in Japanese education.

50

Living in Shizuoka, Japan

Pastor Masuyama and his wife, Fumiko, and other people from Megumi Kyokai (Grace Church), the nearby TEAM church, welcomed us and helped us move in. Among the group were two special ladies, Keiko Sagauchi and Hiroko Sagawa. They spoke fluent English and proved to be caring, helpful, and loving Christian friends.

We were delighted that the university had found us a nice apartment near the church. We quickly settled in and began teaching—Elcho at the Japanese government university and I at Shizuoka Eiwa Girls' Junior and Senior High School.

We were glad to have Bert, Mary Ellen, and Micah living in Kamakura, and we spent at least one weekend a month together. Bert was working for the United States government, and Mary Ellen was in the United States Army Reserves. She was glad to be home with three-year-old Micah. He played nicely by himself when she taught her English ladies' class in their Kamakura home. She also taught a weekly two-hour English night class for Nissan engineers.

Elcho enjoyed teaching at Shizuoka University. He had a big office with a magnificent view of Mt. Fuji and the ocean. His students and fellow professors treated him with great respect. Most of his students were Japanese, with one exception. Fardis, an attractive young lady from Iran, was not as quiet as the Japanese students and came to his office more often.

One day, Elcho told me about her. "I think she's lonely," he said. "Why don't you call and ask her to lunch?" So I did.

We met for lunch in a nice little Japanese cafe. She was happy about our new friendship and seemed to be searching for more meaning in life. From the beginning, we liked each other. I introduced her to young Navigator staff members, and they took her under their wings. I invited her to a revival meeting at our church, and she accepted Christ that night. That was the beginning of Fardis's remarkable journey of faith.

Since Shizuoka Eiwa was a sister school to the Yamanashi Eiwa, where we had been teaching, it had many similarities. The twelve hundred girls in the school wore school uniforms of a specific length, and they had to obey strict rules. The girls could not color or curl their hair or wear makeup. Although it was considered a Christian school, only about 10 percent of the teachers and students were Christians. Attendance at the daily morning chapel services was required, and we Christian teachers took turns in leading them. I was asked to take my turn, and with the help of a translator, I happily did. I taught twenty English conversation classes a week.

In Megumi Church, Hiroko or Keiko translated songs into Romaji (the transliteration of Japanese using the English alphabet) so we could sing along. They also gave us Scripture references to read ahead of time so we could understand more of the sermons without translation.

After the sermon, about fifty of us stayed to eat a tasty, simple meal the ladies prepared. We usually had Japanese curry and rice, a vegetable dish, and fruit and sweets for dessert. After lunch, Elcho taught an English

With Hiroko Sagawa

Bible class for young adults who wanted to improve their English.

Before long, Keiko asked me to teach a ladies' Bible class in our apartment. As Hiroko is an accomplished pianist, we enjoyed singing

English songs. Once a month, we had a potluck together. Although we were foreigners, we felt more at home in this church than in any church in Kofu. This was because many young adults spoke some English and had been in the United States for a period of time. TEAM missionaries Don and Mary McAlpine had established the church. They had started as an English outreach, much like we had been a part of with the Ojiros in Hamamatsu.

As foreign English teachers, both Elcho and I were often asked to be judges in city and statewide English contests. Soon after we arrived in Shizuoka, I was asked to judge a contest in the prestigious Futaba Girls' High School. From the stage, I noticed an attractive lady with a big smile looking at me. After the event, she introduced herself as Christine Unno.

We made an appointment to meet at a nearby coffee shop for lunch the next day, and she told me a little of her story. Christine was a young Chinese Christian from Singapore who married Hiro, a young Christian from a traditional Japanese family in Shizuoka. Hiro had gone to a university in Singapore. One day, out of curiosity, he had gone to a Christian meeting on campus. Christine was active in that group, and they met that day. Hiro heard the gospel message and became a Christian. They fell in love and were now newlyweds living in an apartment near us. Christine was a foreign teacher in Futaba Jogakuin, a Catholic girls' school almost next door to Eiwa. Later, I learned that Christine had just lost her mother. That was the beginning of a close relationship that has grown through the years. I became her "American mom."

One day, Miriam called. "Wanida wants to visit you for a couple of months," she said. "She can spend time with you and also with Mary Ellen, Bert, and Micah. How does that sound?"

That was fine with us. So the next weekend, we drove to Narita Airport to pick up our eight-year-old granddaughter, who had flown by herself from Los Angeles to Tokyo.

Some days, Wanida went to school with me, and the girls and teachers liked to talk with her in English. She was not shy and had good conversations with them. Hiroko, her sister Junko, and Keiko took her sightseeing. Wanida saw Junko's famous cake shop, where she bakes and sells her own cakes. They also took her to the Toro Ruins, a famous tourist attraction, which is the restoration of a farming village of the Yayoi Period, dating

Hiroko's sister, Junko, had a cake and coffee shop where I liked to meet friends. Junko became a good friend and has come with Christine Unno to visit us on two American homestay programs.

back two thousand years. As a piano teacher, Hiroko helped Wanida with piano lessons. She also played a harpsichord beautifully.

Wanida was delighted to spend a day with her grandpa at the University of Shizuoka, especially in his big office with the beautiful view of the ocean and Mt. Fuji. She and I took the Shinkansen bullet train so she could be with the Kubo family in Kamakura for a couple of weeks. I spent the weekend with them and then had to get back to Eiwa for my classes. Later, we met Wanida and the Kubo family at the Toyota resort at the base of Mt. Fuji, where we were the guests of Masahiro and Fumie for the weekend.

Golden Week is a weeklong school holiday in May, so we took a road trip with the Kubo family and Wanida to sightsee. Many historic places have petting zoos and pony rides for children to be entertained while the adults look around. At Karuizawa, we stayed at the TEAM compound in a cottage owned by our friends, DeWitt and Betty Lyon. They had two grand pianos in the cottage, so Mary Ellen and Elcho enjoyed playing and singing together. Finally, we had a good weekend visit with our friends, Ken and Miko Horikawa.

When our schools were out for the summer break,

Elcho and Ken Horikawa wearing yukatas and relaxing at the TEL-GenRad guesthouse in Hakane.

Wanida flew with us to her home in San Diego, California. LeRoy, Carol, and family were living in Colorado Springs, where LeRoy was a pastor and finishing his graduate studies at Denver Theological Seminary. They drove to San Diego for a vacation, and together we went to the beach house that Miriam and Wichit had for their use.

LeRoy and Carol with Liz, Leah, and Levi in 1986.

We had a great time singing, playing games, and being on the beach. The grandkids wanted me to go swimming with them.

One day I went wading, so I left my new, expensive Japanese glasses on. The grandkids kept taking me further and further out when suddenly a big wave knocked me down. My glasses went flying and were never seen again!

Even though we were living and working in Japan, we were able to spend time with our children, grandchildren, and aging parents during our summer breaks.

51

Returnees and Internationals

Soon after getting back to Japan in August 1986, Keiko told me that Mr. and Mrs. Osawa, who lived nearby, wanted to meet us. So Keiko and I went to visit Mrs. Osawa, along with my missionary friend, Betty Lyon, who was visiting from Tokyo. Mrs. Osawa showed us gracious hospitality, including a fabulous meal. She had studied in America, and even though she had no practice in speaking English, she spoke it quite well. The Osawas had a large, traditional Japanese home over one hundred years old. It was much like the original home, only upgraded with modern conveniences. The house was surrounded by a traditional Japanese garden that featured topiary shrubs. We talked about her experiences as an international student studying in the United States and about the need to reach out to students from other countries studying in Japan. She offered her home to us for use in hospitality anytime we wanted.

In October 1986, the world came to Shizuoka and to the Osawa home. About one hundred international students studying in Japan and returnees to Japan from studying abroad came from various parts by bus, train, and car for an ISI retreat. Hiro gave a stirring testimony about how he had found Christ as an international student studying in Singapore. He was now back in Shizuoka and involved in the church there. Some students told about their experiences in the States, many finding Christ as their Savior while there. Mark Komaki did an excellent job of coordinating the retreat, and Elcho was a good emcee and host, as well as accordionist.

Winnie Ritchie was visiting Japan, so she attended the ISI retreat and stayed with us for a week afterwards. She met many of our friends and went with me to my classes at Eiwa. We enjoyed her visit very much.

ISI Japan had a special get-together for returnees and internationals studying in Japan at least four times a year. If someone from ISI headquarters came through, we had something extra. Mark Komaki, Masaki Kagatani, Elcho, and I planned these events. Occasionally, we had a one-day gathering, but at least twice a year, we planned a weekend retreat.

The Shizuoka Eiwa school was much friendlier to us foreign teachers than Yamanashi Eiwa had been. In fact, the city of Shizuoka was friendlier to outsiders than Kofu. Since mountains surround Kofu, it had been more closed to outsiders, even Japanese. The Horikawas, Ogawas, and Hashimotos—our best friends in Kofu—were all outsiders. That is, Kofu was not their hometown, and they felt the same way we did. Our common feeling helped us to be closer friends than we might otherwise have been.

Sports Day, held in October, was a big event in Eiwa. All students participated in some way. Eiwa used the National Olympic Training Sports Arena in Shizuoka. Parents, alumni, and city and school officials came for part of the day. At the end of the eight-hours of sports events and ceremonies, fifteen hundred helium-filled balloons were sent into the sky. I always enjoyed these Sports Day events because students and staff were relaxed and had fun away from the pressure of studies.

The music program at the school was outstanding. In an outdoor stadium, the school band gave a professional-quality performance.

Since Eiwa had Christian traditions, Christmas was special with Christmas music, often accompanied with a bell choir and the only pipe organ in any high school in Japan. At a candlelight service, over a thousand girls sang carols, and the choir sang "The Hallelujah Chorus."

Although big department stores were decorated for Christmas and played carols over their intercoms to encourage people to buy gifts, most people knew nothing about the true meaning of Christmas. At Eiwa, only about ten percent of the students and faculty were Christians, but the story of Jesus' birth was always told in every Christmas program I attended during my six years there.

Megumi Church had a nice Christmas program and church dinner. Our Bible-study group had a Christmas party, and we in ISI held a big dinner party in Tokyo for international students and returnees. We always had the most returnees from the International Christian Fellowship in Escondido, California, where the Maneevones worked. We had met many of them there when we had visited our family.

Because Mary Ellen was in the United States Army Reserves and Bert was working in Japan with the United States government, they arranged for Ken, Miko, Madoka, and us to stay with them at the New Sanno, a United States Armed Forces hotel in Tokyo, over the Christmas holidays. We also joined them on a road trip to Sendai during the New Year's celebrations.

Harry Larson, the missions pastor of Emmanuel Faith Community Church in Escondido, California, and his wife were visiting all their missionaries. They came to us in March 1987, and we showed them around Shizuoka. We had a dinner party for them in a Chinese restaurant and invited our closest friends.

Seiya and Yoriko Kagatani, who were in our English Bible-study group, had a remarkable story. Yoriko, a Christian girl, had recently returned from Oregon after a six-month homestay. She was traveling from her hometown to Tokyo—a thirty-hour journey. Next to her in an assigned seat was Seiya, a science major studying in a Tokyo university. Since he was not a Christian, Yoriko told him about the Lord for most of the long journey. He liked her, but she told him she would never date anyone who was not a Christian. They exchanged addresses and realized they were living near each other in Tokyo.

When Seiya returned to his apartment, he could not get Yoriko and her words out of his mind. He began to study the Bible she had given him. When he had questions about what he was reading, he called Yoriko and asked her questions. He finally decided that this was the truth and accepted Jesus as his Savior. After he became a Christian, they began a serious courtship. When we met them, they were newlyweds living in Shizuoka and were part of Megumi Church. We were glad to have them in Elcho's English Bible study and to get to know them better.

We were surprised one day when Seiya asked if he and Yoriko could have an American homestay with us in our little apartment, since he had never been out of Japan. Of course, we told him we would be pleased to have them, so they came on a Friday evening. We had a typical American dinner and enjoyed singing around the piano with Yoriko as pianist while

Elcho played the accordion. Later, we played table games. We gave them our small bedroom, and we slept in the living room on our futon. On Saturday, we went to a park for a picnic and did the same thing that evening as we had done the night before. Then we attended church on Sunday.

Later, they invited us to their home for a delicious dinner. Yoriko told about her experience in the States, and they showed us their wedding pictures. Seiya was a pharmacist. After their son was born a year later, they went to Dallas, Texas, for Seiya's graduate work, and they spent time with my sister, Sadie, and her husband, Pete, and became good friends. We watched their family grow to include three boys and a girl.

Elcho enjoyed teaching at Shizuoka University, but he was surprised that most students didn't study very hard. They had gotten into the university, and that seemed to be the most important thing. When he would ask what they did the previous night, the most common answer was that they had gotten drunk.

To get to know them better, Elcho invited his students to our home for a dinner party and told them the reason we were in Japan. They brought us gifts, especially flowers. A few of them invited Elcho to visit local attractions with them. He had two students from the People's Republic of China in his classes at Shizuoka University. They were friendly and came to our home and several ISI Japan activities.

ISI Japan had a weekend retreat every spring and fall for internationals studying there and for returnees to Japan. We held our spring retreat in 1987 at a big lodge in Atami. During those relaxing times, we came to know the students better, talked about spiritual things, and made lasting relationships. We had inspirational times of singing and Bible study. Hiroko played the piano beautifully and told how she had found Christ. She also said she had decided to go

Jack (Chen) Mukaiyama and Elcho at the ISI retreat. Jack was a student from Taiwan who later became a Japanese citizen and changed his name to a Japanese name.

to the University of California in Fresno for graduate studies and would be leaving soon.

At the retreat, we had quality time with Jack (Chen) Mukaiyama from Taiwan and with Chen and Grace, the two students from China who were in Elcho's English as a Second Language classes at Shizuoka University. It was interesting to see these three Chinese people from different cultures becoming friends. Another young lady at the retreat, Ayuko, also from our English Bible class, asked for prayer, as she felt that the Lord was leading her to work in China, and she had applied for a job there. She later got the job and left within the next six months.

52

Another Turn in the Path

Elcho's one year at Shizuoka University passed by quickly. Since it was a Japanese government university, he could no longer teach there at age sixty-three. We didn't know what to do next.

We had met the president of Eiwa Tandai (junior college) several times. One evening when we were at a dinner party in the home of mutual friends, he heard that Elcho would have to leave the university because of the age limit. So the president asked him if he would teach at Eiwa Tandai. The junior college was trying to become a university and could use his Ph.D. qualifications. Elcho gladly accepted and agreed to begin teaching there the next semester. Eiwa Tandai was affiliated with Eiwa, the girls' junior and senior high school where I taught.

When we moved to Shizuoka in the spring of 1986, the university rented a nice apartment for us near the church. That was satisfactory for the time being, but it took me more than an hour by two buses to get to Eiwa. In the winter months, it was dark when I left home, and it was dark when I returned. However, I had a small tape player that I could hold in my hand and listen to messages from our home churches with earphones. Those times in the Word were a big help to me, but I could listen to tapes without riding four buses for a couple of hours a day.

When I was walking through a beautiful park during my lunch break one day, I saw new houses under construction. I jotted down a phone number for Elcho to pass on to the Shizuoka Tandai office that would be finding our housing. One home was completed about the same time that Elcho started teaching at Eiwa Tandai, and we moved in. We called it our "dollhouse" because everything was in miniature. We had three small bedrooms upstairs, a small kitchen with a table, and a *tatami* room (a traditional Japanese room with a tatami mat floor) that we used as our living room.

The toilet and place for bathing were separate. A small washing machine stood in a little room before we entered the bath area. The tub area, where we showered before we got into the ofuro (a deep bathtub) was typically Japanese. We dried clothes on poles hung on our upstairs verandah. This was a much better home than the apartment and gave us more room for entertaining.

LeRoy graduated from Denver Theological Seminary with a master's of divinity degree in June 1987. We could not leave our Eiwa classes in Japan to attend his graduation, but we were proud of him and thankful that he was serving the Lord.

I was privileged to give several chapel talks on how to have real joy. The one that got a lot of attention had this message: "J—Jesus first; O—Others next; Y—Yourself last. That is the only way to spell real joy." In addition, I said there is a difference between happiness and joy. Money and material wealth can bring happiness but not necessarily joy.

I was the sponsor of the Christian students club, and

the young people asked me many questions after those chapel services. The assistant chaplain had translated the message for me, and he asked questions about it too. The Christian student club made JOY their motto and placed posters printed with it around the school.

Walking home from Eiwa, I occasionally saw a friendly lady working in her garden who always said hello to me. She seemed to want to be my friend. One day, I stopped to visit with her and learned that she was an English teacher, her husband was a lawyer, and that her name was Toshie (pronounced TOH-shee-ay) Saito. She invited me to have a cup of tea and told me she had two little children, a girl and a boy. I liked her and felt we would be friends. However, I never realized at the time how close she and her family would become.

The Kubo family and I were staying at the United States Navy Officers' Club in Yokosuka, in August 1987, while we waited for Mary Ellen to give birth to their second child. The hospital was just across the street.

Danya Sharon Hanae Kubo was born on August 8, 1987. It was Micah's fourth birthday. Mary Ellen and Danya were released from the hospital and we all celebrated by going to the officers' club for dinner.

Bert, Mary Ellen, Micah, and Danya were in Japan with the U.S. government for five years while we were there.

53

Comings and Goings

We had an inspirational weekend with ISI at Eiwa's retreat center at the base of Mt. Fuji in October 1987. The fifty attendees enjoyed comfortable accommodations, exceptional Japanese food, and beautiful scenery. Alvin Lowe, a guest Bible teacher from Singapore and himself a returnee, brought challenging messages. Everyone took part in the singing and seemed eager to learn more about the Lord.

We were glad that Jack Chen not only came again but also brought three friends with him. We all liked having Mary Ellen and her family there, especially baby Danya and four-year-old Micah. Two Navigator workers from Hawaii helped with the music. Seiya and Yoriko, as well as Hiro and Christine were there and grew spiritually. We felt that the Lord had something special for them to do for Him in Japan, and this has proven to be true.

On Thanksgiving Day in November, Eiwa girls brought flowers, candy, and fresh fruit to school. They took these special treats to people in nursing homes and hospitals. I went with a group of girls to a large nursing home where we gave flowers and treats and sang Christian songs. Later, Elcho and I drove to New Sanno Hotel for a weekend with the Kubos and Horikawas for an American Thanksgiving.

Christmas in 1987 was much like our other Christmases in Japan. It meant great music and pageantry at Eiwa, Christmas activities at Megumi

Church, an ISI Japan Christmas party in Tokyo, and time with family and friends.

Miriam decided to go to India for her Woodstock twenty-year class reunion in June 1988. She stopped in Japan on her way there with daughters, Wanida and Anjuli, to visit us and her sister, Mary Ellen, and family. Miriam spoke to the twelve hundred Eiwa girls during the morning chapel, and she and her daughters visited my classes. It was a good opportunity for my

Miriam, Anjuli, and Wanida visited us in Shizuoka on their way to India for Miriam's twenty-year Woodstock reunion.

Japanese students to practice their English and for my granddaughters to learn more about Japan. Later, we drove them to Tokyo, where we met the Kubos and ate at a traditional Japanese restaurant.

Toshie and her lawyer husband had a little girl, Yuki, in August 1988. Christine and Hiro had a little girl, Sarah, and Yoriko and Seiya had a son, Zen, in September. The church in Japan was growing.

The next few years continued much the same in our teaching at Eiwa—Elcho in the college and I in the high school. We continued to work with Mark Komaki in ISI Japan and to be a small part of Megumi Church. Although everyone was busy, we continued to do things with young families in Shizuoka, our Kofu friends, and Mary Ellen and her family.

In February 1989, my sister, Polly, called and said that our mother had passed away. She had died in Yakima, alone and lonely, and I was sad that I had not been there for her when she needed me.

LeRoy and Carol moved their family to Bellevue, Washington, in June 1989. His cousin, Gerald Redding, lived in the area and helped them settle in. They found a nice home and a good church, and he got involved in the international student outreach. The Navigators were beginning a new work with international students in the Pacific Northwest, and LeRoy was accepted as a provisional staff member to work with Warren and Hilvi Mason in the Seattle area. However, he would have to raise support.

We knew firsthand how much harder it is to raise funds for mission work in America than for overseas missions.

Our family made some very happy memories when we flew home from Japan for our summer break in August 1989. First, we went to Bellevue, Washington, to visit LeRoy and Carol in their new home. It was so good to be in the beautiful Northwest

Geleg Kyarsip, a special young Tibetan man, always came to visit when we visited LeRoy and Carol in Bellevue, Washington.

again. They had reconnected with some of our Tibetan friends, Geleg, Chimie, Gedun, Wangden, and Yungchin, and we were glad that they all came to see us in Bellevue. We liked meeting some of the international students that LeRoy and Carol were working with at the University of Washington when they had a picnic in the park or when they came to LeRoy and Carol's home.

Elcho had always made an effort to see his former Tibetan and Chinese students whenever he was near where they were studying or working. He had seen Shawn and Gary the summer before when they were graduate students at Willamette University in Salem, Oregon. He had encouraged Shawn in

his faith as a believer in Jesus and listened to his big ideas and dreams for the future of China. They went sightseeing and to church together. Elcho introduced Shawn to our longtime friend, Pauline Goodwin, and to Oregon State Senator Mark Hatfield. When Shawn heard that we were visiting LeRoy in Bellevue, he called and asked if he could come and spend the weekend with us. We were delighted to have him come and spend time with all of us. He went with us to Westminster Chapel, the church where LeRoy and his family were now involved in Bellevue.

Our immediate family had a few days together on the Oregon coast before a reunion of Elcho and his four siblings and their families. Four generations of Reddings gathered for four days at the Mountain Lake Bible Camp near Medford, Oregon, in August 1989, to celebrate the seventieth wedding anniversary of Elcho's parents. Since many members of the Redding family are good singers, we had a wonderful time singing around the piano. Elcho's parents renewed their wedding vows in a ceremony, complete with attendants, flower girls, and ring

Shawn came to visit us at LeRoy and Carol's house during our vacation from Japan in 1992. Although Shawn had seen many pictures of the children, this was the first time he met Levi and Leah in person.

bearers. Mary Ellen and Miriam sang a duet, Elcho's cousin Gerald sang a solo, and LeRoy and Elcho conducted the ceremony. The climax of the family reunion was the testimony and baptism of Elcho's sister, Miriam, and her daughter, Nancy. LeRoy and Elcho held the baptism in the swimming pool. Because we had lived overseas most of our adult lives, we had not had much time to be with our siblings and their families, so it was nice to reconnect with the Reddings.

In December 1989, Elcho and Nagai Sensei of the Navigators worked together on a Christmas outreach to university students in Shizuoka. I spent time with Fardis. She continued to grow in her faith and attended Christmas celebrations with us. Since the Kubo family would be leaving Japan soon, we spent the Christmas holidays with them.

In the spring of 1990, our granddaughter Liz, a fifth grader, flew by herself from Bellevue to spend five weeks with us. She enjoyed everything about Japan. Hiroko had returned from her graduate studies in California and entertained Liz while we were teaching. Hiroko played the piano for her, taught her to cook Japanese dishes, and took her to the Toro Ruins

Liz with Christine, Sarah, and Hiro Unno in our home in Shizuoka, Japan

and other places around Shizuoka. Liz liked watching Japanese baseball with her grandpa.

Liz also went with Elcho to Eiwa Tandai and came with me to my school. The Eiwa girls loved having her visit our classes, and some came to our home after school to do things with her. They taught her origami and a few Japanese words. Although they were only seventh graders, they communicated in simple English, and she tried to help them with their English.

The Unno family invited us to their home, where Liz loved holding baby Sarah. She also enjoyed going to downtown Shizuoka with Christine, Sarah, and me and eating at Junko's cake shop.

Later, Liz spent a week with the Kubos. They made reservations for us to stay at the New Sanno Hotel so it would be easier for Mary Ellen and me to take the children to the Tokyo Disneyland.

In the summer of 1990, our Kofu friends gave the Kubo family a big farewell dinner party, since they were moving back to Honolulu, Hawaii. The Horikawas, Ogawas, Hashimotos, and Nonogakis were there. Interestingly enough, they were all professionals who had studied in the United States. Not a single one was from Eiwa School. As usual, we sang

At Hamamatsu Castle with the Kubos and Miko Horikawa

English songs out of books we had made, such as, "You Are My Sunshine," "Home on the Range," "Amazing Grace," "What a Friend We Have in Jesus," and "Abide with Me." Elcho played several marches and a couple of hymns on his accordion, and Mary Ellen sang, "We Shall Behold Him." We were sorry to see Mary Ellen and her family return to Hawaii.

A young Australian man, who was attending Living Way Church, liked Fardis. She was somewhat attracted to him but had reservations. One day we met in town, and she told me about the situation. We talked and prayed. With her graduation from the university coming up soon, she had many decisions to make. She wanted to get married, and she didn't want to go back to Iran. She had no idea what to do after graduation from Shizuoka University, but we knew the Lord did, and together we asked Him to show her.

On our summer vacation in 1991, we flew to California for a family reunion in Escondido at the Maneevone home. With our children and grandchildren, there were seventeen of us. We went to Sea World, the beach, and Wild Animal Park in beautiful San Diego. We made priceless memories as we played games, sang along with instruments, and laughed.

However, we noticed that Elcho was quieter than usual and shuffled his feet when he walked. Miriam arranged for him to see a doctor at the Parkinson's clinic at Scripps, but he refused to go. Later, he regretted that decision.

Our three children never gave us any trouble and always brought us so much joy. They love the Lord and have brought their children up to love and serve Jesus.

54

Friends Along the Path

After LeRoy, Carol, and family returned to Bellevue, Washington, and Bert, Mary Ellen, and family had flown back to Honolulu, Miriam asked me to go with her to Saheed's home. Although he was not a Christian, he seemed to enjoy coming to their home for international student activities. His mother was visiting from India and had invited us for dinner. I not only was eager for authentic Indian food, but I also wanted to see if I could still carry on a conversation in Marathi, which happened to be the language that Saheed's mother spoke.

We had delicious Indian food served on their patio. Among the guests were about twenty young adults. A good-looking fellow with black hair and Arab features caught my eye. I introduced myself to Meridad ("Mark" in America), began talking with him, and found he didn't have a girlfriend.

"What's a handsome guy like you doing without a girlfriend?" I asked.

"No girl in the world has all the qualifications I want in a wife," he said.

"What are those qualifications?"

"Number one, she must be a Christian; number two, she must be Iranian; number three, she must be educated; number four, being attractive would be a big plus," he said.

"I know just the girl that has all those qualities!" I said. "Her name is Fardis."

He couldn't believe it, but I assured him it was true. I gave him Fardis's address and a picture I had brought from Japan of her with a group of other internationals. Then I took a snapshot of him to send to Fardis. I thought they would be a perfect match.

Later, I wrote to Fardis, told her about meeting this young man, and sent the photo I had taken of him. I told her she probably would be getting a letter from him—and she did.

We were happy living near our friends and carrying on our ministry in Japan, but we knew that at sixty-seven years of age, we needed to settle back in our homeland. In all our adult lives, we had only spent twelve years in the States. We were like foreigners in our own land.

Previously, we thought we'd retire in Escondido next to the Maneevones, but we learned that the property on Birch Way could not be divided, and it had a moratorium on building. Moreover, that area, which used to be quiet and peaceful, was now crowded and busy. We also considered moving into the mobile home we had inherited from Aunt Mary Marshburn where TEAM missionaries were now living. But Elcho did not want to live in a crowded mobile home park, so we sold it. Now the question was, where should we retire?

While we pondered, Elcho and I flew to Bellevue, Washington, to visit LeRoy and Carol. We went to Westminster Chapel with them and enjoyed the service and people. We liked the area and the idea of living near LeRoy. When we saw a house on their cul-de-sac for sale, we bought it, and, for the first time in our lives, we owned a home of our own. We rented it to a Christian Russian family until we were able to move there from Japan.

LeRoy and Carol were not able to raise enough funds to stay on staff with Navigators, but they remained involved with internationals. He was now working with the Preferred Risk Insurance Company. We were glad that Geleg, Chimi, Mrs. Taring's daughter, Yang Chen, and other Tibetans came around often, even when Elcho and I weren't visiting. LeRoy's childhood friends were Tibetans. We loved seeing them, and they made us the best *momos*, the popular Tibetan pot stickers.

Since Elcho's mother was in a nursing home in Othello, Washington, LeRoy and his family drove us to see her. She was ninety-one-years old and still played the piano in the home. Elcho's dad was living in their mobile home in Royal City. We had a nice visit, but as we said our good-byes, we had a feeling that we would not see her again until we all get to heaven. She died before her next birthday.

On our way back to Japan, we stopped in Honolulu, Hawaii, to visit Bert, Mary Ellen, and their family. It was good to see them for a couple of days in their own home.

After we arrived in Japan, I visited with Toshie several times, and her little girls seemed curious about me. They were sweet and well behaved, and little Yuki stole my heart. One day over green tea, Toshie and I each had a bilingual New Testament in English and Japanese, and she asked me questions about several verses. Toshie was an excellent cook, so one day she invited Christine and me to her home to teach us how to make sushi. Her sushi rolls were perfect, so neat and trim. But we stuffed ours so full that they were too fat, and when we cut them into slices, they fell apart.

In the fall of 1991, Fardis called and arranged to meet me in Shizuoka. She was happy about the letter that Mark (Meridad) had sent. I told her about Miriam and Wichit and their ICF group in California that Mark attended.

In November, Fardis decided to fly to San Diego for the winter break to see Mark. She stayed with a friend of Miriam's and met him. He showed her the sights of San Diego, and they spent lots of time together. As they got better acquainted, they felt they were meant for each other and that the Lord had brought them together. Fardis would finish her studies at the university in Japan in March, and she would move to California to plan for their August 1992 wedding.

Among our Japanese friends were our landlord, Tadatoshi, and his wife, Fumiko. They were not Christians, but they befriended us. They lived close to us, and Tadatoshi often came over in the evenings to talk to Elcho and practice his English. As Fumiko was a gifted pianist, she gave piano lessons. She was also fluent in English and a big help to us, especially when we needed medical help.

I also liked Tadatoshi's mother very much. I helped her with English once a week, and she often invited me to her home where, in a huge tatami room, she had traditional ladies' dancing classes and tea-ceremony classes. Her house was over one hundred years old and was like an old traditional Japanese home. She also was a member of an exclusive swimming club and often invited me to go with her as her guest.

The ISI retreat in 1991 featured a cruise ship.

Our ISI Japan fall event was lunch on a cruise ship, as fifty of us sailed around Yokohama harbor in September 1991. Since Fardis's mother was visiting her from Iran, I spent much of my time with her and Fardis. She was having a difficult time with her daughter not only becoming a Christian but also planning to establish a home in America. After the cruise, we went to the home of a young pastor who had helped us plan the event. We crowded in, most of us sitting on the floor, and we had a great time of singing and praising the Lord in testimonies and a short message. Fardis translated for her mother, and everyone was very kind to her.

Although Fardis's parents were not happy that she had become a Christian and was going to marry a Christian, they were pleased that her fiance was a well-educated and gainfully employed Iranian. We could not get away from Eiwa in time for their wedding in August 1992, but Miriam was a big help to her. Fardis's folks came from Iran, and Mark's family came from England. They had a beautiful wedding in Emanuel Faith Community Church in Escondido, California. They established a fine Christian home and these days, I like to spend time with them and their two teenage sons when I

Liz, Elcho, Hung Nguyen, and Millie in Escondido, California. Hung was with us when his country of Vietnam fell and has been very special to us through the years.

visit Wichit and Miriam in Escondido. They are involved in the Iranian Christian Fellowship of San Diego. It was a thrill recently to be in their church service and to see their family leading the worship. I shared about knowing Fardis in Japan as a university student, before she became a Christian, and seeing how the Lord had blessed her since she had given her life to Him. As many in the service didn't understand English, she translated for me. When Fardis and Mark visited me in Kirkland, Washington, I was glad to be able to introduce them to Baharam Zahid, who pastors the Iranian Church in Seattle.

55

A California Homestay

Christine and Hiro Unno were due to have another baby after the first of the year. Christine had complications, so she had to be hospitalized for a couple of months with bed rest until the baby was delivered. Eiwa was quite near the hospital, so I tried to visit her as often as possible. A healthy little girl, Elisa Unno, was born to them on February 6, 1992. She is truly a gift from the Lord.

Hiroko and Tetsuya were planning to get married, but in church services, they sat on opposite sides. Pastor Masuyama had asked them not to sit together until their engagement was formally announced as an example to the other young people. A few months later, Hiroko and Tetsuya were married, and Elcho and I were treated royally and given a very prominent part in the wedding ceremony. I am not sure if we were the *omiai*, meaning the "go-between" or the *shounin*, meaning "official witnesses."

Many pastors in Japan are skeptical of young people who become Christians while studying abroad. On the other hand, students who are used to American mega churches and our active International Christian Fellowships (ICFs) are not very tolerant of Japanese traditional churches when they return home. They get discouraged and often just give up. That is why it is so important to properly prepare international students to return to their homelands. In their thirty-seven years of ISI ministry in San Diego, Wichit and Miriam have done a good job of preparing students to return home and in keeping in touch with them wherever they go.

We realize that it is hard for the church in Japan when only one percent of the population is Christian. Japanese traditions and culture are so tied to Buddhism and Shintoism that it is often very difficult for Christians to take a stand.

The *obune* festival is in October when the Japanese go to the graves of their ancestors. Some told us that this was just a time of respect and similar to when we take flowers to the graves of our loved ones. Others told us it was a time of worship. Similar to our Hindu and Buddhist friends in India, they offered food and incense in acts of worship. Hiro decided to go to the grave with his parents. He kept the grave clean and took good care of it, but when it was time for worship, he went down the hill and did not participate in the ceremony.

Graves in Japan are different from those in the States. Cremation is the norm. A large cement underground container has many urns in it. Only pure direct-line ancestors are allowed to have urns in the grave. This is all registered at government offices for inheritance purposes. Christians have separate cemeteries, so it is difficult for them to take a stand against such traditions.

In America, if we don't like certain teaching in the church or don't agree with the pastor on some issues, we can leave and join another church. It is not that easy in Japan with so few churches, especially outside the larger cities like Tokyo and Osaka. Many friends who talked to us about problems in their churches decided to stay and tried to change things.

I knew we were going to be leaving Japan and moving to Bellevue, Washington, when Elcho's contract at Eiwa expired on March 31, 1993.

I had always wanted to do an American English-speaking homestay for Eiwa high-school girls. I asked permission from the school, and they gave their approval. Christine helped me prepare the Eiwa girls, and Miriam found good Christian homes for the girls to stay in. It was a big undertaking but worth the try. I had seen girls go on study tours abroad and knew we could do it better and cheaper. We charged the girls a reasonable fee, which paid all the expenses for two chaperones, rented vans, admission fees for theme parks, stipends to host families, plus their air flights to and from San Diego. I couldn't post the fliers on the Eiwa walls, as the school was not sponsoring it, though it had approved it. So I printed up fliers, announced it in my classes, and told them about the planned activities.

Two very special young mothers were Christin Unno and Toshie Saito. I visited them in their homes and in the park, and they would visit me. They are shown here with their daughters Sarah, Elisa, Kio, and Yuki.

Word spread quickly, and the whole school seemed to be asking me about it. I had no idea how many would sign up, so I was surprised when, within days, almost forty girls came with their application papers filled out. Soon afterward, their parents deposited funds to the special account I had set up at Shizuoka Bank. Two English teachers, Keiko and Yuri, were to go with us. Each girl was allowed one checked bag and one carry-on.

Because Elcho and I would be moving back to the States soon, I frantically packed suitcases and boxes of things I wanted to take home. We only had a few months left, and we could get along without much. I took eighteen suitcases or boxes and one trunk. I bought forty-two Northwest Airlines tickets to San Diego, and the airline allowed us two suitcases each. Since I had suggested each girl only take one good-size suitcase going so she would be able to bring back things from America, I was able to get most of our things to Miriam's home at no added expense. It was quite a hassle at the Narita Airport, but all went surprisingly well.

The Maneevone family and several host families warmly greeted us. Most of them had high-school students who went with us to amusement parks. The two Eiwa teachers, Keiko and Yoko, stayed with a couple of single ladies that they related well to. We went to Disneyland, Sea

World, Universal Studios, Knott's Berry Farm, Wild Animal Park, and church with host families around San Diego, and spent time at the beach. Granddaughters Liz, Anjuli, and Wanida went with us, talking with the girls and making sure that all were doing well. We divided into small groups with one or two persons in charge. We had no cell phones in those days, but we had to make sure not only that they didn't get lost, but also that they had a good time and communicated in English. Keiko and Yoko were helpful, and I am thankful that all went well. We made many pleasant memories for these Japanese high-school girls and for my family as well.

56

A Big Scare and a Glorious Send-Off

In Japan, Elcho began to sit down to teach his classes. He was not feeling well, and I was concerned. One day in February, I got a call at Eiwa that Elcho was in the hospital. He had driven to Eiwa College, gotten out of the car, and his coworker, Lurleen, had found him slumped over the car, babbling incomprehensibly. He could not move and didn't know where he was. She ran to the office, where they called the emergency ambulance and took him to the hospital. Fumie, my fellow English teacher, took me there in her car. We waited and waited, and we were told that he was still having an MRI.

Later, he told me that his MRI was a frightening experience as it was quiet and dark in there. He had not been told what was going on, and he was confused about it. As he was so much larger than any Japanese, it was very tight inside the equipment. He thought they would never get him out, and it was like his tomb.

I asked Fumie if the emergency-room doctor in charge of Elcho would notify our friend, Dr. Morakami, a heart specialist, who was on the staff of that hospital. Dr. Morakami came right away and examined Elcho. I thanked Fumie for her help and told her that she could go back to school now. Dr. Morakami took over Elcho's care and admitted him into the hospital. The doctor told me that Elcho was having a series of transient ischemic attacks, and his heartbeat was not normal.

I called the family and a few special friends and asked them to pray for him. Hiro came in the evening, visited with him, and prayed for him. After several days, Elcho seemed to be quite normal, so he was released from the hospital, and Hiro helped us get him back home. It was a wake-up call, and we knew we needed to get Elcho to the States.

Elcho recovered enough to teach a few classes and to give an early final examination to get his grades in, and Eiwa College agreed to let him go a week early. The English department gave him a nice farewell dinner, and our friends showered us with good-bye gifts. Toshie, Christine, and Fumie brought us meals, which gave me time to finish packing and get ready for the big transition.

More than one hundred Japanese friends, staff, and students from Eiwa College and Eiwa School, Megumi Church friends, neighbors, and special friends were at the train station to see us off for Tokyo.

Our Kofu friends, Ken and Miko Horikawa, Kuni and Yasuko Ogawa, and Kenji and Etsuko Nonogaki had reserved and paid for a suite at the Okura Hotel, not only for them but also for us to stay that night. We had a wonderful dinner and sat around talking and remembering our times together. In the morning, we all enjoyed a scrumptious breakfast buffet then Elcho and I boarded the airport shuttle for Narita and Seattle, Washington. I can still see our friends standing and waving as we drove away.

We made happy memories in Japan. We went temporarily to help a church with their English program and stayed twelve fulfilling years. I know the Lord led us down that path.

Part 7

Retirement

57

Returning to the Pacific Northwest

Aboard a Northwest Airlines flight in March 1993, the reality of settling back in our homeland hit us. As we talked about our future, we knew we could trust the Lord to lead us step by step on the final path He had prepared for us. We briefly stopped in Honolulu, Hawaii, for a few days with Mary Ellen, Bert, and their family before arriving in Seattle where LeRoy, Carol, and their children welcomed us to our new home in Bellevue, Washington.

When I asked Miriam how she would define retirement, she said, "Retirement is the graduate school of life." Retirement is not the end but the beginning of a new chapter. For us, retirement was a continuation of showing hospitality and sharing the love of Jesus with those who crossed our pathway.

We quickly settled into our home on the cul-de-sac next to LeRoy and his family. On Sundays, we went to Westminster Chapel in Bellevue, with them. We liked the teaching, the music, and the people there. Elcho's nephew Gerald and his wife Sharon were also in the church. Sharon was in charge of making the pictorial directory for the church, and she asked me to help. Through this experience, I met many people in a short time.

Thankfully, Elcho was feeling better. With the good care of Dr. Furlong at Kirkland's Virginia Mason Clinic, his heart and the Parkinson's disease seemed under control. Music and laughter filled our home, so it was not hard to settle into life in the beautiful Pacific Northwest.

Elcho and I in 1993 are standing outside of our home in Bellevue, Washington, where we enjoyed happy times showing hospitality to the many who visited us there.

Westminster Chapel was a missions-minded church and supported many career missionaries working around the world. However, even though many internationals lived in the area, none attended the church. Thankfully, this began to change when Dr. Gary Gulbranson came as our senior pastor and Mark Carlson became our missions pastor.

We enjoyed doing things with LeRoy's family. Backyard barbeques, camping in a rented motor home, and sightseeing around the beautiful Northwest were happy times. Elcho especially liked going to grandson Levi's baseball and football games. As a boy, Elcho had played in sports and band concerts, but his dad never came to encourage him.

When we went to an ISI team potluck at the old, elegant home of Dan and Carolyn Brannen on Capitol Hill in Seattle, we met those who reached foreign students at our local colleges and universities. We heard about the Friday night International Christian Fellowship (ICF) meetings at the ISI house near the University of Washington. We liked the ISI staff and volunteers and hoped we could fit into this ministry with them.

Visits with our nine grandchildren were few and far between when we were living in China and Japan. We loved being able to spend more time with them when we moved back to the U.S.

Among the group one evening, we met an interesting couple. He was from Iran, and she was from Japan. We liked Bahram, Keiko, their seven-year-old daughter, Roya, and young son, Amir. We learned that when Bahram was a student at Seattle University, he had occasionally come to Dan's Bible class. After they were married in 1981, Dan and Carolyn invited them to their home for the holidays. They had enjoyed many Thanksgiving and Christmas dinner celebrations with them.

Since I was interested in their fascinating story, I asked Keiko to tell me more. Her family in Japan had some challenges in 1985, so they asked her to come home for a visit. However, because of her immigration status, she could not leave the States. Worried about her parents and pregnant with her first child, she was miserable and spent many sleepless nights.

One day in 1986, soon after Roya had been born, Keiko was holding her little baby. She realized how helpless the baby was. Her baby's life was completely dependent on her to do everything for her. Keiko had been worried about her own frustrating situation, and now she had someone who was completely dependent on her.

Keiko had heard much about the Lord and the Bible, but she hadn't read it. When she started reading it, she came across these verses, "Come to Me, all you who labor and are heavy laden, and I will give you rest. Take My yoke upon you and learn from Me, for I am gentle and lowly in heart, and you will find rest for your souls" (Matthew 11:28–29). Although she didn't know much about Jesus, she decided to follow Him. She prayed, and her heavy burden lifted, but she was afraid to tell her husband. Two months later, when she finally got up enough courage to tell him, he said that he too had decided to follow Jesus but had been afraid to tell her. They got involved in a local church and became volunteers in the ISI ministry of reaching internationals.

Keiko encouraged me to attend the Friday ICF meetings, and I was anxious to get involved. I started meeting students at the local college and at the Crossroads Shopping Center near our home. As we became acquainted, I invited these students to go with me to Seattle for the Friday ICF meetings. We all enjoyed meeting students, ISI staff members, and volunteers like Keiko and Bahram. One couple was from my church. Mark was a lawyer and his lovely wife, Melinda, was a teacher.

Several of us in Westminster Chapel started what we called "Talk Time" on Tuesday evenings. The idea was to help internationals find friends and to feel comfortable in speaking English. These were simple English classes with grammar, pronunciation, and practical things about living in America. It turned out to be more for English as a Second Language (ESL) students and immigrants at first. After each lesson, we divided into groups in the Fireside Room. When mothers with small children came, I took them to the nursery and talked with the mothers while the children played. However, we also were anxious to reach local international college students.

When I became friends with the lady in charge of housing for foreign students at our local college, she told me that Bellevue Community College had a one-year International Business Program (IBP) for Japanese university students. I called the coordinator of the program and invited her for lunch on our patio. Keiko joined us. The coordinator was friendly and appreciative. I told her we would like to help in any way we could, including welcome dinners and finding more host families. This proved to be an open door for us.

I was happy to be involved in the outreach to internationals studying in the colleges and universities in the Seattle area.

When the next group of international business students came to our welcome dinner, we invited them to Talk Time and ICF activities. As most of them didn't have cars at first, we met them at the college in our cars and vans, took them to activities then drove them to their new homes afterwards. Many came to the welcome dinner parties, and a few came regularly to the activities and to our home. Koji, Kazu, Keiko, Kaori, Masami, Hiromi, Akiko, and Mieko—all non-Christians at that time and all from Japan—were among the regulars. They liked to hear about our experiences in Japan, China, and India. We also asked them about their experiences and helped them to adjust to life in America. We helped some to find cars, learn to drive, and get insurance from LeRoy. At that time, Wycliffe Bible Translators was putting on a program in churches, which they called "The Journey," a simulation of missionary life in various countries. When Wycliffe brought "The Journey" to Westminster Chapel, I asked some Japanese students to represent Japan with me. We dressed in *yukatas* (a light-weight garment, a bit like a kimono), decorated the room with Japanese posters, served Japanese snacks, and talked about Japan to those that came through our "country."

During their time of study here, several students accepted the Lord and today are serving Him around the world. Akiko is married to a pastor and living in Indonesia. Kaori got her master's of business administration degree (MBA) in New Zealand, is involved in the Alpha Course (a ten-week exploration of the Christian faith designed for spiritual seekers), and is teaching Japanese in a university there. Masami helps in the Alpha Course at Westminster Chapel in Bellevue. The church still gives welcome dinners for incoming IBP students, and some come to Talk Time and ICF. Jani James took over the leadership, and I enjoyed working with her. It is still going strong today under the capable leadership of Sylvia Ramquist, who is on the staff of Westminster Chapel. Keiko is still involved in the outreach to internationals.

58

Connecting and Reconnecting with Friends

During the next few years, our home was usually filled with family and friends. Not only did our immediate family come, but our international family came as well. Some stayed a few hours and some a few weeks. The Hiro Unno family came from Japan in 1994, and we took them to Victoria, British Columbia. Hiro could only stay for a long weekend, but Christine and the girls stayed for nearly a month and have continued to come almost every year since then. The Mochizuki family, some former Eiwa girls, Hiroko and Tetsuya Watanabe, and many more came from overseas.

Our closest neighbors in Bellevue were newlyweds from Japan. He had a two-year working visa with his Japanese company to run its Seattle office. Yoko and Hiroshi were lonely and not confident in English. So Elcho helped Hiroshi with his English several evenings a week and answered his questions.

One day, Yoko told me she was pregnant and that she missed her family in Japan. I spent time with her and took her to church activities. Her mother came to be with her just before their little boy was born. A few weeks later, ten Japanese new mothers, who were in Yoko's Japanese new-baby classes in Bellevue, came with their babies to her home for a potluck Japanese lunch. Our granddaughter, Liz, and I were invited and realized how many international neighbors wanted to be friends.

We enjoyed reconnecting with missionary friends who had also retired to the Pacific Northwest and Canada. We had become close during our years in India and on the Tibetan border. It was especially good to see Nonie Lindell States, daughter of Jonathan and Evie Lindell, outstanding missionaries to Nepal. Nonie was Mary Ellen and Miriam's classmate in Woodstock School and had spent many weekends and holidays in our home in Mussoorie. Now living in Seattle, she soon became a vital part of our family.

One day early in 1995, a friend and I were driving a van full of internationals to the Seattle ICF when she asked, "Why don't you start an ICF in Bellevue? This van full of students is enough to start our own group."

"That's a great idea," I said. So we seriously prayed about it.

Within a few days, Mark Carlson, the lawyer from the Seattle ICF group who was now our missions pastor at Westminster Chapel, called me. He said that a Christian doctor and his wife, John and Paula Rowland, had a big house they would like to use for an outreach to internationals. That was the beginning of ICF in Bellevue, Washington. It continues today in the home of Gary and Alice Eilers, and Bahram and Keiko still cook and help in many other ways.

Among our missionary friends who retired in the senior community at Warm Beach in Stanwood, Washington, were Dr. Al and Carol Holt. Elcho and Al first met in 1942, at the Church of the Open Door in Los Angeles, and we later worked with Al and Carol in India. Al operated

We were honored guests at Shawn's wedding on January 28, 1995, and, among all the guests who attended the reception, we were the only people who were not Chinese.

on me in a village hospital when the electric generator stopped. He had to stop the surgery to go outside and start the generator again. After they retired, we enjoyed several TEAM reunion lunches in their lovely retirement home. Since Al was an accomplished pianist, we always loved to hear him play.

We were encouraged at one reunion when our friend Les Buhler told us about his recent trip to India. He had visited Dharampur, where we had established seven village schools with Christian Indian teachers. When we were there, several village boys had accepted Christ, but we couldn't follow up with them after we left the field. Les assured us that the church had grown, and when he visited, he helped them put a new roof on the church building. One former teacher had gone on for further education and was now responsible for eighty churches in different part of India.

When another TEAM missionary couple, Charles and Anita Warren, visited us, they brought along Andrew (Andy) David, a handsome, young Christian Indian man who lived near us. Andy's father, an Indian Air Force officer, had been an active member of Delhi Bible Fellowship when Charles was the pastor there. Andy led worship in our newly established Bellevue ICF. He went to work at Microsoft and now has worked his way up to a responsible position. Today he is happily married with three boys and is an elder at Crossroads Bible Church in Bellevue.

Four special Chinese friends came to spend time with us. Kong Mian Jen Cheung, who in 1979-1980 had lived with us in Orange, California, visited us with her daughters. Her parents had been good to us in Shanghai, China. She now has a home in Beverly Hills, California, but lives most of the time in Hong Kong where her husband works. Jane Wang, another friend from Shanghai, and Shawn Chen, our former student in China, also visited us several times.

Then there was Ben. One day we received a letter with the return address written in Chinese. Inside was a letter from Ben Leo, a former student

Kong Mian Jen Cheung visited us several times in Bellevue, and we have enjoyed keeping in contact.

in China. He said he had been searching for us on the Internet and asked us if we were the Elcho Reddings who had taught in China in 1980-1981. "There can only be one Elcho Redding," he wrote. "If you are, I want to tell you that I am now married, and my wife and I are going to church here in China."

We wrote to him, telling him how happy we were to hear from him and about his news. We gave him an invitation to visit us anytime he could. As there was no address to copy in English, I cut the return address written in Chinese and pasted it on the outside of the envelope. Before long, Ben wrote that he was coming to see us. He ran a manufacturing company in China, which was a joint venture with a Detroit company. Since he was coming to Detroit for business meetings, he would stay a weekend with us. It was refreshing to be reunited with Ben and to hear about what had happened to him since we had said good-bye at the Chongqing airport fifteen years before. Ben later became a good friend of the great-grandson of Hudson Taylor, founder of the China Inland Mission, now the Overseas Missionary Fellowship (OMF), and Ben has been a help to their medical team. These days I talk to him often on Skype™.

Elcho was always glad to see his former students. Here he is with Gedun Phunsok and Kalsang Wangden from his Tibetan Tutorial School.

We were glad that when our Tibetan friends were in the Seattle area, they always came to visit us. Mrs. Taring came to visit us when she was ninety-one years old. Betty, Una, and Peggy, her three daughters, all came to visit us at various times. Tenzin, her grandson, spent much time with us when he was a student at the University of Washington. Geleg, the little boy who lived with us in India

328 • Wherever He Leads

Special guests in our home: Sonam Dohma (Bhutan), Isaku (Laddak), Elcho, Tenzin (Tibet), and Jane Wang (China).

and in California, was now living in Seattle with his wife, Chimi, and we always included them in our family gatherings.

August 22, 1997, was our fiftieth wedding anniversary. I wanted a big celebration, but Elcho was not doing well and wanted just our family and the "Tibetan boys." Earlier in August, our family and the Tibetan students that we had brought to America thirty years earlier, all came

On August 22, 1997, we celebrated our fiftieth anniversary very quietly with Elcho's sister Miriam Stanley, LeRoy, and Carol.

together to help us celebrate. They presented us with a beautiful twelve foot by sixteen foot handmade Tibetan carpet that has been in Wichit and Miriam's family room in Escondido since then. On the actual day, LeRoy and Carol took Elcho's sister, Miriam, who was visiting, and us to Salty's, a nice restaurant on Alki Beach, to celebrate the happy occasion.

Sonam was a delightful young Christian lady from Bhutan, who our fellow TEAM missionary, Irma Jean Storr, had sponsored to attend college in the United States. One day she came to visit us with Isaku, a young Christian Lhadaki man whose grandparents, the Elea Phunsogs, had been our good friends in India. We had helped put his father into a good Christian school in India. That same day, Tenzin and Jane Wang were also there. Our home in Bellevue, Washington, saw friends from Bhutan, Lhadakh, China, and Tibet.

We four sisters (Millie, Sadie, Jeane, and Polly) gathered together for a happy reunion in 1995.

I was especially glad to have my three sisters and their husbands visit us for several days. Because my sister, Sadie, and her husband, Pete Ackley, had been missionaries in Africa since 1949, and we'd been overseas then too, this was the first time that we sisters had all been together in over thirty years. We had not only remained married to our first husbands, but we also all celebrated over fifty years of marriage. Sadie died in 2001 and Jeane in 2005.

One day, Miriam called. "We know a Christian young man with a Ph.D. in engineering from New Zealand who has been teaching at the University of California at San Diego," she said. "He is going to teach at the University of Washington in the fall. I told him you would be glad to have him stay with you until he can get his own place. I know you and Dad will really like him. That's okay, isn't it? He's driving up there this weekend."

Our daughter knew us well, and we were glad to have Dr. Greg MacRae live with us for three months while he settled into life in Seattle and

found his own home. He was staying with us when the earthquake occurred in Kobe, Japan, and the University of Washington engineering department sent him there to investigate why buildings collapsed the way they did. He also spent time under the Lake Washington Floating Bridge and told us it was a disaster waiting to happen.

Greg previously had spent a couple of years in Japan and knew the language well, so the Japanese students who came to our home liked to talk with him. He was very good on the harmonica and often played it while we sang around the piano. We were glad to be part of Greg's life for the next ten years before he returned to his homeland. He is now nicely settled with his charming wife, Ing, and their four boys in New Zealand, where he teaches engineering at a university.

In September 1998, Ken, Miko, and Madoka Horikawa, came to visit us for the second time during our retirement. As Ken wanted to visit places where he had been during his days as a graduate student, we drove to Marysville for lunch. While driving home, a lady drove through a stoplight and hit us broadside, totaling our van and sending all five of us to the hospital. We were thankful to be alive, although I was hospitalized with a broken back and was in a body cast for many days.

A medical student from Thailand who was finishing his residency at the University of Washington called us one day in 1999. Mutual friends had told him about us, so he wanted to meet us. We were delighted when Kit Putrakul told us that he was a young Christian and would like to be discipled. When he finished his residency, he moved in with us for several months while he prepared for the next step in life.

One morning, we were having our morning coffee on our deck when I began talking with a slur, and my right side felt different. Kit examined me and called 911, and I was hospitalized with a stroke. My face was twisted, and I was told that I might never smile again. Also, my right side was weak for some weeks. Thankfully, with early detection and good therapy, the effects were minimal.

Kit grew spiritually and dedicated his life to the Lord for His service. He went to work with a Christian organization among the tribes in Northern Thailand, where he met an American nurse named Avery, who soon became his wife. Together with their young son, Lucas, they now work in a medical clinic in Cambodia.

Kit Putrakul from Thailand studied to become a medical doctor at the University of Washington. He became a Christian there, and after his graduation, he lived with us for awhile and was with me when I had my stroke in 1999.

Sonam brought her mother Tsewang, a devout Buddhist who had recently arrived from Bhutan, to visit us. Tsewang wanted to learn English, and I needed help, so she moved in with us for three or four days a week and then took the bus to be with her daughter. Every morning she counted her beads and chanted the mantras in her room. She was interested not only in learning English but also about what we believed as Christians. She only helped us for a couple of months, but we became good friends. She is now fluent in English, has become a devoted Christian, and lives with her daughter, Sonam, and family in the Seattle area. She knit me two beautiful Bhutanese sweaters that I enjoy wearing.

I had a nice visit with Fardis and her little boy in 1999.

59

The Rocky Path and a Victorious Home Going

One day, we went with some of our adult grandchildren to a famous Chinese restaurant in downtown Seattle for lunch. The entrance on Lake Union was up at least fifty stairs. Fortunately, we were able to go to the entrance for the disabled and the restaurant staff. We had a great meal and a happy time eating by the water, but as I was getting into the backseat of the van, I lost my balance and fell backwards into the cement gutter at the bottom of those steps. Malina, our nurse granddaughter, ran up those steps as fast as she could to call 911 and hysterically told the Chinese manager what had happened. He ran out and saw me lying in intense pain at the bottom of the steps and thought that I had fallen down them. Soon the ambulance took me to the nearby Virginia Mason Hospital. I had never had such pain in my life and was not surprised when I was told that I had broken my hip.

LeRoy came right away, and I soon went into surgery to have pins and screws put in. I thought I would never walk again, and rehabilitation was painful. Mary Ellen got an emergency family leave and flew from Honolulu to help. Miriam came from San Diego, and LeRoy brought Elcho to see me at the hospital. My family encouraged me to get out of that hospital bed and do what the physical therapist wanted me to do. It was difficult, but I kept saying, "I can do all things through Christ who strengthens me" (Philippians 4:13). I have no doubt that He helped me, and I had a good recovery.

Elcho loved having his children there while I was in the hospital. I was thankful for friends in the Westminster Chapel care group and our Wednesday Bible study who brought food and helped me when I returned home and my family had gone back to their homes.

In December 2001, Elcho wanted to fly to San Diego, California, to spend the Christmas holidays with Miriam, Wichit, and the girls in Escondido. We knew this would probably be his last opportunity. It was a good Christmas, and we all made happy memories.

Elcho's Parkinson's disease was making it increasingly difficult for him to bathe and dress himself. He also found it hard to get into the van, so I had a special seat installed to make it easier for him. A nurse began coming once a month to take his blood and to check his vital signs, so he didn't have to see Dr. Furlong as often. Fortunately, I was able to get Kitiana, a Christian caregiver from Fiji, to move in and help me with his care.

Although Elcho's body was stiffening and he couldn't move as he wanted, he was a joy to be with. He loved to listen to hymns, choruses, and classical music. It was difficult for him to read, but he liked me to read to him, or he listened to Scripture tapes. He never complained, had a great sense of humor, and was appreciative. He liked to watch television and kept up with the news. But it was difficult for us who loved him to see his earthly body in such obvious decline.

I was thankful that Elcho liked Kitiana. She was a big help and freed me so I could take part in some church and ISI activities. When she had her days off, I cared for him alone. We all liked listening to Bill Gaither videos, and Kitiana asked if we could send some to her son, who was a pastor in Fiji. After we sent the videos to him, he told us that he had gathered the entire village together in an outdoor arena one night and showed the video on a big screen. When Lily, also from Fiji, who sang with the Gaithers, came to Westminster Chapel, she and Kitiana met and became friends. Actually, they looked as if they could have been sisters. In the fall of 2002, Kitiana decided to go home. How would I care for Elcho now? I asked the Lord for wisdom and direction.

At times, Elcho's medication caused dementia and hallucinations. Although he found it difficult to get out of a chair and walk, his mind and attitude remained good. He was always glad to see family and friends. Sadly, I realized that it was physically impossible for me to care for him alone and getting good in-home help seemed hopeless. This was one of the most difficult times in my life. It looked as if I would have to put my dear husband into a nursing home, and he was willing to do anything I decided. Elcho still had his keen mind and sweet spirit, but he was trapped in a body that moved with great difficulty. When our children came to Bellevue, we talked with Dr. Furlong, who told us what we didn't want to hear. Elcho's physical condition would not get better, only worse. Together we looked at nursing homes and tried to figure out the best path to pursue.

Our grandson, Micah, was a freshman at the University of Hawaii. I asked Mary Ellen if he would like to live with us and go to a college or university in our area. He could get his grandfather up, bathe, and dress him, and I could watch Elcho while Micah was at school. We could pay Micah, and that would help with his educational expenses. She talked it over with her family.

Micah came from Honolulu to help me with Elcho's care and go to Northwest University. Christine, Sarah, and Elisa came every summer from Japan to visit as well. Back row, left-to-right: Micah, Danya, Liz, Christine, Millie; front row: Elisa, Sarah, and Elcho.

Mary Ellen could not think of putting her dad in a nursing home, and they felt it would be too much for Micah, so they decided that Mary Ellen, Micah, and Danya would come for a while and help with Elcho's care. Micah enrolled in Northwest University, Danya in Bellevue Christian High School, and Mary Ellen got a nursing job at Valley Medical Center. Bert continued working at his job in Honolulu as a United States government civil servant. This worked out fine for Elcho and me, but separation was hard on Mary Ellen's family.

Things changed in the fall of 2003 when we sold our Bellevue home and, together with the Kubos, purchased a home in Kirkland that had two separate living quarters. Elcho and I lived downstairs, and the Kubo family lived upstairs. Bert sold their home in Hawaii, resigned from his job, and joined his family. It was a big sacrifice for the Kubo family, but I will always be grateful that they gave us four happy years with Elcho at home, surrounded by his loved ones. I was glad to be with Elcho day and night, but one of the Kubos got him up, bathed, and dressed him, and someone was upstairs if I needed help during the day. Mary Ellen, Nonie, and I were able to go to the Wednesday Bible study that we enjoyed, and the girls worked in our garden the rest of the day. Elcho enjoyed sitting outside in his wheelchair, watching them work. Often he held the hose and watered the plants. He enjoyed having Mary Ellen push him around the garden almost every day. He appreciated the little things in life, and the Lord was very close to him.

We had enjoyed living near LeRoy, Carol, and their children for ten years. They were empty nesters and grandparents when LeRoy sold his insurance business in 2004, and accepted the pastorate of the First Mennonite Church in Nampa, Idaho. We all decided to fly there for his installation. Elcho was proud of his only son and glad to see him as a pastor again.

For Mothers' Day in 2005, LeRoy and Carol sent me an airline ticket to visit them for a few days. I needed a break but not the kind I got. Just before I left, I stumbled over the doorstep to the patio, fell hard, and broke my right hip. Four years earlier, I had broken my left hip. When I came to after surgery, I was surprised to see Elcho in his wheelchair, along with Mary Ellen, Geleg, LeRoy, and Miriam. Thankfully, I made it through the surgery and rehabilitation. It was not easy, but who wouldn't succeed with such love and attention?

Some international friends, who visited us in the summer of 2005, were Dr. Kit and Avery who did medical work in Cambodia; Dr. Greg who was moving his family to New Zealand; Shawn Chen and Ben Leo, former students from China; Tibetan and Bhutanese friends; Christine Unno, Toshie Saito and their daughters Yuki, Sarah, and Elisa from Japan. Yuki wanted to finish high school in the States or Canada, so Mary Ellen helped her find a good Christian high school in Victoria, British Columbia, Canada, where she went in the fall. All of our immediate family, including our nine grandchildren with their families, also spent time with us.

Elcho usually enjoyed his family and friends, but at times, he didn't seem to be himself. He was not as interested in people as usual and often was confused. A severe kidney infection put him in the hospital several times. Those of us who loved him were sad to see him trapped in a body that made moving difficult. Nonie spent at least one day a week with us. She and Mary Ellen are longtime, close friends, and they were such an encouragement to us during that time. Elcho liked sitting in the garden and watching

In his last days, one of Elcho's greatest joys was spending time out in the garden. This is the last family picture of the five of us before his death on September 24, 2006.

Mary Ellen and Nonie as they weeded and planted. They also shaved him, cut his hair, and massaged his dry skin and aching body with ointments. Anna Joy, our first great-grandchild, lived near us and always made Elcho smile when her mother, Liz, brought her to visit. I am not sure who loved it the most when she crawled up on his lap and asked him endless questions.

In April of 2006, we were invited to have an audience with the Dalai Lama of Tibet at an ecumenical conference. Although we were not interested in the conference, we wanted to see our friend again. Tashi Wandu, who used

In April 2006, we were asked if we'd like to have an audience with the Dalai Lama in San Francisco, so some of my grandchildren joined Miriam and me there for the special occasion.

to come to our home in the 1960s, was the personal representative of the Dalai Lama in the United States at the time.

Miriam, seven of our grandchildren, and I enjoyed a personal twenty-minute audience with him. I presented him with a book I had put together about our friendship with Tibetans, covering almost five decades. He was interested and took time to look at it and make comments.

I was sorry that Elcho was not up to the trip, but the Dalai Lama asked us to give him his greetings. He told the Tibetan officials and United States security men, "Tibetans owe a great deal to the Reddings for all their help to the Tibetan people." We had given him the traditional white scarf when we had entered his chambers, and as we left, he put others around our necks. He gave me a special scarf to give to Elcho.

Tashi told us later that he was grateful to have spent so much time in our home as a teenager and often remembers singing hymns around our piano in Mussoorie. We feel that the Tibetans and their leader respect us as Christians. We were thankful to have been in the right place at the right time in the 1960s to help them and show them the love of Jesus our Lord. Later that summer, some of our former Tibetan students, who we had helped come to the United States, gathered from New York, California, and Canada, for a special reunion in Seattle to visit Elcho.

When Elcho was hospitalized again in August 2006, with a high fever, Dr. Furlong met with us as a family and told us that Elcho should go into hospice care. It was not the news that a wife and children wanted to hear, especially on our fifty-ninth wedding anniversary. Elcho kept saying that he wanted to go home. We repeatedly told him that he was now home. But a hospice person explained that Elcho was saying he wanted to go to his heavenly home, and we needed to give him permission. It was not easy to do, but we did.

September 2, 2006 was Elcho's eighty-second birthday. Although he was confused all day, he finally realized it was his birthday and seemed happy to celebrate with the Kubo family and Nonie. He even sat at the table and ate a little chocolate cake and ice cream.

The hospice people told us that he might still be with us at Christmas, but we who spent twenty-four hours a day with him had our doubts. Mary Ellen, Nonie, and I spent many sleepless nights by his bedside as he lingered between death and life. He loved to listen to music, especially hymns and classical music. The Lord was very real to him, and he was not fearful. He knew where he was going, and he was ready to meet the Lord, whom he had served all of his life.

LeRoy came from Nampa, Idaho, and Miriam came from Escondido, California, to be near their father during his last days. Some of the grandkids joined us. Although Elcho enjoyed listening to hymns and classical music, he especially loved to hear his family singing around the piano, and he often sang along. He enjoyed many songs, but "Great Is Thy Faithfulness" and "I Will Sing of the Mercies of the Lord" were his all-time favorites.

While heaven seemed closer during those days, so was our grief. We realized we didn't have long to enjoy his presence on earth. One evening, I was sitting by his bed when he looked at me and said, "Why are you crying, honey?" He was about to leave me, and he asked me why I was crying! Before I could think of an answer, he weakly whispered, "It's all right. The Lord will take care of you." I knew that but still couldn't stop the tears.

Mary Ellen described his last words in a letter she wrote about her dad's last days:

> Just a couple of days before Dad went to be with the Lord, being very frail and knowing he was soon to leave us, we were singing together from one of his favorite passages in Psalms, "I will sing of the mercies of the Lord forever; with my mouth will I make known Thy faithfulness to all generations" (Psalm 89:1), only he intentionally changed the word *faithfulness* to *preciousness*. I was surprised and corrected him. His reply was, "Oh, but He has been precious to me!" The Lord is both faithful and precious to His children, to those who love, trust, and obey Him. That is a legacy that my dad left me and my family.

I will be forever thankful to Mary Ellen and her family for their help in taking care of Elcho at home so he never had to spend one day in a nursing home. Elcho's final days are precious memories to us. Although his body was weak, he was alert at times, quoting Scripture and softly singing along with us. He made us laugh, and he made us cry. His sense of humor and wisdom astounded us. He had taught us how to live, and now he taught us how to die. Surrounded by his loved ones, just before midnight on September 24, 2006, he went to be with the Lord. He was "absent from the body and present with the Lord."

I asked LeRoy if he would lead the memorial service. He said he thought it would be too difficult, so Pastor Gary, our senior pastor at Westminster Chapel, agreed to do it. After a couple of days, however, LeRoy changed his mind. Since he knew his dad better than anyone else, he felt he should do it. Pastor Gary was on standby, but LeRoy did a beautiful job of officiating both at the Sunset Hills graveside service and at his dad's memorial service at Westminster Chapel.

All of our immediate family, including the spouses of our grandchildren, Elcho's sister, Miriam, his brother, Dallas, other family members, fellow missionaries in TEAM and ISI, Tibetans, and other international friends came from Canada and California for a great service remembering

Elcho's life. "Precious in the sight of the Lord is the death of His saints" (Psalm 116:15). "Eye has not seen, nor ear heard, nor have entered into the heart of man the things which God has prepared for those who love Him" (1 Corinthians 2:9). Our children and grandchildren all had part in the service, and I am thankful for each one of them. Two of our favorite songs, "Great Is Thy Faithfulness" and "Because He Lives," were sung at the service. The third verse is so meaningful.

> And then one day, I'll cross the river,
> I'll fight life's final war with pain;
> And then, as death gives way to vict'ry,
> I'll see the lights of glory—and I'll know He lives.

—William and Gloria Gaither

Elcho, who had been a vital part of my life for over six decades, was now home with the Lord he loved and served all his life. He had fought a good fight and finished his course on earth. He left a lasting legacy for his family and friends. LeRoy changed the name of his insurance company in memory of his dad (EZR Insurance, "Making Insurance Easier.") Even our little great-granddaughter, Anna, often asks me if I miss Great Papa. Then, she says she does too. Our adult grandchildren often tell me how they still miss and think of him. What a joy and comfort that is to me. When I visited our oldest granddaughter, Leonie, recently, I was surprised to see only one framed picture on her desk. It was a picture of her as a baby with Grandpa Redding.

60

God's Miraculous Fruit in China

In an annual Christmas card from Shawn Chen, one of our former Chinese students, he enclosed this letter that encouraged and blessed me.

> I just returned from China this week. When I got back to my Los Angeles office this afternoon, I found your letter on my desk. After I read it, I still couldn't believe that Dr. Redding was gone. How sad I am today. Dr. Redding was one of the most important people in my life. When my life was very different from what it is today, it was Dr. Redding who led me to the Lord. I can't help thinking of the good times we had together. He was the first one to get me to ride in a car, fly in an airplane, and wear a down coat from Hong Kong. In 1980, that was a big luxury for a kid in Chongqing, China. He took me traveling with him to many cities in China and gave me many colored pictures of myself. He made me feel special. These days I am blessed with so much of everything, and I have a desire to serve the Lord.

> I will definitely miss him so much, but I know he is with the Lord now. One thing that I regret is that I didn't have the opportunity to show him what I have accomplished in China. Dr. Redding went to China twenty-six years ago to share the gospel. Through the years, Dr. Redding encouraged me to carry on his work in China. I have established SIAS University

with fifteen thousand students, with about one hundred international students and one hundred American teachers. So Dr. Redding's work in China didn't die but is being carried on.

Since Dr. Redding didn't have a chance to see what I have done in China, can you come and see the continuation of his work through me? How is your health these days? You look very healthy in your Christmas letter. I will make the arrangements and take good care of you. I don't think you can even imagine the changes that have come to China since you were last here. How exciting it will be if I can show you China again! Let's discuss the details and make a schedule for you to come.

When Ben Leo, another of our former students in Chongqing University, heard that I was going to China, he wanted me to come to his graduation from Singapore Bible College. Ben had given up a successful business career to study the Scriptures. Ben didn't want me to travel by myself and offered to send funds for tickets for our three children to come with me. I could scarcely believe it, as nothing like this had ever happened to us before. I had gone to China reluctantly in 1980, and now, twenty-seven years later, I was reaping the fruit of that year.

Dr. Furlong would not give me clearance to go until my heart doctor gave his okay. He gave me various stress tests, even altitude tests, and I passed them all. He said that if someone had told him a year ago that he would be giving clearance for me to go to China and Tibet, he would have said they were crazy, but I had his complete approval. Dr. Furlong jokingly said that he thought I should take my doctor with me.

How is it possible that my reluctant "yes" to Elcho's question, "Are you willing for us to move to China?" twenty-seven years before would bring so much joy to me and his children after he had gone? The story of the life that Elcho and I shared would not be complete without telling about this sentimental journey in 2007.

This expense-paid, two-month adventure to Japan, Singapore, China, and Lhasa, Tibet, was at the invitation of two of our former Chinese students, Ben and Shawn, who are having a significant influence in China today. They were both aware that the help and encouragement Elcho gave them as university students in China twenty-seven years earlier played a significant part in their success.

When I looked at our tickets, I saw that we could break our journey in Japan for no extra charge, so that is what we did. One Sunday in April 2007, LeRoy preached at the morning service at Lakeview Bible Church in Nampa, Idaho, where he was the pastor, and then flew to Seattle. The next morning, he and I flew to Japan, where Hiro and Christine Unno met us at Narita Airport and drove us in their new van to Shizuoka, Japan, a five-hour trip. They put us up in the best hotel in Shizuoka, where it was easy to meet people who came to see us. Hiro took vacation time to show us around, and he arranged for us to see the people and places that had been important to Elcho and me.

LeRoy preached in the church were Hiro was involved. Even though many church members were on a retreat, it worked out fine because people wanted to see me and to meet LeRoy. In Shizuoka, the church was packed. As was their custom, we enjoyed a nice lunch together after the service. I was glad that LeRoy could hear how his dad had blessed so many. The next day, about twenty young adults, who had been in Elcho's English Bible class, met at a Chinese restaurant in the hotel. Around the table, each one told what the Bible classes twenty years earlier had meant to them. Junko gave LeRoy a notebook filled with her notes of Elcho's study on the book of Galatians in both English and Japanese. One day, we went to Shizuoka University and Eiwa University where Elcho had taught and to Eiwa High School where I had taught. Every evening we had dinner with the Unno family, including their teenage daughters, Sarah and Elisa. They are all committed Christians and treated us like their own family.

We also spent an enjoyable day with Yuki's parents, Toshie, and her lawyer husband in their lodge in the Japanese Alps. Yuki was a senior in a Canadian high school and growing in her walk with the Lord. One day we took the bullet train to Atami to spend the day with our friend, Junko Sagawa, the cake lady, in her sixteenth-floor penthouse overlooking the Japanese Sea.

LeRoy and I took the train to Kawasaki where our good friends, Ken, Miko, and Madoka Horikawa, met us. Their home became our home and headquarters for the next ten days. The Horikawas, like the Unnos, were anxious to show LeRoy the places and people that had been an important part of his dad's life during our twelve years in Japan. Ken arranged for us to go to Hakone to stay at the TEL-GenRad guesthouse, with a visit to a traditional Japanese spa, a fabulous dinner, and an evening of karaoke. The next day we enjoyed a beautiful drive around Mt. Fuji to Kofu, where we visited with Kuni Ogawa's widow and daughter. We also saw the Eiwa high school, where we had taught for six years.

Ken and Miko Horikawa are our very best friends from our days in Kofu, Japan. When I returned to Japan with LeRoy in 2007, we stayed with them, and they showed LeRoy all of his dad's favorite places.

Ken and Miko had designed their lovely home themselves. It was disabled-friendly, even with an elevator that took us to the second floor. We went through several photo books of shared memories, and Madoka gave us a tour of Tokyo.

We took the train to Gunma to visit Tetsuya and Hiroko Watanabe for a couple of days. Also, Seiya Kagatani came from Saitama to take us to be with his

Seiya and Yoriko Kagatani had us in their home for several days.

family for several days. It was good to see Yoriko and the children again. These longtime friends had been part of our English Bible study and helped in the ISI Japan retreats. LeRoy already knew them, as both families had visited us in Bellevue. Many years ago, Seiya had done his Ph.D. studies in Dallas, Texas, and Pete and Sadie (my sister) Ackley had been their American hosts. Seiya and LeRoy talked about the difficulties of being a Japanese Christian father. Since Seiya's work was very demanding, much of the burden of raising three teenage boys was left up to Yoriko. Sunday was often the only day he had at home with the family. Mandatory school activities were often planned on Sunday, which made it difficult to go to church together as a family. We did, however, enjoy going to church with them on the Sunday we were there. Afterwards, the church members ate together. I sat next to the director of World Vision in Japan. He said that, although Japan is less than one percent Christian, Japanese people gave generously to World Vision in the sponsorship of needy children.

Hiroko joined us for the train ride back to Keio Plaza in Tokyo where we met Keiko Sagauchi; Lan and Fumie Mochizuki; Jordon Nogaki; Akiko Arai; and Ken, Miko, and Madoka for a farewell dinner. I was thankful that LeRoy could share this memorable time in Japan with me.

LeRoy and I in 2007 with Ben, his sons Aaron and Abel, and Pastor Ng Lian "Moses" Wen in Ben and Han Jin's home in Singapore.

We flew to Singapore where Ben met us at one thirty in the morning! It was great to see him again and to meet his lovely wife, Han Jin, and their two young sons, Abel and Aaron. They were gracious hosts, but Singapore was hot and humid. Ben showed us around a Singapore that had certainly changed a great deal since we had been there on our return trip to India when LeRoy was two years old.

Miriam arrived from California the day before Ben's graduation. That night, we attended a buffet dinner in his honor at the community center of his condominium association. Many of his best friends were there,

and we met some of his fellow classmates at Singapore Bible College and the staff of Medical Service International (MSI), a Christian NGO of Overseas Missionary Service. They liked looking at a book I had written about our year in China, with hundreds of pictures of Ben and his classmates. His friends were surprised that he was forty-seven years old and had been my student in China in 1980, twenty-seven years before.

It was a thrill to be at Ben's graduation and to realize that he had such a positive testimony. LeRoy, Miriam, and I talked about how proud Elcho would have been of Ben. At the reception, I sat next to the board chairman, a successful Singapore businessman. I asked him when he had become a Christian and was pleased to hear that an ISI volunteer had led him to Christ in Orange County, California, when we were on staff there. After graduation, LeRoy flew home, Miriam and I flew to Beijing, and Ben moved his family back home to Chengdu, China.

Craig Chen, another former student at Chongqing University, now a teacher at the International School in Beijing, met us in Beijing and took us to the hotel that Shawn had arranged for us. Dr. Tim, a research scientist and another former student, took us to walk on the Great Wall of China the next day. Several Chinese students, who had been a part of Miriam's ICF group in California, came to our hotel to see us. For the next three days, Tim, Craig, and their wives showed us many interesting places around the city.

It was a one-hour flight to Zhengzhou, Henan, where Shawn Chen's SIAS University is. Miriam and I were treated like celebrities from the minute we arrived at Zhengzhou Airport. I would not have believed what Shawn had accomplished in the previous nine years if I had not seen it with my own eyes. We were there for the special homecoming week.

At that time, SIAS International University had twenty thousand students, one hundred international students, one hundred international teachers, fabulous facilities, and the most beautiful campus one could imagine. We were there for five wonderful days. Shawn's parents were also visiting, and we were glad to see each other again. His parents, Miriam, and I were given a special tram with our own driver to take us around the campus and to and from the activities. The American teachers and the staff in founder and president Shawn's office were amazed to see my book with pictures of Shawn as our student nearly three decades earlier.

My time with both Ben and Shawn in China was very emotional for me. Many years ago as a high-school student in Yakima, Washington, I had chosen John 15:16 as my life verse: "You did not choose Me, but I chose you and appointed you that you should go and bear fruit, and that your fruit should remain." I had gone to the uttermost parts of the earth, and I had tried to witness for my Lord. However, in the past, I seemed to have seen little fruit. During those days in Singapore and in Zhengzhou, China, I was thankful I had reluctantly left the comforts of Orange, California, to go with Elcho to China. Although we were there only one year, I finally saw glorious fruit, and it was far above anything we could have thought! I thanked the Lord and gave Him the glory.

61

A Lifelong Dream Comes True

The purpose of our fabulous trip to Asia was to be at Ben's graduation and at Shawn's SIAS International University for the homecoming celebrations. However, we were also going to Chengdu to spend more time with Ben and Han Jin and for a reunion that Ben was planning with more of our former Chinese students. We also wanted to see our good friends, Kris and Stephanie Rubish, so Kris arranged for us to go into Lhasa, Tibet, for several days.

Miriam and I flew back to Beijing where grandson Micah (in place of his mother) arrived to go with us into Tibet. Then we flew to Chengdu where Kris met us at the airport to give us our travel permits, air tickets, and reservations for accommodations and tours in Lhasa. To obtain our travel documents, we had to buy a tour package with a van and driver and an English-speaking guide. It also included entrance fees to the historical sites that we wanted to see. We left our suitcases with Kris, and we each took a small bag for our days in Tibet. Miriam also took a large child's car seat as a gift for Dawa, a returnee, who had been her guest in California.

Miriam, Micah, and I had a nice flight from Chengdu to the new Lhasa Gonggar Airport. Our tour guide and driver met us with a comfortable van, and we rode for an hour on a new highway from the airport to our hotel in the heart of the city. Lhasa, Tibet, at an altitude of 11,800 feet, is one of the highest cities in the world. It contains many culturally significant Tibetan sites, such as the Potala and Norbulingka, the former homes of our friend, the fourteenth Dalai Lama. Elcho and I had talked about visiting this place for years, and now I was there with Miriam and Micah. Of course, working with hundreds of Tibetans in India during the 1960s and continuing their friendship through the years, we had heard many stories about Tibet. The Dalai Lama escaped from the Norbulingka, his summer palace, in March 1959, just before we saw him for the first time.

Dawa and her husband, Deyang, a charming Tibetan couple, soon came to our quaint Tibetan hotel to welcome us with scarves, a case of bottled water, and a big bouquet of roses from their garden. They took Micah and Miriam to dinner, but I opted to watch the people below my hotel window. Actually, I was glad to see so many Tibetan people in Lhasa, as I had heard that the Chinese had taken it over. I found out later that this was a special Tibetan holiday, and Tibetans had come from surrounding areas for meetings in the temples.

It was exciting for me to be in Lhasa, Tibet, for five busy days. Elcho and I had talked about this trip for years, and we had heard many stories about this place. The Potala, the former home of the Dalai Lama, is now a museum. Rising one thousand feet above the city, it was just a few blocks

down the street from our hotel. Miriam and Micah climbed the two hundred fifty steps to the top, but I decided not to attempt it when I was told there was no turning back and the stairs were narrow, winding, and steep. While they were climbing, I walked around the base and remembered stories that Jigme and Mary Taring had told us about their lives in Lhasa before 1959, and then later what their family had gone through after they had fled to India. I looked for their home at the foot of the Potala, but a guard stopped me and sent me back to the front of the building. All the places that we visited—the Potala palace, the Norbulingka, the Sera monastery, and the Jokhang temple—were damaged during the 1959 uprising and the Cultural Revolution. But now they have been restored and are UNESCO world heritage sites.

Ben met us back in Chengdu and took us to his home, a fifteenth-floor condominium. He and his family had just moved back to China after two years in Singapore, but he had notified our former students in the Chengdu and Chongqing areas that I was coming. During the next few days, twelve former students came to see us. They enjoyed looking at my China book with pictures of them as university students almost three decades earlier. They could not believe how much better their lives were now than what they were then. I understood, as for me it was unbelievable to see the economic improvement in Chengdu.

Kris and Stephanie Rubish lived in a rented apartment in Chengdu while they were studying Chinese and Tibetan. We enjoyed spending time with them and meeting some of their friends. They had completed their language studies and now were planning to move further up into the mountains to Kandaling to open a guest hostel.

Friends Reena, Yuki, Millie, Paul, Sarah, Christine and Toshie at Danya Kubo and Scott Lee's wedding reception, February 14, 2009

In my home in Kirkland, March 2010, with two special friends from China, Dr. George Chin and Ben Leo, and three Japanese adopted "granddaughters," Yuki, Sarah, and Elisa

Ben told Micah about a Christian NGO medical team that was going into a remote area of Tibet that needed someone to help the Swiss doctor. Micah changed his ticket and stayed behind in Chengdu awhile longer. He helped the Rubishes move to their new mountain home, took a crash course in Tibetan, and then went with the medical team further into the mountains. Miriam and I flew back to Beijing and home to America.

It was a wonderful six-week journey with LeRoy, Miriam, and Mary Ellen's son, Micah, in Japan, Singapore, China, and Tibet. It was a joy to show our children that lives had been changed because of Elcho's life and work. When Micah helped take care of his grandfather during his last days, he had heard many stories about these people and places. I was glad that he was able to stay on to help a medical team in eastern Tibet, a part of the world Elcho had always dreamed of going to but never did.

As I retrace my spiritual journey, I remember my high-school years in Yakima, Washington, when I dedicated my life to Jesus Christ. I was fortunate to hear outstanding Bible teachers and missionaries. Since I knew that I wanted to be a missionary, I decided to attend the Bible Institute of Los Angeles (now Biola University). I not only prepared for my future by studying hard under godly professors, but I matured in my Christian faith and met Elcho, the young man who would walk with me on this path. We had a good life together in India, the Tibetan border, California, China, Japan, and the Pacific Northwest.

Two of the first verses I memorized as a girl was Romans 10:9–10, "If you confess with your mouth the Lord Jesus and believe in your heart that God has raised Him from the dead, you will be saved. For with the heart one believes unto righteousness, and with the mouth confession is made unto salvation." As a teenager, I decided to follow Christ and I have never regretted it. The Lord Jesus Christ has led and guided me all these years. And when I have wandered, I am glad He has graciously brought me back to the right path. It brings me comfort to know that despite our faults, our children are carrying on our legacy and serving the Lord.

In 2008, Dr. Doug Shaw president of International Students, Inc. (ISI), presented me with the first Spiritual Legacy award during our international conference in New York City. The plaque states: "Presented to Millie Redding for her dedication and love for international students."

In April 2010, the Lord led me again down an unexpected path when I moved to Idaho to be near LeRoy and Carol. He miraculously supplied a lovely home in a senior community with a big indoor heated swimming pool. I remain very happy living in Idaho.

I had a wonderful eighty-fifth birthday in 2010 when all my children, grandchildren, and great-grandchildren came to my new home and helped me celebrate!

I am glad that family and friends make the effort to visit me in Idaho. Special friends from Japan have visited me several times. But in this age of the Internet, I am also grateful to be able to keep up with family and friends around the world with my cell phone, Skype™ on my MacBook, and my iPad.

The Lord tells us to remember what He has taught us and to pass this on to the generations that follow. It brings me joy to see our children, our grandchildren, and even our great-grandchildren making the right choices and serving Jesus. I love the verses that talk about God's faithfulness to all generations: "Your faithfulness endures to all generations" (Psalm 119:90). "The Lord is good; His mercy is everlasting, and His truth endures to all generations" (Psalm 100:5). I am reminded of the words that Elcho sang in his last days of his life here on earth, "I will sing of the mercies of the Lord forever; with my mouth I will make known Your faithfulness [preciousness] to all generations" (Psalm 89:1).

While I miss Elcho on this path I am walking now on earth, I know I will see him again because he is with the Lord he loved and served. I am grateful that I have seen some positive marks God has allowed us to leave not only on our children, grandchildren, and great-grandchildren but also on countless people around the world. Jesus says, "If anyone serves Me, let him follow Me; and where I am, there My servant will be also. If anyone serves Me, him My Father will honor" (John 12:26).

I am thankful that Elcho and I followed the Lord Jesus wherever He led. And as He leads me forward, I intend to follow Him until He calls me home to be with Himself.

I hope that as you have read this book, you have seen God's faithfulness, love, and guidance throughout our lives. That is my reason for telling this story, and it's to Him I give all the praise and glory.

Follow Me
Ira E. Stanphill

I traveled down a lonely road, and no one seemed to care.
The burden on my weary back had bowed me to despair.
I oft complained to Jesus how folks were treating me,
And then I heard Him say so tenderly,
"My feet were also weary on the Calvary Road.
The cross became so heavy. I fell beneath the load.
Be faithful, weary pilgrim, the morning I can see.
Just lift your cross and follow close to Me."

"I work so hard for Jesus," I often boast and say,
"I've sacrificed a lot of things to walk the narrow way.
I gave up fame and fortune; I'm worth a lot to Thee.
And then I hear Him gently say to me,
"I left the throne of glory and counted it but loss.
My hands were nailed in anger upon a cruel cross.
But now we'll make the journey with your hand safe in mine,
So lift your cross and follow close to Me."

O Jesus, if I die upon a foreign field someday,
'Twould be no more than love demands, no less could I repay.
"No greater love hath mortal man than for a friend to die."
These are the words He gently spoke to me.
"If just a cup of water I place within your hand,
Then just a cup of water is all that I demand."
But if by death to living they can Thy glory see,
I'll take my cross and follow close to Thee.

Made in the USA
Charleston, SC
22 May 2013